Being Young in Super-Aging Japan

Japan is not only the oldest society in the world today, but also the oldest society to have ever existed. This aging trend, however, presents many challenges to contemporary Japan, as it permeates all areas of life, from the economy and welfare to social cohesion and population decline. Nobody is more affected by these changes than the young generation.

This book studies Japanese youth in the aging society in detail. It analyzes formative events and cultural reactions. Themes include employment, parenthood, sexuality, but also art, literature, and language, thus demonstrating how the younger generation can provide insights into the future of Japanese society more generally. This book argues that the prolonged crisis resulted in a commonly shared destabilization of thoughts and attitudes and that this has shaped a new generation that is unlike any other in post-war Japan.

Presenting an inter-disciplinary approach to the study of the aging trend and what it implies for young Japanese, this book will be useful to students and scholars of Japanese culture and society, as well cultural anthropology and demography.

Patrick Heinrich is Associate Professor at Ca' Foscari University in Venice, Italy. His recent publications include (with Dick Smakman) *Urban Sociolinguistics* (Routledge 2017) and *The Making of Monolingual Japan* (2012).

Christian Galan is Professor at Toulouse-Jean Jaurès University, France and researcher at the CEJ-Inalco in Paris. His recent publications include (with E. Lozerand) *La Famille japonaise moderne (1868–1926)* (2011) and (with J.-M. Olivier) *Histoire du & au Japon* (2016).

Routledge Contemporary Japan Series

69 Local Politics and National Policy
Multi-level Conflicts in Japan and Beyond
Ken Victor Leonard Hijino

70 Trauma, Dissociation and Re-enactment in Japanese Literature and Film
David C. Stahl

71 Rethinking Japanese Studies: Eurocentrism and the Asia-Pacific Region
Edited by Kaori Okano and Yoshio Sugimoto

72 Japan's Quest for Stability in Southeast Asia
Navigating the Turning Points in Postwar Asia
Taizo Miyagi

73 Gender and the Koeski in Contemporary Japan
Surname, Power and Privilege
Linda White

74 Being Young in Super-Aging Japan
Formative Events and Cultural Reactions
Edited by Patrick Heinrich and Christian Galan

75 The Japanese Communist Party
Permanent Opposition, but Moral Compass
Peter Berton with Sam Atherton

76 Japan's Colonial Moment in Southeast Asia 1942–1945
The Occupiers' Experience
Satoshi Nakano

For more information about this series, please visit: www.routledge.com/Routledge-Contemporary-Japan-Series/book-series/SE0002

Being Young in Super-Aging Japan

Formative Events and Cultural Reactions

Edited by
**Patrick Heinrich and
Christian Galan**

LONDON AND NEW YORK

First published 2018 by Routledge

2 Park Square, Milton Park, Abingdon, Oxon OX14 4RN
605 Third Avenue, New York, NY 10017

Routledge is an imprint of the Taylor & Francis Group, an informa business

First issued in paperback 2021

Copyright © 2018 selection and editorial matter, Patrick Heinrich and Christian Galan; individual chapters, the contributors

The right of Patrick Heinrich and Christian Galan to be identified as the authors of the editorial material, and of the authors for their individual chapters, has been asserted in accordance with sections 77 and 78 of the Copyright, Designs and Patents Act 1988.

All rights reserved. No part of this book may be reprinted or reproduced or utilised in any form or by any electronic, mechanical, or other means, now known or hereafter invented, including photocopying and recording, or in any information storage or retrieval system, without permission in writing from the publishers.

Notice:
Product or corporate names may be trademarks or registered trademarks, and are used only for identification and explanation without intent to infringe.

Publisher's Note

The publisher has gone to great lengths to ensure the quality of this reprint but points out that some imperfections in the original copies may be apparent.

British Library Cataloguing-in-Publication Data
A catalogue record for this book is available from the British Library

Library of Congress Cataloging-in-Publication Data
A catalog record for this book has been requested

ISBN: 978-1-138-49497-8 (hbk)
ISBN: 978-0-367-44518-8 (pbk)

Typeset in Times New Roman
by Apex CoVantage, LLC

For Satsuki and Emil

Contents

List of figures	ix
List of tables	x
List of contributors	xi
Acknowledgments	xiv
Conventions	xvi

1 Introduction: studying the young generation in super-aging Japan   1
PATRICK HEINRICH AND CHRISTIAN GALAN

PART I
Formative events   15

2 The political economy of the declining birthrate   17
YUIKO IMAMURA

3 From youth to non-adulthood in Japan: the role of education   32
CHRISTIAN GALAN

4 Youth sexuality under the spotlight in a super-aged society with too few children   51
BEVERLEY ANNE YAMAMOTO

5 Raising children and the emergence of new fatherhood in a super-aging society   69
MASAKO ISHII-KUNTZ

viii *Contents*

6 Struggling men in emasculated life-courses: non-regular employment among young men 84
JUN IMAI

7 The Fukushima event, or the birth of a politicized generation 102
ANNE GONON

PART II
Cultural and emotional reactions 117

8 "How average am I?" Youths in a super-aged society 119
FLORIAN COULMAS

9 The structure of happiness: why young Japanese might be happy after all 132
CAROLA HOMMERICH AND TIM TIEFENBACH

10 Life on the small screen: Japan's Digital Natives 150
HIDENORI MASIKO (TRANSLATED BY YUKA ANDO)

11 Dialect cosplay: language use by the young generation 166
PATRICK HEINRICH

12 No family, no school: young people in literature by young Japanese writers 183
DAN FUJIWARA

13 Visualizing elders by young artists: age and generational differences 198
GUNHILD BORGGREEN

Conclusions 215

14 Social rejuvenation and change: the resilient generation of the Heisei period 217
CHRISTIAN GALAN AND PATRICK HEINRICH

Index 229

Figures

2.1	Voter turnout for the 45th Lower House general election in 2009 and the 46th Lower House general election in 2012	23
2.2	Proportion of the vote by age groups for the 46th Lower House general election in 2012	24
2.3	Proportion of working women according to industry and age	27
2.4	Proportion of female employees aged 15–29 according to education degree and employment status	27
2.5	Proportion of female employees aged 15 and over according to education degree and employment status	28
3.1	The dichotomization of Japan's university system	38
3.2	The evolution of "generational units" in terms of their educational paths	39
4.1	Percentage of students reporting experience of sexual intercourse, 1974–2011	53
4.2	Trends towards sexlessness among Japanese couples, 2002–2016	60
4.3	Percentage of men and women reporting no interest in or dislike of sex by age group, 2016	61
5.1	Percentage of fathers and mothers taking childcare leave, 2010–2015	73
6.1	Percentage of non-regular employment among men by age	85
8.1	Percentage change in the world's population by age, 2010–2050	128
9.1	Life satisfaction across age groups, 1970–2015	133
9.2	Happiness of middle and high school students, 1982–2012	135
9.3	Mean levels of happiness by age group	140
9.4	Mean levels of domain satisfaction by age group	141
9.5	Subjective importance of domains for happiness evaluation by age group	141
11.1	How much do you appreciate your dialect and the standard language?	173

Tables

2.1	Issues of concern by generation	25
2.2	Proportion of female employees aged 15 and over according to education degree and industry	26
8.1	Life expectancy in Italy, Japan, and Germany, 1900–2013	120
8.2	Total fertility rates in Japan, Italy, and Germany	120
8.3	The super-aged society	120
8.4	Life stages conceptualized in three languages	122
8.5	Italian terms from a popular Italian website	122
8.6	Age of consent (the legal age to have sex) across selected countries	122
8.7	First experiences and transitions	123
8.8	Percentage of young adults living with their parents	124
8.9	Median age in selected countries and the world	125
8.10	Wealth, age, and crime	126
8.11	Population projection for Japan until 2060 with medium, high, and low fertility	127
8.12	Satisfaction with present life and society	129
8.13	Dissatisfied with present life because of . . .	129
8.14	Sense of insecurity about the future	129
9.1	Results of OLS-regression on happiness	143
9.2	Mean levels of domain satisfaction by age group	146
9.3	Subjective importance of domains for happiness evaluation by age group	146
10.1	Classifications of digital habitus formation	153
11.1	*Kayra gobi* and associated stereotypes	175

Contributors

Yuka Ando is Lecturer of Japanese Language at Duisburg-Essen University. Prior to joining Duisburg-Essen University in 1999, she worked at the University of Hawai'i in Manoa. Ando is specialized in teaching material development and language teaching pedagogy. Her research focuses on cognitive linguistics and the acquisition of Japanese case particles among foreign language learners.

Gunhild Borggreen is Associate Professor at the University of Copenhagen. Her research and teaching focus on contemporary art and visual culture with special attention to "the social turn" in contemporary Japanese visual arts, as well as topics such as performance, national identity and gender. Borggreen is a co-founder and project manager of the research network ROCA (Robot Culture and Aesthetics). Publications include "Art and Consumption in Post-Bubble Japan" in *Consuming Life in Post-Bubble Japan* (2017), "Cute and Cool in Contemporary Japan" in *Social Aesthetics: Between Experiencing and Imagining* (Brill, 2015), and "Drawing Disasters: Manga Responses to the Great Eastern Japan Earthquake" in *Comic and Power* (2015).

Florian Coulmas is Senior Professor of Japanese Society and Sociolinguistics at Duisburg-Essen University. He is associate editor of the *International Journal of the Sociology of Language* and author of more than 20 books, among them *Population Decline and Ageing in Japan: The Social Consequences* (Routledge, 2009). Among his many edited books, there is *The Demographic Challenge: A Handbook about Japan* (Brill, 2008).

Dan Fujiwara is Associate Professor at the University Toulouse-Jean Jaurès and member of the Centre for Japanese Studies (CEJ-INALCO). His research focuses on modern and contemporary Japanese literature, representations of family, adolescence and childhood, border-crossing literature (*ekkyō bungaku*) and post-Fukushima literature. He has published "L'endroit et l'envers des couples mariés dans les romans de Natsume Sōseki" in *La Famille japonaise moderne (1868–1926): Discours et débats* (2011); "L'adolescent par lui-même: une nouvelle figure de la literature japonaise contemporaine?" in *Japon pluriel* 9 (2013); "Radioactivité et imaginaire littéraire" in *Cahiers d'histoire immédiate* (2015). He is currently interested in the works of Rībi Hideo, Tawada

xii *Contributors*

Yōko and Mizumura Minae, as well as in the topic of "fourteen-year-olds" in contemporary Japanese novels.

Christian Galan is Professor of Japanese Studies at the University Toulouse-Jean Jaurès, researcher at the INALCO Center of Japanese Studies in Paris and co-director of the Collection Japon at Belles Lettres. He specializes in the history of education in Japan and the Japanese educational system. Publications include *L'Enseignement de la lecture au Japon* (2001), *I'm Learning Japanese* (2010), and as co-editor, amongst others, *La Famille japonaise moderne (1868–1926): Discours et débats* (2011), *Language Life in Japan* (Routledge, 2011), *Individu-s et démocratie au Japon* (2015), and *Histoire du & au Japon* (2016).

Anne Gonon is Professor at the Graduate School of Global Studies at Doshisha University in Kyōto. She participated in an International Associated Laboratory on "Human Protection and Disaster Response: Intensive Care in Industrial Societies". She is a scientific coordinator of an International Scientific Coordination Network (GDRI) on "Vulnerability and Forms of Life", in association with the French Centre National pour la Recherche Scientifique. Her works concentrate primarily on care and social violence theory. She published *Précarité et isolement social – le monde des travailleurs journaliers japonais* (Maison Franco-japonaise, 1995); *La vie japonaise* (1996), "Vulnerability in times of disaster" in *Iride* (2013), and was co-editor of *Le monde comme horizon: état des sciences humaines et sociales au Japon* (2009).

Patrick Heinrich is Associate Professor at the Department of Asian and Mediterranean African Studies at Ca' Foscari University of Venice. His present research interests focus on language in the city and on language endangerment and revitalization. His regional focus is Japan. Edited books include *Handbook of the Ryukyuan Languages* (2015, Mouton de Gruyter) and *Urban Sociolinguistics* (2017, Routledge). His latest monograph is *The Making of Monolingual Japan* (2012).

Carola Hommerich is Associate Professor of Sociology at Hokkaido University in Sapporo, Japan. She studies social and subjective wellbeing in the context of social inequality. In 2008, she received her Ph.D. in sociology from the University of Cologne, comparing work values of young non-regular employees in Germany and Japan. In her current research, she focuses on the interrelations of objective precarity, status anxiety and feelings of social isolation, and analyzes their impact on the behavioral outcome as well as on subjective wellbeing. Recent publications include *Social Inequality in Post-Growth Japan: Transformation during Economic and Demographic Stagnation* (2017, Routledge, co-edited with David Chiavacci) and "Analyzing the Relationship between Social Capital and Subjective Well-Being: The Mediating Role of Social Capital" in *Journal of Happiness Studies* (2017, with Tim Tiefenbach), among others.

Jun Imai is Professor of Sociology at Sophia University in Tokyo, Japan. His research is about employment relations and its impact on social inequality

Contributors xiii

from a comparative and economic sociological perspective. His major publications in English include *The Transformation of Japanese Employment Relations: Reform without Labour* (2011) and *Japan's New Inequality: Intersection of Employment Reforms and Welfare Arrangements* (2011, co-edited with Yoshimichi Sato). He has recently been working on projects about changing masculinity in Japan, and also on the development of cross-border labor mobility in East and South-East Asia.

Yuiko Imamura (MSc in Public Policy, Queen Mary University of London) is a Ph.D. student of the Graduate School of Political Science at Waseda University in Tokyo. Her research focuses on the politics of welfare-state reform, in particular on declining birthrates and female participation in the labor market in Japan. Her master's thesis was on the subject of the declining birthrate and the scarcity of daycare services in Japan.

Masako Ishii-Kuntz, Ph.D., is Professor of Social Sciences and Family Studies at Ochanomizu University in Tokyo. Prior to her appointment at Ochanomizu, she taught sociology courses at the University of California, Riverside for 20 years. She is an author and co-editor of many books and articles including *Ikumen genshō no shakaigaku* (2013) and *Family Violence in Japan* (2016). Her most recent research projects include examining the use of Internet technologies and social media services in fathering, mothering and grandparenting practices in Japan, Korea, the US and Sweden. In recognition of her contribution to the international research and teaching of family sociology, she received the 2012 Jan Trost Award from the National Council on Family Relations. Currently, she serves as the president of the Japan Society of Family Sociology.

Hidenori Masiko is Professor of Sociology at Chūkyō University in Nagoya, Japan. He earned his Ph.D. at Tokyo University. His research focuses on the sociology of language and on images of Japan. He is a co-editor of the journals *Kotoba to shakai* and *Shakei gengogaku*. He has written many books, including *Ideorogī to shite no nihon* (1997) and *Chi no seiji keizaigaku* (2010).

Tim Tiefenbach holds a Ph.D. in Economics from the University of Bayreuth. He is a well-published scholar on happiness in Japan and a former senior research fellow of the German Institute of Japanese Studies. His research is based on the microeconomic analysis of large-scale household surveys with a focus on subjective variables, especially subjective wellbeing. He has published in internationally renowned journals in economics and psychology such as the *Journal of Population Economics*, *Personality and Individual Differences*, the *Journal of Economic Psychology* and the *Journal of Happiness Studies*.

Beverley Anne Yamamoto is Professor at the Graduate School of Human Sciences at Osaka University. She holds a Ph.D. from Sheffield University. Her research focuses on youth sexuality, the sociology of education and medical sociology, and she has widely published on these topics. She translated Chizuko Ueno's *Nashonarizumu to gendā* into the English version *Nationalism and Gender* (2004) and is the author of *The Sexual Behavior of Japanese Youth* (Routledge, 2017).

Acknowledgments

It is no exaggeration to say that this book was not planned. It seems more as if this book came to us. After moving from Japan to Italy in 2014, Patrick thought it was a good occasion to expand his work from sociolinguistics and considered the problem of generations as a possible topic to focus on. Since researching youth involves studying new and fresh developments by definition, this topic fitted in nicely with his long-standing interest in social change in Japan. Change, albeit with a focus on language, had also been the topic of a book that both of us had edited together some years ago, *Language Life in Japan: Transformations and Prospects*. It thus made much sense to ask Christian whether he would also be available to explore the young generation in present-day Japan. Christian has studied childhood in Japan for three decades now and, having just concluded a number of volumes on this topic, Japanese youth presented a welcome occasion to expand attention from childhood to youth.

In order to produce a book that would focus on what it means to be young in a super-aging society, we departed from Karl Mannheim's famous article on "the problem of generation", and accordingly looked for colleagues to join us and to help address the many aspects of Japanese youth we wanted to cover. We were aware from the start that this would result in a volume that integrates views from many different disciplines and that the authors would have to adapt the styles and conventions in which they usually write. It implied for everyone to work differently from the usual routine. We are glad that all authors collected in this volume took a leap of faith and provided a fresh contribution to our understanding of contemporary Japanese youth. We are grateful for their courage and for providing a chapter that was not easy to write. We all strove to create a volume where the entire book would amount to more than the sum of its parts. Ultimately, it is up to the reader to decide whether we have succeeded in this or not, but we as editors are confident that this book provides for a pioneering and rich portrayal of a new generation in Japan.

We started getting serious about compiling a book with a symposium at Ca' Foscari University of Venice in 2015. The symposium was generously supported by a Grant for Intellectual Exchange Conferences from the Japan Foundation (Ref. No. 10097134), and it received additional funding from the Department of Asian and African Studies at Ca' Foscari University. We gratefully acknowledge

Acknowledgments xv

their support. As with our first jointly edited book, we are glad to publish it with Routledge, and we are grateful to Stephanie Rodgers and others at Routledge for their support and assistance along the way of turning a bunch of files on our computers into a coherent volume.

It took almost three years to produce this book, and it sometimes developed quickly and at times stalled, as we were all involved in various other projects at the same time. And then there was life keeping us busy – in the most general and in the most literal sense. During the time this book was produced, two babies were born in Japan by two of our authors. With their birth, the rejuvenation of Japanese society is moving on also within our small group of authors. We are more than happy to dedicate this book to them.

Satsuki and Emil – we welcome you, and we salute you!

Patrick Heinrich and Christian Galan
Venice and Toulouse

Conventions

A quick word on conventions: Japanese words are transcribed in the modified Hepburn system, and Japanese names are given in the established Japanese order, family names first. All translations from Japanese are by the authors, unless otherwise specified. There are two exceptions from these simple conventions. We chose to treat Tokyo as an English word and therefore do not indicate the long vowels with a macron, i.e., we write Tokyo instead of Tōkyō. Furthermore, Masiko prefers and uses the Kunrei transcriptions of his name in the Latin alphabet – hence it is transcribed as Masiko and not as Mashiko. We often refer to the modern Japanese periods in this book but refrained from putting the respective dates of the western calendar in parenthesis every time. The Meiji period lasted from 1868 to 1912, the Taishō period from 1912 to 1926, the Shōwa period from 1926 to 1989, and the current Heisei period, in which this book is focused, started in 1989.

1 Introduction

Studying the young generation in super-aging Japan

Patrick Heinrich and Christian Galan

Introduction

The young are no longer what they used to be. They never were. Being different from one's parents is a major issue for the young. For parents, on the other hand, getting old involves the difficulty in understanding attitudes and behaviors of the young. For parents, youth often entails "problems" which call out for a "solution" – for the young, older generations are seen to not "really" be up-to-date. Any book devoted to what it means to be young is well advised to declare how it confronts such multifaceted views on youth.

In this book, we attempt to tackle present-day youth in Japan in a twofold way. We will, firstly, focus on generation-making mechanisms, and secondly on how young Japanese themselves "make sense" of their present situation. This introduction outlines what we mean by this in concrete terms. Towards this end, we will first sketch out the socioeconomic situation into which young Japanese were born, familiarize readers with existing research and terminology on Japanese youth, delineate how to study generation-making mechanisms, and finally turn towards how to study youth from the perspective of the young themselves. As a whole, this book seeks to show that present-day Japanese youth is remarkably different from other Japanese generations, and that this, in turn, implies the naissance of a society that is dissimilar from the Japanese post-war society as we knew it. Heisei is a new period in many ways.

Something happened

When the Heisei period began on 8 January 1989, the Nikkei Index had just passed 30,000 points, and it was heading straight on towards the 40,000 mark. For many, Japan was on the top of the world. The Nikkei Index reached 38,000 in December 1989. It started slipping back towards the 30,000 mark when Satō Ryōei made worldwide headlines 1990 for buying Van Gogh's *Portrait of Dr. Gachet* for 82 million dollars and Renoir's *Au Moulin de la Galette* for 78 million dollars two days later. There was no awareness then that the dropping Nikkei Index was not simply on a "course correction". It would continue its decline for many more years. In June 1995, the Nikkei dropped below 15,000 and went on

2 Patrick Heinrich and Christian Galan

straight towards the 10,000 mark. By then it was clear that the days of "Japan as Number One" were over. This was a serious economic crisis. At the end of the 1990s, the crisis remained unresolved. In an attempt to leave it behind, once and forever, and to make a fresh start into the new millennium, Prime Minister Mori Yoshirō's advisor coined the term "lost decade" (*ushinawareta jūnen*). However, the past would not go away. The economic crisis lingered on, and at the end of the zero years the term "two lost decades" (*ushinawareta nijūnen*) appeared. There will be no need to coin a term for "three lost decades". Economic stagnation, growing public debt, and deflation have become the new normality for Japan. The past, the economic bubble, and everything that came along with it, is the anomalous today. For no one is this truer than for those who have been born after the bubble burst.

There is more to the Heisei period. The second fundamental change made fewer headlines, though, as its effects were seen to be less pressing at the start. Nonetheless, the degree of change is extraordinary here as well. In 1989, the Japanese population was growing by more than 1,100 persons a day – in 2017 it is shrinking by 1,000 people day. In 1989, 12 percent of the total population was older than 65 – in 2017, 26 percent of the population is older than 65 (Countrymeters 2017). Japan's population decline is irreversible. It will continue for many decades to come (Coulmas 2007), unless Japan fundamentally changes its immigration regime, for which there is no sign at the present. Japan has undergone the process of social aging faster than most other societies. Today, it is the oldest society in the world, making it also the oldest society to have ever existed in history. Japan transformed itself from an "aging society" (8 percent of the population older than 65) to an "aged society" (14 percent older than 65) in a record-setting pace of 24 years. Japan's aging and declining population has far-reaching ramifications. It affects Japan's economy, welfare, social cohesion, education, and on an international plane its competitiveness, exchange and relations to other countries.

Beyond these figures lies profound social change, and young Japanese have been most crucially shaped by it. Growing up in an economically stagnant and socially aging Japan, they were socialized in a very different setting from that of their parents or grandparents. For young Japanese, "Japan as Number One" is a distant tale from the past – unconnected to their experiences and lives. Social aging also affects the young by increasing the "passive part" of the population, which in turn enhances the duties and the obligations of the "active part". Already in 2020, two "active people" will correspond to one "passive person". Moreover, due to social aging, the young generation is exposed to deeper layers of past attitudes and experiences than ever before. Put simply, more past is part of the present, or more past is "made to fit" the present.

The generation born between the end of the 1980s and the 1990s differs from previous generations, in that its membership does not simply rely on age as the sole criterion, in the sense of "young people are no longer what they used to be!" The generational ruptures are played out on a different level now. It's more like "society is no longer what it used to be!" The young have been dealt a different "set of cards" than their parents and grandparents. The present and the future are no longer

Introduction 3

safe or guaranteed, as it had been before. Social trajectories have become blurred and uncertain (except for elites). Any society, writes Mauger (2015: 3, translation ours) on inter-generational continuity, requires the "biological reproduction of the group, the production of the quantity of goods needed for its subsistence, and inseparably, the reproduction of social structures, where such reproduction takes place." If we place Mauger's idea in the contexts of Japan's super-aged society, and consider the relations between the young and the older generations, we realize that Japanese society is undermined on each of these three points. The sustenance of Japanese society as it was formed in the post-war period is under threat.

The social and economic changes of the Heisei period are far-reaching. Personal economic decline is more than a "potential source" of anxiety. Surveys reveal that 37 percent have personally experienced social decline in the past ten years (Hommerich 2014: 457). Japan has today the second highest level of poverty of all OECD countries – only the US has a higher percentage. More than 15 percent of the population, that is more than 20 million people, are officially poor. One third of the employees are irregularly employed and do not receive the social, economic and psychological benefits that come along with regular employment. Being poor is the rule rather than the exception among the non-regular employed. The young are most severely affected from non-regular employment and its many social consequences (Sato and Imai 2011). Unsurprisingly, therefore, young adults have a lower average monthly consumption than retired people, despite the fact that retirees are supposed to be "set up" and also no longer have work related expenditures (Matsuura 2011: 163).

In contrast to the generation of their parents and grandparents, many young Japanese will not succeed in living an ordinary life (*hitonami no seikatsu*), i.e., graduate, enter the workforce, marry, have children and raise them safely. The young fare worse than their parents, and they know this. The idea of an all-middle-class society (*sōchūryū shakai*) or a super-stable society (*chō-antei shakai*) no longer applies. Japan is today a society of socioeconomic difference (*kakusa shakai*), and young people can neither ignore nor bypass this fact. There also exists inter-generational inequity (*sedai-kan kakusa*) with far-reaching consequences (Shigeyuki, Oguro and Takahashi 2010). Japanese society is liquidizing and is transforming itself into a relationless society (*muen shakai*). Increasingly often, group membership simply entails responsibilities, but individuals are left "on their own" in case of difficulties. Unsurprisingly, therefore, we find a fervent carving for security among the young. Allison (2013: 68) reports that 85 percent of young women aspire to become full-time homemakers (*sengyō shufu*), but young men who could offer such a lifestyle to their young wives are few and far between today. Furuichi Noritoshi (2011) also has a point in writing that "if the standard for becoming an adult is becoming a '*seishain*' [regular worker] or '*sengyō shufu* [. . .], then more and more young people will not be able to become adults. They'll stay disconnected from age altogether, or simply stay [forever] young" (quoted from Allison 2013: 261–262).

Making sense of the Heisei period requires new adaptions, a task for which young Japanese have not been prepared. A large part of Japan's young generation

4   *Patrick Heinrich and Christian Galan*

is, voluntarily or involuntarily, not well integrated into society. There are ±700,000 *hikikomori* and ±1.5 million potentially being tempted by this type of social withdrawal. To add, there are 1.8 million *freeter* and ± 760,000 young or young adults between 15 and 34 years who are NEET (Not in Employment, Education or Training).[1] Such lack of participation in society is a matter of concern for a country, which has the oldest society of all OECD states.

A survey conducted for the Japanese Cabinet Office (Naikakufu 2010) showed that 83 percent of the *hikikomori* declared to see themselves as having no or almost no talent at birth, against 67 percent for the control group. 71 percent of those who thought to have no talent also declared that there were many things for which they had to apologize to their family, against only 32 percent for the control group. 34 percent of those who saw themselves to be without talent also declared that they had nobody or almost nobody in whom they could trust in the past, against 7 percent for the control group. The concern of the government is, however, less about insecurity or public health. It is mostly concerned with the negative economic impact of *hikikomori* as a long-term phenomenon. Nonetheless, the problem is more complex than inactivity negatively affecting the economy. NEET and also the under-employed, job-hopping *freeters* often are not in this situation entirely by their own choice. Many of them are only given an option between withdrawal, on the one hand, or low-paid, insecure and demeaning employment, on the other hand (Genda 2011: 89). They see little reason to be positive about their futures. Most famously, perhaps, this mood has been articulated by novelist and social commentator Murakami Ryū (2000) in his bestselling novel *Kibō no kuni no ekosodasu* (The Exodus of a Country of Hope).

A French survey conducted in 25 countries on the "youth of the world" found that Japanese turned out to be more negative and pessimistic than the youth of any other country (Reynié 2011). Here are some findings of this study. Only 43 percent expressed to find their own future promising, and only 24 percent thought that the future of Japan was promising. 74 percent were dissatisfied with the economic situation, and 60 percent with their own work. 32 percent hoped that their work situation would improve in the future. 61 percent declared to be dissatisfied with the epoch they were living in. A lack of inter-generational solidarity becomes apparent with only 35 percent declaring that they support the idea of paying for the pensions of the older generations, and with 50 percent strictly opposing this idea. Furthermore, the Japanese youth showed the lowest rate on a number of factors such as the importance of time spent with the family (79 percent), the importance of the family for the construction of the personal identity (73 percent), and only 69 percent expressed satisfaction with the family they were born into. Only 26 percent considered establishing a family of their own a top-priority for a satisfactory life, and only 37 percent declared that having children was a part of their top-three priorities in the next 15 years. Somewhat hard to relate to these attitudes is the fact that 52 percent of the Japanese youth thought sexual relations should only take place in marriage (fifth position after Morocco, India, South Africa and Turkey). As a general conclusion, this international comparative survey revealed, "when most of the young people are

Introduction   5

dissatisfied of the general situation of their country, they declare, on the other hand, that they are satisfied with the epoch they are living in" (Reynié 2011: 10, translation ours). There is one exception to this trend. In Japan, young people are both dissatisfied with the general situation and with epoch they are living in. Another somewhat contradictory finding was that only 46 percent of the young Japanese have the conviction that they are able to make their own life decisions, but 70 percent believed that "people can change society by their choices and their actions". These contradictions must be understood as a manifestation of changing attitudes among the young.

The current evolution of Japanese society amounts to nothing less than a question of the survival of a society that developed after 1945 and stabilized from the 1960s until the early 1990s. This social change is being pushed ahead by economic stagnation, social aging and population decline, on the one hand, and it is further accelerated by the neoliberal policies pursued all across Japan since the late 1990s, on the other hand. What does it mean to be young in such a situation? We argue that the socio-economic changes of the Heisei period led to a commonly shared destabilization of thoughts and attitudes. As an effect, the generational break between those born in the post-war period and those born during the Heisei period is stronger than the "habitual destabilization" between generations.

We are not the first to write about young generations in Japan. There exists a whole genre, *wakamono-ron* ("theories on the young"), with a long history devoted to this topic in Japan.[2] This genre has generated a large number of ascriptions and labels for Japanese "young generations". Upon inspection, however, many of these designations turn out to be nothing more than media buzzwords, absent of sociological or historical considerations. A common weakness of them is that labels are simply superimposed on a specific age cohort. It is therefore questionable whether these labels actually designate "generations as social groups" in a serious sociological or historical sense. It is nevertheless instructive to recapitulate the most well-known of these designations, because they offer a perspective on how "being young" is thought to differ across time. For the sake of brevity, we will start our review in the 1970s.

A genealogy of young generations

Since the early 1970s, we can attest an intensive discussion of young generations in Japanese scholarship and the Japanese public (Furuichi 2011: 65–69). Prominent scholars include the sociologist Inoue Shun, who first outlined the field of youth sociology in Japan. Other experts of the field such as Miyadai Shinji are well-known public figures in Japanese mass media. They, and many others, have compiled a large corpus of literature on Japanese youth over the years. When reviewing this literature, one finds a new catchword – seen to capture the essence of the young generation – in every new decade. As an effect, the generations portrayed correspond, more or less, to age cohorts comprising ten years (Ichikawa 2003). Furthermore, some generations, like the *shirake sedai* ("Apathic generation") of the 1970s, have not left much impression, while others are said to have

6 Patrick Heinrich and Christian Galan

introduced entirely new attitudes and behaviors to Japanese society. The *shinjinrui* ("new breeds") are seen as an example of the latter type of generation.

The *shinjinrui* were the first who had not experienced foreign occupation or the restrictions of the post-war reconstruction years. Born between 1961 and 1970, they were identified as "new breeds" when the first of them reached adolescence in the late 1970s. The term diffused in the 1980s and actually became "word of the year" in 1986. *Shinjinrui* referred to young middle-class Japanese in the then new Japanese consumer society. They were said to have developed behaviors and values that appeared disruptive to older generations. The term itself retains an ambiguous character, oscillating between the positive and the negative. It was mainly used to describe a new mode of consumption, using, as it did, marketing vocabulary to refer to them. The catchy "new breed" was only one of many terms that existed at the time, but all others have slipped into oblivion. *Shinjinrui* flourished in the media, both in Japan and overseas. Abroad, the term was often misunderstood, especially because of its Nietzschean ring and the prominent discourse of "Japan as Number One" in the 1980s. The *shinjinrui* saw the appearance and development of *otaku* ("obsessive fandom") culture, a term first used in this sense in 1983 by social commentator Nakamori Akio. *Otaku*, in its early manifestations, referred to individualistic and frantic consumers who spent their childhood, adolescence, and the start of adult life in the secure cocoon of the economic bubble.

The term *shinjinrui* was not intended as a criticism, nor was it an ironic reference to a generation who played *Space Invaders*. It was sought to point out to a new type of "salaryman" – a new type of employee or social being, who would primarily be defined by their consumer behavior. The "new breeds" were the first to seek brand clothes and objects in order to express their hedonism. Being up-to-date, or "nowy" (*naui*) as they called it, set them apart from older generations. New information technology was one of their many interests. It were the "new breeds" who spread information technology from the spheres of the corporate world into private life, and technology then turned out to be pivotal for further radicalizing *otaku* culture. The *shinjinrui* were also the first for whom staying single was regarded a possible lifestyle choice, because single life allowed them to continue pursuing their consumer interests.

The *shinjinrui* gave way to the *dankai junior* (literally, "baby boomer junior"), that is, a second baby-boom generation. They were the children of the first baby boomers, who had been born immediately after WW II. The *dankai juniors* were thus born in the first half of the 1970s, and they have also experienced and benefited from the strong economy in their childhood and during adolescence. They were raised in the comforts of a rich and at times overconfident Japan. The "baby boomer juniors" were the first new generation to experience the beginning of the digital revolution and, upon entering adulthood, the transformation of Japan into an information society. They were subsidized by their parents, and made modest, non-flamboyant marriage ceremonies in restaurants, etc. fashionable. They were portrayed as being self-absorbed, as lacking self-constraint, and as seeking self-actualization (*jibun-sagashi*). They also became associated with social ills such as compensated dating (*enjo kōsai*).

Introduction 7

The *dankai juniors* were then succeeded by the so-called *dansō junior* (literally, "displaced junior"). This generation was further divided into two groups – the *posutobaburu* ("post-bubbles"), i.e., those born in the second half of the 1970s who experienced the burst of the bubble as young adults, and the *eitīzu* ("eighties") born in the first half of the 1980s with only a faint memory of the economic heydays. The "post-bubbles" are the first generation to have fallen victim to the economic crisis. They grew up in affluence during childhood and the first years of adolescence, but then came to feel effects of the economic crisis. They have experienced various watershed moments in Japanese post-war history, such as the end of a period marked by the death of Emperor Hirohito in 1989, the Great Hanshin Earthquake in Kobe in 1995, the poison gas attacks on the Tokyo subway system by the Aum Shinrikyō Sect in the same year, the glacial age of non-hiring between 1995 and 2000, and the arrival of unemployment und precarity. The "eighties", too, experienced the comforts of the economic boom in their early childhood, but saw the social divide and the economic crisis arrive already in their teenage years. They were the first generation growing up with the Internet, digital culture, and the mobile phone.

Last but not least, there are the *shin-shinjinrui* ("new new breeds"), a label for an age cohort, which is more or less congruent with that which is at the center of this book. We will, nevertheless, refrain from applying this term here for reasons explained below. The *shin-shinjinrui* are the children of the *shinjinrui*. They were born between the mid-1980s and the mid-1990s, and they amount for some 13 million people, or 10 percent of the Japanese population. The "new new breeds" have never experienced an economically confident or otherwise triumphant Japan, nor have they ever known a society as stable and secure as the society their parents knew in their youth. The *shin-shinjinrui* are the children of the demographic and economic crisis. While they often received enormous amounts of pocket money – they usually lack siblings and, due to longevity of their grandparents, receive money from "six pockets". They have, however, also experienced the effects of poverty and other difficulties in various contexts. We will elaborate in detail on this aspect in this book.

As illustrative as these above labels may be for introductive purposes, we can nevertheless note a number of limitations. To start with, the young generation is portrayed from the perspective of older generations – they are being "othered" from the older generations. The findings from such efforts are actually "discourses on the young" rather than meticulously researched facts. No attempt is made to distinguish for whom exactly these characterizations apply, i.e., there is no distinction between regions, rural or urban or social class differences; there are also no considerations for "how deep" the generational divide is. Furthermore, the focus has been placed on "alarming deviances" such as, for example, an inclination to use consumer credits for shopping, to engage in "compensated dating", or to be prone to extreme *otaku* behavior, sweeping thereby more mundane characteristics or constitutive behaviors of the young under the carpet. What is needed in the study of the young generation is therefore research illuminating to what extent the young actually form "a generation" in a sociological and historical sense, how a divide between generations has come about, and how it manifests in everyday life.

On generation-making mechanisms

We are currently witnessing a far-reaching "reshuffling of cards" between the generations in Japan. Already in the above recapitulation of *wakamono* and their particularities since the 1970, we recognize that all those considered to be "young" today are defined on the basis of the economic crisis, i.e., of having or not having grown up in an affluent Japan. *Shinjinrui* is hardly used anymore, and there is a very obvious reason for this. With the hindsight of history, we recognize that this marketing terminology did not fit to this generation. In comparison to their children (the *shin-shinjinrui*), the "new breeds" do not appear to be so different from their parents in terms of values, experiences and life plans. The real divide runs between "new breeds", born during the economic heyday, and their children, the "new new breeds", who were born and raised during the economic crisis.

Research on Japanese society supports the view that the post-bubble generation experienced a Japanese society with remarkable differences to the society their parents and grandparents knew when they were young (e.g., Funabashi and Kushner 2015). Despite these social changes, the values, discourses, and attitudes of the older generation did not change dramatically. They remain more or less the same today. While the parents of the young generation live in the same present-day Japanese society, they continue relying in large parts on attitudes and behavioral patterns acquired in their youth. It is revealing that older generations call Japan's economic stasis "two lost decades", i.e., regard it as a lamentable "divergence" to a strong economy, although an economic stagnation of more than 20 years is rather a stable condition, and despite the fact that all signs are set for this situation to further extent into the future. For the young generation, who grew up in a society of zero-economic growth and of demographic decline, the present situation is not and cannot be "exceptional", because it is all that they have ever experienced. The young are therefore more "up-to-date" to this situation and, one might add, also more realistic about Japan's future prospects.

Individuals are crucially and forever shaped by the experiences of their youth. How shared experience forms individuals in similar ways is therefore the departure point for any treatment of generation as an "analytic category". When studying the young generation, considerable attention needs to be placed on how sociocultural history forms individuals into a "social generation". Labeling age cohorts as a generation is insufficient towards this end, because the biological rhythm of life (birth, youth, adolescence, adulthood, old age and death) works itself through the medium of social events. The sociological study of generation must therefore simultaneously account for biological and historical time. It is of utmost importance to experience specific events at a similar age, because the participation of the same "present" is stratified differently according to the biological age of individuals. For the young generation, the present cannot but be formative, while the older generations have already made formative experiences before. The fact that youth lacks experience facilitates them to adapt to a changing world.[3]

According to Mannheim, experiencing the same time at a similar age is not sufficient for forming a "social generation". "Generation as an actuality" (Mannheim

Introduction 9

1998[1923]: 181–184) emerges only in the case that thoughts and attitudes are fundamentally destabilized, and this is more likely to happen the "quicker the tempo of social and cultural change" (Mannheim 1998[1923]: 190). A generation as an actuality may then actually involve different groups, that is, reacts differently to the same process of destabilization and form "generation units" (Mannheim 1998[1923]: 184–193). It is the fact that they react and come up with new attitudes and behaviors that makes them a generation – and not necessarily shared values and behaviors.

Japan's present young generation is not "simply new" – like any new grouping of an age cohort – but it is "new in novel ways". Consequently, the relation between generations in Japan today is no longer a simple matter of calculating the difference in age between parents and children, nor simply of studying biological maturity, or of investigating how psychological maturity is socially constructed. There is Fukushima, of course, but Fukushima itself has not made a new generation. In order to study generations, one needs to study the years and events that preceded, accompanied or followed Fukushima, and study to what extent the triple disaster of March 2011 proved a lasting event in the formation of attitudes. We argue that the young generation has been made by "a period effect", which includes multiple historical events and socioeconomic factors such as demographic decline, economic and social consequences of the burst bubble, poverty, breaking the pact for education, consequences of neoliberal policies, political choices by the government, the triple disaster of Fukushima, but also the evolution of the outside world and international society. Something happened in the Heisei period, and we seek to explore "what has happened" and "to what effects" for the young generation in this book.

Emic perspectives on the young generation

How is young Japanese identity built in a situation of a generational divide, which involves an absence of credible role models for the situation young people today find themselves in? Through what kind of solidarities, ideals and references can young Japanese build a social identity as Japanese? The problem is that the "short history" of the young and the "long history" of older generations are quite diverse. The life-worlds of adults do not correspond to the reality the young are experiencing. What then is identity for the young, and how does it remain "Japanese"? How do young Japanese individuals construct a coherent representation of themselves in a society and a family environment, where the former benchmarks, be they social, economic, psychological, or otherwise have suffered, if not altogether lost relevance? Attempts to identify are blocked in all directions. "Upstream", so to say, they are blocked by obsolete representations of their parents, while they are disturbed "downstream" by uncertain, unclear and unstable new representations.

The normative and structural crisis of adolescence usually allows teenagers to gradually find their ideals and to ensure consistency in relation to themselves, others and the society in which they live (Erikson 1968). This includes many facets of everyday life, orientation of and access to sexuality, relations to work, learning

10   *Patrick Heinrich and Christian Galan*

to place value on the company and its interests, and many other criteria, which mark the transition to adulthood. How to continue to behave and act in a society, where all central markers of reference for building identity have been devalued, undermined or displaced, all the while one pretends that they are still available and valid? Clearly, young people in Japan have to deal with some amount of inconsistency and conflict, which cannot but make them more reflexive about themselves, about society, and about their place within this society.

On an ideological, sexual or professional plane, growing mature and access to maturity – attitudes expected from adults – can no longer be taken for granted. Growing mature can no longer follow the paths that were available to older generations. However, these paths continue to exist in values, ideologies and expectations. Hence, the values, beliefs and goals, which young people are expected to explore, and the "real problems" they have to confront in order to make "their choices" do not correspond. Young people are faced with expectations, which can no longer be realized, and they are prepared for battles, which are no longer fought. For the young generation, the future is spelled out differently, their attitudes and expectations for the future have changed, but many institutions do not seem to pay attention to this. There is a notable tendency to stick to ideologies of the foregone Shōwa world *à la* "Japan is back again", "resurrect Japan", or "Tokyo Olympics 2020" as an effigy of Tokyo Olympics 1964.

The assumption from which we depart in this book is that for the young, a sense of belonging to a generation is not simply one of chronological time and a configuration of specific tastes, brands, aspirations and hobbies as it was the case for the generation of their parents. Being part of the young generation today also encompasses subjective matters – one is part of the young generation because one *feels* to be part of it, because one *feels* to have been "dealt different cards" than the generation before. It is for these reasons that the objective of this book is to examine the specific historical and social developments that led to this situation, and to examine the specific cultural reactions to these changes by the young. Awareness of "being dealt a different set of cards" is what makes a generation in the Mannheimian sense – not the different attributes or habits such as "the acceleration of time" or "the digital revolution", etc.

The figures on Japanese economic stagnation, population decline and youth pessimism make it easy to either fall into the trap of "pitying" Japanese youth (see Ebihara 2010 for a discussion), or of devising schemes for how to make them "more confident" or "more positive". In his review of Furuichi's 2011 book *Zetsubō no kuni no kōfuku na wakamono-tachi* (*The Happy Youth of a Desperate Country*), Toivonen is therefore critical of seeing Japanese youth either simply as the main "victims" of the lost decade and population decline or as "weak". He asks the excellent question, "[w]hat if young people are not the losers they are made out to be, hanging desperately on the margins of a society that denies them access to jobs and all forms of success?" (Toivonen et al. 2012). 1985-born Furuichi Noritoshi's work on the present-day young generation has drawn a lot of attention for declaring that large parts of Japanese youth are actually happy, despite being aware of their difficult situation and their rather bleak prospects. Furuichi's (2011: 129) main thesis is squarely based upon the presentation of data

Introduction 11

showing that Japanese youths today are happier than in former periods of time. One needs to note, however, that the same data shows a very sharp decline in happiness for those being in their 30s, 40s and 50s today, leaving the view of a "desperate country" intact. Taking such a finding seriously, Furuichi engages in an emic perspective on youth. Consider, in a longer passage, how he first accounts for the difficult circumstances in which the young generation finds itself, and immediately afterwards provides for an inside view of how happiness remains largely unaffected by these circumstances for young Japanese.

> Whatever way you look at it, the number of children will not increase any time soon, and however much you may criticize the policies of the past, this will not improve Japan's current situation either. Even if inter-generational inequity is not at the heart of the problem [because there is also desperation among the old and middle-aged, PH/CG], it does not change the fact that Japan's future is desperate. There is also no doubt about the fact that young people and children will ultimately have to live longer than everyone else in this desperate future. In 2012, the Babyboomers are reaching the age of retirement. While the economic market is still doing well due to its "let's aim at the Babyboomers" approach, most of the Babyboomers will have exited the consumer market in 20 years [. . .]. In 2030, those called the "lost generation" will be seeing their 60s. *Hikikomori* and NEET will then be a youth problem and an elderly problem at the same time. The Babyboomers as a motor of the consumption market will no longer be around, and the question emerges whether the active part of society will then be able to support the growing number of those being part of the "lost generation"? In view of these delusions about a dire future, the Japan of 2011 is still carefree. How are young people able to exist happily in such a desperate situation? [. . .] Article 25 of the Japanese Constitution stipulates that "all people shall have the right to maintain the minimum standards of wholesome and cultured living". While it depends on the period of time and on the societal situation what "the minimum standards of wholesome and cultured living" implies, I think that for me "living a life playing Wii with a lover or a friend" or "a life where you enjoy playing Monster Hunter" would be an adequate answer. I think that most would consider themselves to be happy in an economic situation where you can afford to buy a Wii or PSP and where you have social relations, which allow you to enjoy playing these in their company.
>
> (Furuichi 2011: 331–332, translation ours)

In this passage Furuichi pushes for intrinsic or emic accounts of what it means to be young and happy in present-day Japan. Research on the young generation – the terms of transition from childhood and adolescence to adulthood, and the integration of young people into adult society – has generally been considered from the perspective of adults. However, in view of institutional change, young people have been left alone to figure out how to deal with a changed Japanese society on their own. They are, therefore, best studied as a social system in their own right, that is, studied from an emic perspective.

12 *Patrick Heinrich and Christian Galan*

In order to study youth from an emic perspective, it is beneficial to consider their life ecology. After all, all authors assembled in this book are not part of Japanese youth. Turning towards an ecological orientation is a helpful tool to reconstruct what it means to be young *for the young*. The Greek word "οἶκος" (*oikos*) is the root of both "ecology" and "economy". Literally it means "house" or "environment", and the study of both economy and ecology share the fact that they are concerned with "the best ways to manage what is available in your environment" (i.e., house). The various elements or phenomena that make up an environment interact thereby in various ways, constituting, in so doing, different systems. It is not difficult to apply the metaphor of *oikos* to the study of "generation as an actuality" or "generation units", as these are nothing but different orders stemming from a differing socio-cultural environment. The obvious strength of "thinking ecologically" about generations is that one has to move beyond singular explanations in accounts on what defines and what makes a generation. An ecological perspective can account for phenomena, which are both biological (e.g., age) and social (e.g., roles). It highlights the idea of "resources", "niches", or "adaptations", and it shifts attentions from facts to processes such as the "management of resources", "forms of human interaction", or "patterns of population decline". Ecological approaches to youth studies have already been conducted, focusing on problems such as youth violence (Moon, Patton and Rao 2010). The biggest strength of such an approach is that it shifts focus from individuals to ecology. Hence, no longer somehow "noteworthy individuals and their attitudes" are taken *pars pro toto* to represent "a generation", but one is forced to indeed consider everyone. And with these ambitions and objectives, let us now turn to studying how Japanese youth forms a generation and how they have responded culturally and emotionally to the events that have shaped them.

Notes

1 *Hikikomori*, literally "those who stay inside", are persons seeking extreme isolation and social seclusion for an extended period of time.

Freeter is a blend between "free agent" and "*arbeiter*" (workers), referring to people who are underemployed and work in low-paid and low-skilled jobs. Students and housewives are not included in this category.

NEET. The number of young Japanese not or marginally participating in society are hard to exactly verify and some individuals may have entered the above figures twice. There is no doubt that these numbers are alarming in either case.

2 As for English publications, Goodman, Imoto and Toivonen (2012) need to be mentioned. *Japanese Youth Sociology* is an analysis of how specific youth problems are constructed and circulated in media discourses at specific periods of time, a topic not prominently addressed by scholarship in Japan.

3 Migrants or social climbers may also come into first contact with a specific sociocultural environment, but this contact is nevertheless different from that of the young, because migrants and social climbers have already made formative experiences before.

References

Allison, Anne (2013) *Precarious Japan*. Durham: Duke University Press.
Coulmas, Florian (2007) *Population Decline and Ageing in Japan*. London: Routledge.

Introduction 13

Countrymeters (2017) *Japan Population Clock.* Online available at: http://countrymeters. info/en/japan (accessed 22 September 2017).

Ebihara, Tsuguo (2010) *"Wakamono wa kawaisō-ron" no uso* [Lies About "Youth Being Pitiful"]. Tokyo: Fusōsha.

Erikson, Erik H. (1968) *Identity, Youth and Crisis.* New York: Newton.

Funabashi, Yōichi and Barak Kushner (2015) *Examining Japan's Lost Decades.* London: Routledge.

Furuichi, Noritoshi (2011) *Zetsubō no kuni no kōfuku na wakamono-tachi* [The Happy Youth of a Desperate Country]. Tokyo: Kōdansha.

Genda, Yūji (2011) Young, Japanese, and Not in Education, Employment or Training: Japan's Experience with the NEET Phenomenon. In: *Demographic Change and Inequality in Japan.* Sawako Shirahase (ed.), 76–97. Melbourne: Trans Pacific Press.

Goodman, Roger, Yuki Imoto and Tuukka Toivonen (eds.) (2012) *A Sociology of Japanese Youth: From Returnees to NEETs.* London: Routledge.

Hommerich, Carola (2014) Neue Risiken, neue Ungleichheiten: Wie gespalten ist Japans Gesellschaft? In: *Länderbericht Japan: Die Erarbeitung der Zukunft.* Raimund Wördemann and Karin Yamaguchi (eds.), 445–460. Bonn: Bundeszentrale für politische Bildung.

Ichikawa, Kōichi (2003) "Wakamono-ron no keifu: Wakamono wa dō katareta-ka" [A Genealogy of Youth Studies: How Have Young People Been Portrayed?]. *Bulletin of Human Science* (Bunkyo University) 25: 123–130.

Mannheim, Karl (1998 [1923]) The Sociological Problem of Generations. In: *Essays on the Sociology of Language.* Paul Kecskemeti (ed.), 163–195. London: Routledge.

Matsuura, Katsumi (2011) Inheritance, Pensions, Childbirth, Childrearing and the Inequalities they Bring: A Case Study of Impact on Net Financial Assessts. In: *Demographic Change and Inequality in Japan.* Sawako Shirahase (ed.), 151–180. Melbourne: Trans Pacific Press.

Mauger, Gérard (2015) *Âges et Generations* [Age and Generation]. Paris: La Découverte.

Moon, Sung Seek, Joy Patton and Rao Uma (2010) An Ecological Approach to Understanding Youth Violence. *Journal of Human Behavior in the Social Environment* 20(7): 839–856.

Murakami, Ryū (2000) *Kibō no kuni no ekosodasu* [The Exodus of a Country of Hope]. Tokyo: Bungei Shunjū.

Naikakufu (2010) *Wakamono no ishiki ni kansuru chōsa (hikikomori ni kansuru jittai chōsa)* [Survey on the Attitudes of Young People (Survey on the Situation of *hikikomori*)]. Online available at: www8.cao.go.jp/youth/kenkyu/hikikomori/pdf_index.html (accessed 22 September 2017).

Reynié, Dominique (2011) *La jeunesse du monde: Une enquête planétaire de la Fondation pour l'innovation politique* [The Youth of the World: A Global Survey of the Foundation for Political Innovation]. Paris: Fondation pour l'Innovation Politique.

Sato, Yoshimichi and Jun Imai (2011) Regular and Non-Regular Employment as an Additional Duality in Japanese Labor Market. In: *Japan's New Inequality.* Yochimichi Sato and Jun Imai (eds.), 1–31. Melbourne: Trans Pacific Press.

Shigeyuki, Jo, Kazumasu Oguro and Ryohei Takahashi (2010) *Sedai-kan kakusa tte nanda?* [What Is Inter-Generation Inequity?] Tokyo: PhP Shinso.

Toivonen, Tuukka, Noritoshi Furuichi, Mikoto Terachi and Tomu Ogawa (2012) Japanese Youth: An Interactive Dialogue. *The Asia-Pacific Journal – Japan Times* 10.35(3). Online available at: http://apjjf.org/2012/10/35/Tuukka-Toivonen/3816/article.html (accessed 22 September 2017).

Part I

Formative events

2 The political economy of the declining birthrate

Yuiko Imamura

Introduction

The declining birthrate is at the heart of social aging, population loss and economic stasis in Japan. The political economy is crucial when analyzing both the ongoing population decline and the current inability to implement political reforms in order to reverse this trend. The question looms why voters have been electing governments that have not addressed these problems – problems that affect, in particular, the young. In this chapter, I outline the political economy of declining birthrates in order to provide information on the emergence of a generation that has been socialized under governments not addressing their immediate and future interests. Quite to the contrary, governments continue to impose burdens on the future life of the young generation.

Policy stasis and the resulting generation gap

Japanese society dramatically changed during the high-growth period, and this transformation continued after Japan entered a low-growth period in the 1970s. At the same time, the institutions that had played important roles in the post-war period did not fundamentally change. The so-called "1955 system" that had secured the dominance of the Liberal Democratic Party (henceforth, LDP) lasted until 1993 when the LDP lost power for one year. Even when it returned to power, the LDP kept sticking to its politics of redistributing economic gains in society, although this became increasingly problematic under conditions of low economic growth. It also became difficult to guarantee full employment, which is the very basis for maintaining the Japanese "standard family" with the male breadwinner. Consequently, "new social risks"[1] emerged in the sphere of family and work, and the low birthrate became an increasingly prominent issue.

The declining birthrate led to dramatic changes in the Japanese population structure. Recent projections suggest that by 2060 the share of the population aged 65 and over will reach 40 percent, and that the total population will decrease by 30 percent (NIPSSR 2012). Many studies point out the negative effects resulting from such demographic change. One such problem is the growth of what is called the "generation gap" (Kato 2011). The generation gap is analyzed by

18   *Yuiko Imamura*

calculating the total benefit and payment throughout one's life for each age cohort. It calculates the balance between the benefits an individual receives on average from the government (pension, medical care and education, etc.), and how much one has to contribute to the state (tax, social security expenses, etc.). According to Nikkei Shinbun (2010), people aged 60 and older receive about 40 million yen more benefit than they actually pay, while those who were younger than 20 in 2010 will have to provide 83 million yen more than they will receive. Accordingly, the "generation gap" between the elderly and the young Japanese amounts to more or less 120 million yen. Although the result of these calculations varies depending on a number of preconditions, and the number and type of services and items included, there is no doubt that the young Japanese will have to shoulder a heavy burden. The level of generation inequality in Japan is high in international comparison (Kato 2011: 31). This trend is to continue and accelerate because the Japanese social security system is based on a "pay-as-you-go system", where the younger generations provide the fiscal resources needed for the support of the old generation. Therefore, as the young population decreases as an effect of the declining birthrate, the burden per person will inevitably rise. The present social security system was established during the high economic growth period under the assumption that the young population would continue to increase. Demographic change such as a shrinking of the young generation could be compensated through an ever-increasing income. However, the current young generation is facing an unstable situation in the labor market due to the slowdown of the economy, the rise of temporary employment and changes in employment practices that now frequently include non-regular work. Furthermore, the mounting debt of the government adds to the generation gap.[2] All of this results in a heavy burden for the young. As of 2011, 2-year-old children were born with an amount of more than seven million yen government debt per person, a number that stood only at 148,000 yen at the time those aged 65 today were born. The debt will continue to increase, and the younger generation has to shoulder an ever-heavier burden – all the while having to work for a longer period of time (Kato 2011: 33).

Another problem of contemporary Japanese society is the growing concentration of population around the Tokyo metropolitan area and the emergence of rural "endangered municipalities" due to outmigration (Masuda 2014). Young people mainly drive this kind of migration. So far, there have been three large waves of rural outmigration. The first and the second wave occurred as pull-effects of youth employment opportunities in the metropolitan areas during economic growth periods, while the third wave in the new millennium is due to push-effects of a deteriorating rural economy (Masuda 2014: 17–22). Assuming that the current trend continues, about half of the nation's 1,800 municipalities will experience a drop of 50 percent in the number of female residents of childbearing age (20–39) by 2040. This makes it impossible for those municipalities to stop the population decline, and they are facing collapse as a consequence. While the share of the young in rural areas will continue to decline, the total fertility rate (henceforth TFR) of the metropolitan area remains at a low level. The TFR for Tokyo stood at 1.15 in 2014, the lowest rate in Japan. For a number of reasons, the metropolitan area is

The political economy of the declining birthrate   19

not an ideal environment for marriage and childrearing. Non-regular employment is increasing there, too. Social aging due to the declining birthrate requires huge costs of supporting the elderly, and these financial resources are then lacking for childrearing support. All in all, it seems unlikely to realize a significant improvement of the TFR in the future. The generation gap is set to grow further.

The problems sketched out above deeply affect the lives of young Japanese. These problems are caused by a number of factors that include the structure of social institutions, policy failures, and the slowing or absence of economic growth. Measures to address these problems require a number of broad and sweeping reforms.

Enhancing the birthrate is inevitable to stop the population decline, and this in turn is a key factor for both reviving the economy and for maintaining the sustainability of the social security system. In order to deal with the declining birthrate, the government has to simultaneously address two problems. It needs to secure the labor force, and it needs to ensure the reproduction of the population. Women are the key for both issues. Only if an environment is established that better enables the balance between work and family, similar to that existing in developed countries with relatively high birthrates, both the expansion of the female labor participation (henceforth, FLP) and the increase of the birthrate can be expected. Towards this end, the government needs to realize gender equality, remove sexual discrimination embedded in social systems and employment practices, revise social security systems that are disproportionally inclined to pensions and medical care, and provide better childrearing support. This requires that the government abandon its stance of familism, i.e., an ideology that emphasizes the importance of the spirit of self-help and cooperation among families and local communities. A much stronger socialization of childrearing is needed instead.

Japan is not alone to face such problems. Declining birthrates became a common phenomenon across many European countries during their transformations into post-industrial societies. In order to deal with the challenges arising from the emergence of "new social risks" and changes in values, national policymakers in western Europe have developed "new social policies" in the field of active labor market policies, childcare and paid parental leave in the last two decades. In doing so, they shifted the family model centering on a male breadwinner towards a dual-earner model (Bonoli 2012: 12). The reason why some western European countries were able to recover birthrates is that these policies enhance the family-work balance, and that they have thereby mitigated the negative effect of FLP on birthrates. Such types of policies remain scarce in Japan, but the expansion of new social policies can provide for a good opportunity for welfare policies in Japan, too.

The effects of neoliberal reforms

In the 1980s, neoliberalism emerged in many economically advanced countries in order to recover from the financial crisis that had followed the oil shock. Efforts of deregulation and welfare retrenchment became important policy objectives. In

20 *Yuiko Imamura*

Japan, administrative and tax reforms were conducted under the Nakasone government following the slogan of "financial reconstruction without tax increase". This policy led to growing financial deficits. At the time, the view spread among the urban middle-class that economic regulations and the tax system excessively privileged the low-productivity sector and rural residents (Miyamoto 2008: 135). Therefore, the government conducted an administrative reform aiming at "small government" in order to cater to urban voters. This reform was caused by the need of the LDP to reach out for urban voters in order to compensate the decline in support from traditional constituencies that were shrinking as an effect of urbanization and economic transformations (Miyamoto 2008: 96).

This system came to end when a non-LDP coalition government was formed in 1993. However, the LDP returned to power already in the following year of 1994, and the Japan Socialist Party (JSP) who had secured power in 1993 disappeared altogether in 1996. In its place, the Democratic Party of Japan (DPJ) took over the JSP's constituencies and emerged as the largest opposition party. At the start, the LDP was reluctant to conduct neoliberal reforms, because the opposition parties had originally advocated them.[3] However, the fact that businesses and voters approved of neoliberal reforms turned the LDP into a "party of reform" (Matoba 2012: 164), and in the 2000s the Koizumi government pursued drastic neoliberal reforms. The Diet became dominated by neoliberal ideologies, and this led to fierce competition in reform efforts between the LDP and the DPJ (Matoba 2012: 169). The Koizumi government claimed that structural reforms would increase the competitiveness of large firms in high-productivity sectors, and that this would lead to an overall improvement of living standards in Japan (Miyamoto 2008: 168). The government deregulated the labor market and increased the flexibility of employment in order to respond to the intensification of global economic competition. The Japanese-style management established in the period of high economic growth was dismantled. That is to say, the LDP sought to expand its support among urban voters and employees of large companies at the expense of traditional constituencies such as farmers, the self-employed and rural residents. Although these neoliberal reforms were to some extent effective in fostering economic growth, the benefits did not affect all social strata equally, resulting in a widening income gap and in an increasing spread of poverty (Miyamoto 2008: 142). This notwithstanding, the reforms did not result in a setback for the LDP. After all, voters were not given alternative choices. There were only two major parties, the LDP and the DPJ, and both were led by neoliberal reformers. When the negative aspects of the reforms became more prominent, the DPJ presented a welfare-centered "manifesto" and took control of the government after the 2009 general election. However, DPJ dominance only lasted for three years. In 2012, the LDP was back in the government, and it has been pursuing a policy of economic growth by sticking to neoliberal ideology ever since.

Addressing the declining birthrate

The problem of the declining birthrate started to receive attention on the political agenda after the so-called "1.57 shock" of 1990.[4] In order to respond to this

The political economy of the declining birthrate   21

problem, a partial expansion of welfare, i.e., new social policies were promoted. Under the Hashimoto government, it was now claimed that breaking away from the social system based on the male breadwinner model and promoting a gender-equal society was a key issue for addressing the problem (Osawa 2007). In 1994, the so-called "Angel Plan" was devised, aiming at an increase in the daycare quota and the diversification of daycare services. A "New Angel Plan" was formulated in 1999. It included issues related to daycare services but also approaches to employment, maternal and child health, consultation and education. Daycare services were further enhanced by implementing an "anti-waiting-lists for new entrants strategy" in 2001, as a means to tackle the problem of long waiting lists for daycare centers, especially in metropolitan areas. The "Declining Birthrate Countermeasure Plus One" plan was created in 2002 in order to expand the range of measures, including a "review of work patterns" and "childrearing support by the local communities". In 2003, the "Declining Birthrate Society Countermeasures Basic Act" and the "Next Generation Nurturing Support Measures Promotion Act" were implemented. These plans required companies and local governments to formulate an action plan to support a better balance of work and childcare. The "Childcare Leave Law" was introduced in 1991. This law and the employment insurance law have been revised several times since then. Parents can take a maximum leave of one and a half years with a benefit of 67 percent of their previous salary for the first 180 days since 2014. Needless to say, the repeated formulation and implementation of such plans highlight the fact that none of them was successful in reversing the trend of low birthrates.

Countermeasures against the declining birthrate started from the increase of daycare services and focused on support for better balancing work and childcare. As a result, these measures mainly benefit the regular full-time female employees with preschool children, especially those working in large farms (Hagiwara 2006; Matsuda 2013). On the other hand, financial support has not sufficiently been provided due to fiscal shortages. As an effect, the feeling that childrearing imposes a heavy economic burden has not been mitigated. Moreover, the youth employment situation has not improved. The present situation is considered an obstacle for marriage and childbirth. The Japanese government has been taking countermeasures against the declining birthrate for more than 20 years now, and the birthrate has become an important issue on the political agenda, but the birthrate of 1.42 in 2014 remains below that of the time when these policy efforts started. The number of childbirths continues to decrease year by year. This indicates that the social environment to have children has not yet improved.

In Japan, a limited daycare service is provided selectively, because the "small welfare state" based on the ideology of familism remains in place. New policies aimed at the realization of a gender-equal society were supposed to support reforms for a universal welfare system and the socialization of childrearing (Miyamoto 2008: 158), but severe pressures caused by financial austerity have made it politically difficult to expand budgets for promoting a socialization of childrearing. Rather, strategies of privatization and deregulation were employed in order to expand daycare service at low cost.

22   *Yuiko Imamura*

The "Declining Birthrate Society Countermeasures Basic Act" of 2003 confirmed the importance of the family. The LDP had fiercely criticized the socialization of childcare when the DPJ proposed it, because principles of "self-help" and "family" are central in its party platform (LDP 2011). Their emphasis on family rests upon the fact that the LDP appeals to traditional values. Secondly, the LDP seeks to avoid expensive daycare services due to Japan's fiscal crisis.[5] Despite efforts to increase daycare capacities, there still remain more than two million children on the waiting lists for daycare centers. Needless to say, this constitutes a major obstacle to the employment of the mothers of these children. Although the FLP has been increasing and now 56 percent of women are employed as non-regular part-time workers (MHLW 2016: 15–16), the wage gap between regular and part-time workers has not been reduced over the past 25 years. The wage-per-hour of part-time workers remains at 70 percent of the wages of regular workers. What is more, this gap grows with increasing age. This rate stands at 82 percent for part-time workers aged 20–24, but declines to 63 percent among part-timers aged 45–49 (MHLW 2015: 7–8). Unlike the case of regular workers, it is difficult for non-regular workers to access subsidized daycare services and childcare leave, since the systems are set up for regular full-time workers. As a result, about 60 percent of mothers leave their job after childbirth. This number underlines the lack of support for working mothers.

Since the implementation of policies addressing the declining birthrate is essential for the revival of the Japanese economy and the maintenance of social security systems, it is in the long run beneficial for all citizens. At the same time, the implementation of such policies clashes with the interests of LDP constituencies in the short run. Unsurprisingly, perhaps, many political actors seeking re-election tend to focus more on short-term political effects. As neoliberal reforms prioritize the interests of large enterprises and promote small government, the interests of young women tend to be brushed aside. While employers recognize the importance of making the best use of the female labor force already in order to combat labor shortages, there is also a strong motivation to retain the female work force as cheap and flexible labor. In order to create an environment that enables a balance between work and childcare, companies must bear the costs of providing various welfare services and review employment practices. Furthermore, male regular employees may be opposed to increases in the number of the female regular workforce, out of fear that women may threaten their position. In order to expand new welfare policies by the government, a cutback in existing programs or a tax increase is needed. Both options involve risks. Tax increases are unpopular. A study by Kabashima and Takenaka (1996) revealed that most Japanese had inconsistent views. They support, at the same time, small government and substantial social welfare. They think that providing welfare is important (old-age pensions, medical care for those who cannot work, etc.), but that it is not appropriate to rely on public welfare when people can work (Kabashima and Takenaka 1996: 256). Unlike the welfare for older generations, there exists little support for an expansion of welfare addressing the needs of the young generation.

The LDP and silver democracy

Elderly voters show higher support for the LDP than the young. What is more, the declining birthrate and the social aging of the population have increased the share of the elderly in the electorate. This strengthens the trend of the so-called "silver democracy", i.e., the prioritization of the interest of the elderly. The elderly show higher political consciousness, higher voter turnout and stronger support for the LDP. The young show the opposite tendency. More specifically, only 14 percent of the young under the age of 30 were "highly interested" in elections, while 36 percent of them state to be "somewhat interested" (APFE 2013a: 22). Due to this low political activation (Figure 2.1), more than half of those in their 20s and 30s claim to have "no party to support" or to "don't know" any party that supports their interests (APFE 2013a: 27). Therefore, voter turnout of the young in their 20s for the 46th Lower House general election in 2012 was only about half the voter turnout for people in their 50s to 70s (Figure 2.1). Note also that there is a notable correlation between voter turnout and educational background among the young. 68 percent of Japanese in their 20s-30s with higher education casted a ballot, but only 43 percent of junior college graduates and people with a lower educational degree went to the polls (APFE 2013a: 29).

Figure 2.2 depicts the share of the vote by age group. It illustrates the reality of silver democracy in contemporary Japan. People aged 50 and over hold 62 percent of total votes and those aged 40 and older amount to 78 percent of the electorate. That is to say, the young generation will never win under majority rule. Even if the political consciousness and voter turnout increases among the young, it is

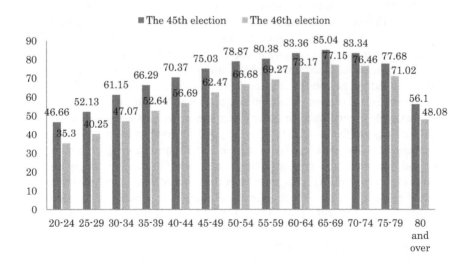

Figure 2.1 Voter turnout for the 45th Lower House general election in 2009 and the 46th Lower House general election in 2012

Source: APFE (2013a: 17)

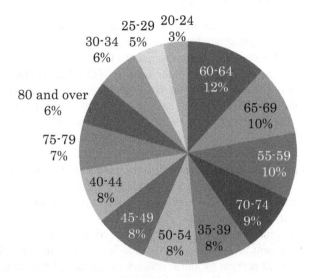

Figure 2.2 Proportion of the vote by age groups for the 46th Lower House general election in 2012
Source: APFE (2013a: 17); Statistics Bureau (2010b)

impossible to reverse the trend of silver democracy. Furthermore, the young are faced with the trend that the share of the young population is constantly decreasing. The revision of the public office election law in 2015 lowered the voting age from 20 to 18 years of age and this meant an increase of about 2.4 million young voters. However, even this reform did not change the fact that the young are dramatically outnumbered. In addition, these new young voters do not have high political consciousness and, therefore, constitute little pressure on policy makers. Almost by nature, politicians craft policies addressing the interests of the older generations, and at present nothing indicates a reversal of this trend.

A survey on voters' concerns shows that they choose issues closely related to their own stage in the life cycle (Table 2.1). All generations are highly interested in economic and tax policies. Those in their 20s-30s are also interested in "childcare and education" (38 percent) while voters over 60 show much less interest on this topic (19 percent). This means that the share of voters who are interested in child-related policy is altogether small. However, numerical strength does not necessarily correlate with political influence.[6] Even if the young are in a minority position, taking positive action could increase their presence and enable the young generation to have a stronger political impact. In order to improve childcare policy and to accelerate the measures combating the declining birthrate, the young would obviously need to be more active in claiming their requests. The problem is that they are not politically united.

The political economy of the declining birthrate 25

Table 2.1 Issues of concern by generation

	20s–30s		40s–50s		60s and over	
1	Economic measures	55.7	Economic measures	70.5	Economic measures	59.5
2	Tax increase	39.8	Tax increase	39.9	Pension	57.9
3	Childrearing/ education	38.1	Pension	38.9	Healthcare/ welfare	56.9
4	Recovery from the earthquake	31.3	Recovery from the earthquake	37.5	Tax increase	37.6
5	Employment	28.5	Employment	35.1	New clear power/ natural resources	37.4
6	Healthcare/ welfare	25.6	Healthcare/ welfare	33.4	Recovery from the earthquake	36.8
7	Pension	25.2	New clear power/ natural resources	31.5	Diplomacy/ defence	32.9
8	New clear power/ natural resources	25.2	Childrearing/ education	27.9	Employment	26.1
9	Diplomacy/ defence	20.7	Diplomacy/ defence	25.8	Participation for TPP	20
10	Participation for TPP	14.6	Participation for TPP	16.1	Childrearing/ education	18.7

Source: APFE (2013a: 56)

Women divided

"Women" do not constitute a unitary and monolithic social group. Therefore, the interests and the "needs of young Japanese women" do not constitute a well-defined cluster of issues either. There are socio-economic differences between women and between their political views. This part illustrates differences in the socio-economic status of women in order to show how their political interests vary.

In 2010, the rate of female labor participation (FLP) stood at 49 percent. It has been hovering around 50 percent since the 1950s. If those aged younger than 20 and older than 65 are excluded, then the FLP stands at about 70 percent. The number of young and middle-aged women in the labor market has been increasing. As an effect, the so-called "M-curve" shape of the FLP rate has become less pronounced. The first peak of FLP rate moved from those aged 20–24 to those between 25–29, while the bottom of it shifted from aged 30–34 to 35–39. This is the effect of the popularization of higher education,

26 *Yuiko Imamura*

an increase in the number of unmarried people, and an increase of those who are "delaying" marriage.

A fundamental change with regard to women is the increase of female graduates from college or university in the past 50 years. In 1970, only 3.8 percent of women graduated from "junior college or higher professional school" and 1.2 percent graduated from "college, university or graduate school". In 2010, these figures stood at 19.2 percent and 11.1 percent, respectively. The proportion of women who have completed tertiary education is highest (30.8 percent) in the age group of 25–29 (Statistics Bureau 2010a: 41, 2010b: 63).

The educational background has implications for the employment, the work career, and the lifestyles of women. Table 2.2, Figure 2.3 and Figure 2.4 indicate that the academic background is closely linked to the choice of industry and employment status. Female universities and college graduates tend to work in the field of "education and learning support" (20.7 percent), "medical, health care and welfare" (16.6 percent), or to engage in other professional, administrative and managerial work. Those having a lower formal education level are more likely to work in wholesales, retail trade, services, and manufacturing. The situation of academic background and industry of employment is very much the same for all age groups (Table 2.2). One noteworthy exception is the primary industrial sector where 80 percent of all female workers are aged 50 and over. This is of course

Table 2.2 Proportion of female employees aged 15 and over according to education degree and industry

	Primary or junior high school	*Senior high school or middle school (under the old system of education)*	*Junior college or higher professional school*	*College, university, or graduate school*
1	Services 28.69% (2.46%)	Wholesales and retail trade 23.5% (3.40%)	Medical, health care, and welfare 33.48% (7.79%)	Education, leaning support 20.7% (3.81%)
2	Manufacturing 17.7% (1.84%)	Services 21.44% (3.02%)	Wholesales and retail trade 16.76% (3.28%)	Medical, health care, and welfare 16.6% (5.24%)
3	Wholesales and retail trade 15.9% (1.73%)	Manufacturing 15.4% (2.28%)	Services 15.11% (3.24%)	Wholesales and retail trade 15.7% (5.31%)
4	Agriculture and forestry 13.9% (0.2%)	Medical, health care, and welfare 14.3% (1.83%)	Manufacturing 7.8% (1.15%)	Services 10.39% (3.42%)

Source: Statistics Bureau (2010b: 66–67, 2010c)

Figures in brackets show the proportion of female employees aged 15–29.

"Services" stands for the total proportion of "Accommodations, eating and drinking services", "Living-related and personal services and amusement services", "Compound services", and "Services, N.E.C."

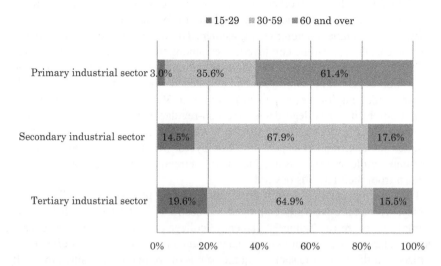

Figure 2.3 Proportion of working women according to industry and age
Source: Adapted from Statistics Bureau (2010c)

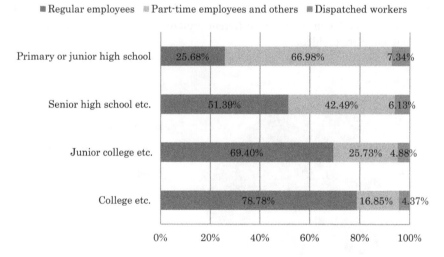

Figure 2.4 Proportion of female employees aged 15–29 according to education degree and employment status
Source: Adapted from Statistics Bureau (2010c)

due to the fact that this sector has dramatically shrunk since 1945. The percentage of women engaging in the secondary sector (15.2 percent) is comparatively small and much lower than that of male workers (32.6 percent). This leaves 80.9 percent of women working in the tertiary sector.

87 percent of female workers are employees today. The proportion of regular employment rises in concert with the level of formal education. This trend is particularly prominent among young women. There are more regular employees (56 percent) than part-time employees even among those who have not studied at university or college (Figure 2.5). However, within the total female workforce, the proportion of part-time employees and dispatched workers (54 percent) exceeds that of regular employees (45 percent). Moreover, 30 percent of female graduates with a university or college degree are non-regular employees. This number is influenced by the fact that many women leave work due to childrearing and later re-enter the labor market as part-time employees. Accordingly, the proportion of part-time employees rises as age increases – a trend that is most pronounced for women from their late 30s onwards.

This data hints at a number of important issues for the topic under discussion. Firstly, women are basically employed as cheap labor. The fact that half of the employed women (including 30 percent of college and university graduates) are non-regular employees implies that female human resources are not effectively utilized. Furthermore, the socioeconomic status of women is diversified today. It was quite uniform in the post-war period as most women worked in the agricultural sector after graduating from junior high school, got married and had children in their 20s. Familism was the basic norm then. Today, women with these life-courses and values coexist with younger women who have a different life trajectory and who also no longer subscribe to the ideology of familism. Women in contemporary Japan have very different preferences. This creates a situation where women are divided.

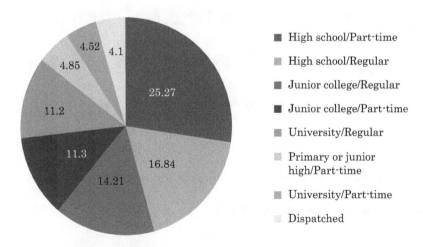

Figure 2.5 Proportion of female employees aged 15 and over according to education degree and employment status

Source: Adapted from Statistics Bureau (2010c)

In order to devise effective measures against the declining birthrate, it is important to implement policies in the field of welfare and employment. It is also important to link these two fields to a coherent concept. Until now, however, the government has not formulated such a comprehensive vision. Given the increase of women with higher education, the rise in FLP rate no longer simply implies an increase in the labor force, but also the acquisition of highly skilled labor. Despite the increase in FLP among young and middle-aged women, female empowerment has not progressed. Gender equality has not been achieved, neither at the workplace nor in the family. Family care responsibility still largely rests solely on women. The LDP has not succeeded to develop a new growth model that involves the activation of women. The prioritization of business interests and the unequal distribution of voters across age cohorts are obstacles that block policies that would pave the way for such changes.

Outlook

This study has discussed how the interests of the young generation are reflected in Japan's political economy in order to analyze declining birthrates. We saw how the LDP established a one-party dominance over a long period of time. It succeeded in doing so by gaining broad support from various social groups. However, with the end of economic growth and the transformation into a post-industrial society, the familial welfare state and the growth model created under LDP rule have become dysfunctional. This mismatch results in declining birthrates. Together with the subsequent aging and shrinking of the population, the declining birthrate threatens economic growth and the sustainability of numerous socio-economic institutions. This in turn results in a widening gap between generations, and in an ever-increasing burden on the young. In order to minimize these demographic constraints and in order to restore economic vitality, female empowerment is pivotal. As it stands, women are not used as skilled human resources despite their high education. It is possible to increase the FLP and the birthrate by creating an environment that allows improving the balance between work and family. However, the LDP has failed to implement effective welfare and economic policies based on a consistent vision towards this end. One major cause for this is that the LDP has not placed political importance on the young for two reasons. Firstly, the young are not the main support basis of the party and, secondly, older voters outnumber them. Unsurprisingly, given these circumstances, many young people show little political interest. This reinforces the trend that most politicians treat the specific interests of the young generation rather lightly.

This chapter has also shown that young women are not politically united in their political objectives due to their different socio-economic background. This notwithstanding, it is important for the government to immediately tackle the declining birthrate because the effects will take a long time to realize. Since political actors tend to not have such long time horizons in their political agenda, it is important for the young generation to participate more actively in politics and to increase their presence there.

30 *Yuiko Imamura*

Let me emphasize here that this study does not seek to raise conflicts. It aims to point out at the necessity of a comprehensive and long-term perspective. Increasing attention on the young generation and their political participation contribute to improve the welfare for all. Crafting and implementing economic policies that generate greater opportunities for women at work while allowing them to balance work and family would result in a strong economy and restore a sustainable society. Sidestepping these issues is not possible, and there is a real urgency to act.

Notes

1 These are "situations in which individuals experience welfare losses and which have arisen as a result of the socio-economic transformations [. . .] [and] post-industrialisation" (Bonoli 2013: 15–16). More specifically, these situations include reconciling work and family life, single parenthood, having a frail relative, possessing low or obsolete skills, and insufficient social security coverage (Bonoli 2013: 16–17).

2 The government planned to enforce a tax hike in October 2015 in order to improve the fiscal situation. However, the tax hike was postponed until October 2019 in order to avoid slipping into an economic recession. In the meantime, the government has to borrow more money to cover fiscal shortages.

3 Neoliberal reform was pursued by the Japan New Party group and *Shinseitō* (Japan Renewal Party) led by Ozawa Ichiro in a non-LDP government.

4 In 1990, the figure of the total fertility rate of 1,57 for 1989 was released by the government. It marked the lowest rate in history and shocked the nation as the rate was even lower than in 1966, the inauspicious year of *hinoe uma* (fire horse) when many people refrained from having a baby.

5 The cost of daycare paid by the public for an infant younger than 1 year is the highest (168,000 yen per month); it is higher than the cost of either a 1–2-year-old (80,000 yen) or an over-3-year-old (35,000 yen).

6 For example, in western countries, governments attempted neoliberal reforms based on social coalitions centred on the skilled middle-class while excluding the working-class (Amable and Palombarini 2014).

References

Amable, Bruno and Stefano Palombarini (2014) The Bloc Bourgeois in France and Italy. In: *Economic Crises and Policy Regimes*. Hideko Magara (ed.), 177–216. Cheltenham: Edward Elgar Publishing.

APFE = Association For Promoting Fair Elections (2013a) *The Survey on Attitude Toward the 46th Lower House General Election*. Online available at: www.akaruisenkyo.or.jp/wp/wp-content/uploads/2013/06/070seihon1.pdf (accessed 19 May 2017).

Bonoli, Giuliano (2013) *The Origins of Active Social Policy*. Oxford: Oxford University Press.Bonoli, Giuliano and David Natali (2012) The Politics of the New Welfare States: Analysing Reforms in Western Europe. In: *The Politics of the New Welfare State*. Giuliano Bonoli and David Natali (eds.), 3–17. Oxford: Oxford University Press.

Hagiwara, Kumiko (2006) *Meisō suru ko-sodate shien* [Straying Childrearing Support]. Tokyo: Taro Jiro-sha Editus.

Kabashima, Ikuo and Yoshihiko Takenaka (1996) *Gendai nihonjin no ideorogi* [Contemporary Japanese Ideology]. Tokyo: University of Tokyo Press.

Kato, Hisakazu (2011) *Sedaikan kakusa* [Generation Gap]. Tokyo: Chikuma Shinsho.

LDP (2011) *Revival of Japan*. Online available at: https://www.jimin.jp/news/policy/130216.html (accessed 24 September 2016).

Masuda, Hiroya (ed.) (2014) *Chihō shōmetsu* [Endangered Municipalities]. Tokyo: Chūō Kōron Shinsha.

Matoba, Toshihiro (2012) *Sengo nihon seitō seijishi-ron* [Post-War Partisan Politics in Japan]. Kyoto: Minerva.

Matsuda, Shigeki (2013) *Shoshika-ron* [The Study on Declining Birthrate]. Tokyo: Keiso Shobō.

MHLW = Ministry of Health, Labour and Welfare (2015) *Tanjikan rōdōsha taisaku kihonhō hōshin (an) – deta-shū sankō shiryō* [Basic Policy on Measures for Part-Time Workers (Plan). Data Collection Reference Materials]. Online available at: www.mhlw.go.jp/stf/shingi2/0000074362.html (accessed 15 May 2017).

───── (2016) *Heisei 27-nenban hataraku josei no jitsujō* [Actual Situation of Working Women in 2015]. Online available at: www.mhlw.go.jp/bunya/koyoukintou/josei-jitsujo/15.html (accessed 15 May 2017).

Miyamoto, Taro (2008) *Fukushi seiji* [Welfare Politics]. Tokyo: Yuhikaku Publishing.

Nikkei Shinbun (2010) Tax, Pension . . . Trial Calculation of Life-Time Total Balance: Shrinking Benefit for Young Generation, Excess Burden 1.8 Times During the Past 5 Years. *Nikkei Shinbun* (6 August).

NIPSSR = National Institute of Population and Social Security Research (2012) *Population Projection in Japan*. Online available at: www.ipss.go.jp/syoushika/tohkei/new est04/sh2401top.html (accessed 19 May 2017).

Osawa, Mari (2007) *Gendai nihon no seikatsu hoshō shisutemu* [Contemporary Japanese Livelihood Protection System]. Tokyo: Iwanami Shoten.

Statistics Bureau, Ministry of Internal Affairs and Communication Japan (2010a) *Population and Households of Japan 2010*. Online available at: www.stat.go.jp/english/data/kokusei/2010/poj/mokuji.htm (accessed 19 May 2017).

───── (2010b) *Kokusei chōsa kaisetsu shirizu (no.2) – wagakuni jinkō/setai no gaikan* [National Census Analytical Series no. 2: Overview of Population and Households of Japan]. Online available at: www.stat.go.jp/data/kokusei/2010/wagakuni.htm (accessed 19 May 2017).

───── (2010c) *Heisei 22-nen kokusei chōsa – kihon shukei* [National Census 2010 Survey Result]. Online available at: www.stat.go.jp/data/kokusei/2010/ (accessed 13 May 2017).

3 From youth to non-adulthood in Japan

The role of education

Christian Galan

Introduction

Japan's current young generation, born between the mid-1980s and the late 1990s, is characterized by two main education-related phenomena. The first, which also applied to previous generations, concerns the school system they passed through, which from the end of the 1950s had been designed to be "cut off from the real world" (Galan 2010). In other words, this system intentionally placed school outside of society, away from its failings and disorderliness, but also untouched by its developments. This supervised and controlled school system felt safe and appeared to prepare students for an idealized Japanese society that was itself safe and harmonious – it was reassuring because, among other things, it was uniform, monolingual and "monoethnic" (Galan 2010). Of course, this idealized society never existed, but the framework continued to function until the end of the 1980s, at which point children and young people increasingly began to develop a certain number of strategies for refusing to enter the "real world" (Galan 2014).

Over the decades, these strategies – *futōkō* (school non-attendance), *hikikomori* (social withdrawal), *furitā* (engaging in temporary or part-time work by choice), and so on – have appeared to be the only means Japanese teenagers and young adults have of demonstrating their refusal to play by the rules regarding a world or future that was not as adults had promised or led them to expect, or which they quite simply rejected. In this sense, as I have written elsewhere (Galan 2014), the *hikikomori* phenomenon can also be seen as a less radical way – compared to suicide or extreme violence – for young people to resolve their struggle to "go out" into the world by showing their inability to accomplish this very process.

The second phenomenon to affect the young generation is the evolution of Japan's educational reality following the country's demographic decline and the introduction of neoliberal reforms, two processes that began in the late 1990s and continue to this day. Both have profoundly changed the nature, goals and philosophy underpinning the Japanese education system. The incremental reforms adopted by the government were not immediately apparent to the population, yet they have disorientated both youths and parents, ultimately eroding their faith in the education system. This situation has been exacerbated by the previously mentioned demographic decline and the recession experienced by Japan for more than two decades now.

From youth to non-adulthood in Japan   33

The consequence for Japan has been that the current young generation has discovered an unprecedented educational context, one for which it was poorly prepared and which – as I will argue here – appears to be both a source of generation-making mechanisms and an obstacle to entering adulthood. I will present four of these mechanisms over the following pages.

The era of open access to higher education

The first of these mechanisms could be described as the advent of the era of open access to university (*daigaku zennyū jidai*). For the first time in several decades, and perhaps in the entire history of modern Japan since the Meiji period, the generation born from the mid-1980s onwards does not have to fight or invest any particular effort in order to enroll at university. Of course, "enrolling at university" can refer to a number of different situations, and I will return to this point later. This generation is the first to experience the open-access era, meaning the era in which university places outnumber university applicants. This came as a surprise to young people.

Japan's population of 18-year-olds, which corresponds to the final year of secondary school and the entry into tertiary education, has been in steady decline since the early 1990s. In concrete terms, the number of 18-year-olds shrunk by almost half over a 20-year period, falling from approximately 2.1 million in 1992 to 1.2 million in 2014.[1] Paradoxically, until 2009–2010 this decline was not accompanied by a drop in the number of students entering university, but by an increase. Between 1992 and 2014, the number of Japanese students at university (*daigaku*) jumped from roughly 540,000 to 610,000.

There are two explanations for this. First, the number of university places increased through the creation of new institutions, a result of the newly liberalized and simplified process for creating private universities.[2] From 523 universities in Japan in 1992, there are now (in 2015) 779 institutions, including 86 national, 89 public and 604 private (MEXT 2015a). Furthermore, with the majority of universities requiring ever-greater numbers of students to break even (a problem that is particularly acute at private universities, where enrolment fees are the only financial resource for virtually all institutions), there has been an increase in the number of places on offer. At four-year universities[3] the number of places rose from approximately 473,000 in 1992 to 584,000 in 2013. Accordingly, whereas in 1966, for example, there were 2.63 candidates competing for each university place and 2.15 candidates in 1976, this proportion dropped to less than two in 1992 (1.94 to be exact), and to little more than one (1.16) in 2013 (MEXT 2013a).

The second explanation I will examine in greater detail further on is that access to university has become easier due to the competition between universities to attract the number of students they require to break even or to make a profit.

This twofold phenomenon (a reduction in the number of under-18-year-olds and increase in the number of students) has led quite logically to an increase in the proportion of a given age group entering university, particularly if we widen the category to include any type of higher education establishment. This proportion,

34   *Christian Galan*

which has risen consistently since the late 1980s, now stands at 56.7 percent for universities and junior colleges, and 80 percent if we include all higher education institutions (universities, junior colleges and professional training colleges, *senmon gakkō*). To rephrase, in 2014, 80 percent of 18-year-olds entered higher education, of which 56.7 percent joined a university (51.5 percent at four-year institutions and 5.2 percent at junior colleges).

Another instructive figure is the proportion of applicants being accepted at universities and junior colleges. This figure rose from approximately 65 percent in 1992 to 93 percent in 2014. In other words, less than 10 percent of those wishing to go to university now fail the application process (Maita 2014). This figure illustrates the extent to which Japan's higher education system has reached saturation. Nonetheless, experts believe that following a short period of respite caused by a stabilization in the number of 18-year-olds since 2010 (which stands at approximately 1.2 million people), the percentage of applicants failing to gain entry will diminish even further as of 2018–2019, when the population of 18-year-olds begins to shrink dramatically (Cabinet Office, Government of Japan 2014), reaching 1.06 million in 2024 and dropping below the one million mark in 2031. The continued fall in the number of 18-year-olds will cause a proportional contraction in the number of students, and thus in the number of universities.

In fact, this problem of a resumed decline in Japan's youth population – and thus in the pool of potential university applicants – in 2018 is dubbed *nisenjūhachi-nen mondai* ("2018 problem") by the university exam industry, for whom the phenomenon will have a disastrous impact on revenue, even with acceptance rates nearing 100 percent. Universities will also inevitably be forced to close. The financial consequences for universities and, more widely, for Japan's higher education sector, will be dramatic. However, that is not the focus of this chapter. The main point, and one that I believe constitutes a generation-making mechanism, is that any young Japanese person wanting to go to university can now do so, providing, as we shall see later, that he or she has the financial means. This universal access to university education has other consequences that are themselves generation-making and will be examined in the following section.

A two-tier university system

The second mechanism I wish to describe, which results from the aforementioned era of open access, is that the generation born from the mid-1980s onwards can and does enroll at university without passing the general admissions exam.

This is one of the main consequences of Japan's declining population, which affects both the way higher education institutions are run and the quality of the courses they offer. As we have already seen, Japanese universities – in particular private ones – have been engaged in fierce competition to attract the maximum number of "clients" (i.e., students) since the early 1990s. The dwindling number of potential candidates has thus caused these institutions to relax their entrance requirements. Although the aim is still to select the best candidates possible, universities cannot afford for student numbers to drop below what is necessary to

From youth to non-adulthood in Japan 35

achieve financial viability. Over the past 20 years, university entrance requirements have thus become significantly more diverse and in the process have changed their nature and function, notably by ceasing to act as a social filter (in part at least, as we will see later).

Until recently, the main method of enrolling at university was via the general admissions exam (*ippan nyūshi*). This was based on the common first-stage examination (*kyōtsū ichiji*), introduced in 1979 and renamed the National Center Test for University Admissions (*daigaku nyūshi sentā shiken*) in 1990, and on a second exam specific to the university in question. It was this type of admission procedure that was described as highly competitive, rigidly inflexible, overly dependent on a knowledge-centered exam and standardized test scores, and criticized for causing the exam hell (*shiken jigoku*) experienced by applicants.

There are now other ways of enrolling at university, and while my aim is not to analyze them in detail, a brief description is necessary if we are to understand in what way they are generation-making and how they differ from those available to previous generations. Among these alternative procedures, the main two I will cover here are known as *suisen nyūshi* ("admission by recommendation") and *AO nyūshi* ("selection by the admissions office").

With *suisen nyūshi*, secondary schools are supposed to recommend students to affiliated universities. This recommendation is then examined via an application package submitted by the candidate and perhaps supplemented by a written test, oral exam, essay or interview. It is completely unconnected to the general admissions exam (*ippan nyūshi*) and provides an alternative to this route. Although this recruitment method has always existed in Japan, few people used it in the past because it was not the standard means of entering university and thus had a negative image. Many excellent students who would have been eligible to benefit from this procedure chose instead to sit the exam for reasons of prestige. This is no longer the case today and *suisen nyūshi* is now one of the main routes by which young Japanese enroll at university, as we will see later.

In contrast, *AO nyūshi* consists of a simple examination of the candidate's application by the admissions office and may be accompanied by various individualized tests. Like *suisen nyūshi*, it is completely unconnected to the general admissions exam (*ippan nyūshi*). Candidates must submit a range of supporting documents that vary by university. These may include a personal statement describing the student's personal goals and originality as well as their motivations and reasons for applying to that particular institution. In the place of traditional written tests, this method of recruitment focuses on high school transcripts and interviews (the two most utilized methods), activity reports, competency tests, oral presentations, or essays. It is designed to gauge the personality and motivation of prospective students. Although it generally requires a letter from the student's high school and one or more letters from other "adults", in 2012, 8.5 percent of applicants who successfully enrolled via the *AO nyūshi* system (48,558) were recruited solely on the basis of their application file (MEXT 2013a).

This "selection" method relying on the admissions office was first introduced at Keiō University in 1990. In 2000, only three national universities had adopted it

36   *Christian Galan*

(Tōhoku, Tsukuba and Kyūshū), but by 2012 it was being employed at 47 national universities, 23 public, and 460 private! Officially introduced as a means of providing access to candidates with atypical profiles and seen as epitomizing the new recruitment procedures designed to escape the exam-focused selection methods that had dominated until then, the *AO nyūshi* system has nonetheless deviated from its original purpose. With the exception of the most prestigious universities, where it continues to fulfill its role of recruiting talented candidates with non-academic profiles, this selection method is now chosen not for the reasons that first led to its introduction (attracting new profiles, originality, creativity, etc.), but by default, i.e., as a means of achieving student quotas and compensating for the failures produced by the general admissions exam. Accordingly, it is seen by many today as a third-rate selection method that reflects (and reinforces) a real or imagined decline in academic standards. In reality, however, it indicated above all the vital need for universities to secure sufficient student numbers, leading them to recruit young people who previously would never have attended university because they did not have the required academic abilities.

To provide a concrete comparison, in 2000, 65.8 percent of students (389,851) were accepted at university via the general admissions exam, 31.7 percent (188,083) on recommendation and 1.4 percent (8,117) via *AO nyūshi* (with 1.7 percent entering via some other means) (MEXT 2013a). Fifteen years later, however, in 2015, only 56.2 percent of students (340,974) entered via the general admissions exam compared to 34.7 percent (211,005) on recommendation and 8.8 percent (53,485) via *AO nyūshi* (and 0.5 percent via other means) (MEXT 2015b, 2015c). This evolution becomes even more spectacular if we distinguish between national and public universities, on the one hand, and private institutions, on the other. Whereas in 2015, 85 percent (84,308) of students entered the former via exam, 12.1 percent (12,096) on recommendation and 2.7 percent (2,679) via *AO nyūshi*, only 49 percent (234,172) sat entrance tests at private universities, while 40.1 percent (191,548) were admitted on recommendation[4] and 10.5 percent (50,143) via *AO nyūshi* (MEXT 2015b, 2015c).

What this signifies is that in 2015 almost half of all successful candidates were accepted at university without sitting the general admissions test and that, while exams remain the main means of entering national and public institutions (accounting for 84.1 percent and 73.3 percent of admissions, respectively), this is no longer the case at private universities, since this method was chosen by less than half of all candidates (MEXT 2013a).

There is fierce debate in Japan over the future of the university entrance exam, and in fact, the current government has announced that it will introduce a new testing method in 2020. (I will not go into the details of these changes, as they do not change the point I wish to make here). The main consequence of this situation is that the entrance exam as we know it has becoming obsolete. It no longer fulfills the same role (for society and businesses), no longer serves the same purpose (for students and universities), nor is used by the same people. This fact alone is generation-making, but what is more – and this is the second point I would like to highlight – this change in the purpose, role, and end-user of the exam has

From youth to non-adulthood in Japan 37

created a dichotomy within the new generations, a clear division that is in itself generation-making.

Until recently in Japan, a person's alma mater was a key social criterion determining the rest of their lives in personal, interpersonal, and hierarchical matters. The fact that anyone wishing to attend university can now do so is in itself generation-making, but what is even more generation-making is that attending university no longer provides any measurable or quantifiable guarantee either of students' intellectual ability or of their personal and psychological qualities, such as their spirit of self-sacrifice or ability to work hard. In the *AO nyūshi* system, for example, there is no evaluation or comparison of candidates either against each other or against a pre-determined benchmark. In short, the scale or measuring tool which made it possible to rank individuals within a single generation, but which also linked them both to one another and to previous and future generations, has been shattered.

Of course, in doing so Japan has brought itself gradually into line with other industrialized countries, but the main subject here is not the nature of the university admissions system but rather the role it has played in Japanese society and in the coming-of-age process – a role it no longer fulfills. The general admissions exam was the keystone of Japan's *gakureki shakai* ("credentialist society" or "education-conscious society"). More than just a gauge of a person's education level or intellectual ability, it was also, and perhaps above all, a guarantee of their personality (strong, determined, capable of effort), of their capacity for work, and even of their ability to put ego aside and concentrate on the end goal. In short, it guaranteed what was seen as the peculiar (and outside Japan much mythicized) identity of the Japanese, or more precisely, of the type of employee sought out by Japanese companies large and small, with each one targeting a specific profile and/or set of abilities, but all of them certain of obtaining individuals who had successfully passed the same tests (in every sense) and been through the same filter. *Yontō goraku* – "sleep four hours, pass; sleep five hours, fail" – was seen as the key not only to successfully entering university but also to obtain the kind of individuals whom the Japanese employment market considered being the ideal workers.

For young Japanese, university entrance exams were the first (and maybe only) major challenge in their lives. This selection process created a hierarchy among young Japanese, separating those who had chosen to go to university from those who had abandoned the idea. The notion that university is an important rite of passage in the lives of Japanese youths and adults, almost like a trait of Japaneseness, is so ingrained in the national and international imagination that many people are surprised to discover that, until 1990, less than a quarter of young people (approximately 24.5 percent) went to university (*daigaku*), and just over half (approximately 53 percent) entered higher education in general (*daigaku, tanki daigaku* and *senmon gakkō*).[5] Until this period, the objective had been clear to both parents and children from an early age. The only way of improving one's chances of securing a good job and salary at a top company, and gaining the respect of one's own family and society as a whole, was to enter the best (i.e., the most prestigious) university possible, whatever the subject studied or the department chosen.

Successfully passing the entrance exam at a Japanese university – whether public or private – almost automatically determined an individual's future employment and salary. Ever since the 1960s, being accepted at the "best university possible" had been the ultimate goal of families in their education strategy, a kind of national obsession. Children were brought up with this in mind. Entering a university ranked 400th was better than entering one ranked 500th; entering one ranked 300th was better than one ranked 350th; entering one ranked 200th was better than one ranked 220th; and entering one ranked 150th was better than one 151st, and so on. The financial investment for families was huge and often came at a catastrophic price in terms of lost childhood years and stunted personal development, but at the end of it all, employment was guaranteed (usually for life) and, above all, the rules of the game (university entrance exams as the key to one's professional future) were known to everyone and accepted by the entire population as "egalitarian" and "fair".

Does this mean that all this has passed and that academic competition in Japan is dead? Clearly not, but today this situation no longer applies to all Japanese children and teenagers – only to those whose families have embarked on a highly elitist path – and it has narrowed to become focused on the most "prestigious universities". In fact, Japan has entered into a "two-tier university" system (see Figure 3.1). The process of selecting or ranking individuals, which duplicated the

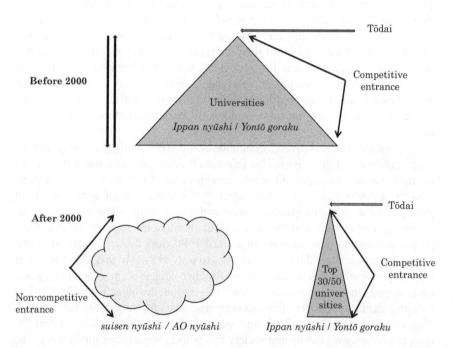

Figure 3.1 The dichotomization of Japan's university system

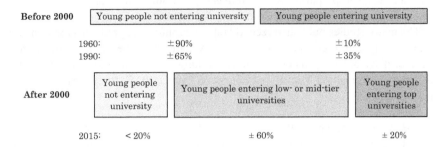

Figure 3.2 The evolution of "generational units" in terms of their educational paths

ranking of universities and previously applied to all students, now concerns only those who aim for and successfully enter a university in the top 30 or top 50.

In the past, it was essentially possible to divide each generation into two groups between those who went to university (or to any higher education institution) and those who did not, the ratio being one in ten in the 1960s and two or three in ten in the 1990s. Today the 1960s ratio has been inverted, with eight in ten people continuing on to higher education. In reality, however, this figure of eight hides another ratio of two in eight, consisting of those who went to a prestigious institution and those who simply went to "other kinds" of university (see Figure 3.2).

For the young generation born between the mid-1980s and the late 1990s, which experienced this change and were taken by surprise, the impact was severe. It generated stress, disappointment and a general loss of reference points. Reality suddenly bore no relation to what their parents and family had described to them and trained them for since childhood. For the first time since the 1960s, the "initial contract" or project on which their schooling had been predicated collapsed, not for all of them but for the majority.

Responsibility for their own careers

The third mechanism I would like to present here results from those previously described and from the financial crisis that has now weighed on Japan for more than 20 years. One of the consequences of this financial crisis is that, for the first time in Japan, a university degree no longer automatically guarantees access to a secure and well-salaried professional life. The bursting of the financial bubble in the early 1990s and the ensuing recession, the loss of social reference points, the rise in unemployment, the declining job security, and so on, have all profoundly changed Japanese society and its professional world, transforming the very essence of the country's education system. Businesses are recruiting fewer workers, salaries have fallen and long-term guarantees have become less certain. The relationship between families and universities or, more widely, the entire education system, has thus degenerated into a breakdown of trust. Rapidly summarized, this situation is essentially linked to a growing doubt on behalf of those concerned as to the necessity of making the sacrifices implicit – for both children

40   *Christian Galan*

and families – in preparing for the university entrance exam, since passing this test no longer provides any guarantees for the future.

The many studies published recently on the evolution of graduate employment rates merely reinforce the concerns held by parents of the young generations. Indeed, if we analyze this evolution over a long period using the statistics published by the Japanese Ministry of Education (Maita 2015), three clearly distinct periods emerge:

- Between 1955 and 1995, graduate employment rates stood at around 80%. If we include the number of students continuing on to postgraduate study (*daigakuin*), we obtain a rate of almost 90–95% of students being successfully "placed" at the end of a four-year university course; in 1965, for example, 83.4% of the 162,349 new graduates found employment immediately after leaving university, with 4.9% continuing on to postgraduate study.
- Between 1995 and 2005 the graduate employment rate fell regularly to almost 55%; this percentage, which was, for example, still at 81% in 1990 out of 400,103 new graduates (6.8% of whom continued with their studies), dropped in 2001 to 57.3% out of 545,512 new graduates (with 10.8% continuing on to postgraduate studies) (MEXT 2008).
- Since 2005, graduate employment rates have regularly improved to reach almost 70% once again (MEXT 2008). However, this is mainly for structural reasons linked to Japan's declining population and the shortage of labor. And employment conditions are radically different to those seen prior to 1995, involving jobs that are essentially temporary, insecure and less well-paid. Turnover rates on first employment have also risen significantly to reach around 30% of young men and 46% of young women in 2014 (Nakajima 2014).[6]

Of course, in Japan as elsewhere, having a university degree ensures better job prospects than not having one, but today no longer to the same extent as for previous generations. Any "competition" for university places now concerns only those students whose families are keen to set their children on an elite path by having them enter a prestigious university. The situation in Japan may soon resemble the French dichotomy of universities versus *grandes écoles*, which in Japan would signify a division between low- and mid-ranked universities, on one side, and those ranked in the top 30 or top 50, on the other.

The structure of Japan's labor market, which makes entering the world of work a more uncertain endeavor, only encourages such a change. The following analysis was taken from an OECD report published in 2009 (Newby/OECD 2009: 65–66, emphasis added by CG):

> Japanese labour markets in general – and the graduate labour market in particular – are *beginning to change. These changes do not appear to be ephemeral, but rather part of a wider and more enduring change in labour practices in Japan, in which "corporations have come to put less emphasis*

From youth to non-adulthood in Japan 41

on long-term employment, and [. . .] individuals are [increasingly] respon-
sible for establishing their own careers."

(MEXT 2006, paragraph 58)

The report then goes on to identify the following major changes with regard to
so-called "irregular workers" (Newby/OECD 2009: 65–66):

Firms have increasingly relied upon these workers both to reduce personnel
costs [. . .] and to enhance the specialized skills available to them [. . .]. A rising share of tertiary graduates begins their careers in temporary, rather than
permanent employment [. . .].

One reason for this change was the growth of so-called "dispatched workers" – workers under contract to a dispatching agency who are entrusted with
specific duties by the companies to which they are assigned. [. . .] This category of workers grew from 144 000 in 1986 to 2.13 million in 2002, among
whom graduates now constitute about 46% of workers.

The problem here is that "individuals [now being] responsible for their own
careers" was not at all the initial objective of the education strategies employed by
parents or by students embarking in good faith on the path of academic competition. And nothing had prepared young people for this reality. This situation has led
Japanese parents and their children to question the pertinence of their education-
related decisions by asking: What is the point? Is it worth it in terms of families' financial investment, children's mental health, and lost childhoods? In fact,
it seems likely that for some young Japanese people, the answer is clearly "no",
particularly if we consider the constantly rising dropout rates of recent years. And
the fact that many more students drop out at private universities than at national
and public ones confirms this hypothesis.

Although the dropout rate at Japanese universities remains one of the lowest of
the OECD countries (Ishiguro 2012), it is rising constantly and is now estimated
to be around 8.1 percent at the end of four-year university courses. A survey
conducted by MEXT (2014a) estimated the number of dropouts to be 79,311, or
2.65 percent of 2,991,573 students (10,467 at national universities, 2,373 at public
universities, 65,066 at private universities, and 1,405 at technology colleges, *sen-*
mon gakkō). For comparison, in 2007 the dropout rate stood at 2.41 percent. The
reasons given by students were as follows: poor academic performance 14.5 percent, maladjustment to student life 4.4 percent, joining the labor market 13.4 percent, transferring to another university 15.4 percent, going abroad 0.7 percent,
death, health problems or physical or mental fatigue 5.8 percent, financial difficulties 20.4 percent, and other reasons 25.3 percent.

The same survey also estimated the number of *kyūgakusha* ("temporarily
absent students" who have not dropped out but are not attending classes) to be
67,654, which represents 2.3 percent of 2,991,573 students (20,491 at national
universities, 3,897 at public universities, 42,798 at private universities and 468 at
technology colleges). This rate was 1.7 percent in 2007. The reasons advanced by

42   *Christian Galan*

students were: poor academic performance 4.4 percent, maladjustment to student life 3 percent, going abroad 15 percent, health problems 14.6 percent, financial difficulties 15.5 percent, and other reasons 47.6 percent.

Another study (Daigaku Chūtaisha no Shūshoku Shien Saito 2016), which solely compared different faculties of economics, found that while the dropout rate was 0.3 percent for the economics department at Tōdai and 0.8 percent at Kyōdai, it was 3.4 percent at Meiji University and 3.5 percent at Hōsei University. The study stressed that while all universities experience students dropping out, this is much more frequent at private universities. Among the causes leading students to drop out, the study showed that 21 percent abandoned in order to transfer to another university, 18.6 percent for financial reasons, 14.2 percent because they were no longer motivated to continue studying, 12.3 percent to take up employment, 5.4 percent because they lacked the required academic level, 2.4 percent due to health problems, 1.9 percent due to mental or physical fatigue, and 23.4 percent for other reasons (Ide 2014).

It also showed that the dropout rate was correlated with the university's *hensachi* ("standard score") rating, which indicates the level of difficulty of its entrance exam – the higher the *hensachi*, the lower the dropout rate, and vice versa. Thus, the dropout rate at the economics department of Keiō (*hensachi* 68) is 2.8 percent and at Shiga (*hensachi* 65), 4.2 percent; this increases to 9.5 percent at the economics department of Tōkyō Keizai Daigaku (*hensachi* 50) and 13.1 percent at Teikyō University (*hensachi* 49). The author of the study also points out that when the *hensachi* of a university falls below 50, the dropout rate tends to exceed 10 percent, even reaching 20 percent in some cases.

If we disregard those students simply changing university, 80 percent of dropouts occur for "negative" reasons and mainly at low- or mid-ranking private universities recruiting the least talented, least motivated students, those whose future after graduation is the most uncertain; in other words, those whose future (and present) fails to match their or their families' expectations. This is particularly the case for "newcomers to university", who, to quote Pierre Bourdieu (1984: 143), were "led, by the mere fact of having access to it, to expect it to give them what it gave others at a time when they themselves were still excluded from it". I will return to this point in my conclusion.

The decision to drop out can be regarded as an escape strategy, similar to *futōkō* (school non-attendance), *hikikomori* (social recluse), *kyūgaku* (temporary absences), *ryūgaku* (sabbatical year abroad), and so forth, which share all but one of the same characteristics, namely the financial difficulties, which for me constitute another generation-making factor, the final one I will discuss here.

Poverty as an obstacle to tertiary education

The final generation-making mechanism I would like to present here relates to the growing awareness or discovery – perhaps even first-hand – by Japan's youth that for the first time in decades, poverty or low parental income may prevent them from progressing as far as they would like with their education, particularly into tertiary education.

The cost of education has come to weigh increasingly heavily on household finances over the past two decades, although, as we saw, the investment made by parents no longer secures the desired results. There are two reasons for this.

First, tuition fees have risen across the board, even at public and national universities (MEXT 2004). Educating a child in the public education system, from preschool to university, now costs around 7.7 million yen (approximately 67,000 €), and in private institutions at least 22 million yen (approximately 192,000 €).[7] University alone costs families 2.7 million yen (approximately 23,500 €) at a national university or at a public university, and on average 5.3 million yen (46,000 €) in the private sector (MEXT 2014b).

Second, household incomes fell consistently throughout the last two decades, with the average income falling by almost one million yen (around 8,800 €) in the ten years from 1998 to 2007. Given that the "average family" does not exist and that the wealthiest section of the Japanese population has seen a rise in income, it is the lower and above all middle classes that have seen their incomes decline – significantly in the case of many families (Japanese Ministry of Health, Labour and Welfare 2007).

This newfound awareness among young Japanese people that financial constraints can bar access to education is apparent at two stages in their schooling, at the end of secondary education and/or after their enrolment at university. Financial problems and/or the absence of sufficient income have thus become an important factor in the decision of Japanese high school students to abandon their hopes of continuing on to higher education.

A survey on the future of Japanese secondary school students was conducted in 2005 and 2006 by the Graduate School of Education at the University of Tokyo (Daigaku Keiei Seisaku Kenkyū Sentā 2007). It revealed that "household finances" was the third-most important factor (59.7 percent) in students' decision on whether to pursue their studies after secondary school, and that "high tuition fees at university" was the third-most frequently cited reason by students (56.4 percent) to explain why they chose to find a job after graduating from school (Daigaku Keiei Seisaku Kenkyū Sentā 2007: 15, 17).

Moreover, 34 percent believed that even entering a nearby national university would be financially difficult (25.5 percent), if not extremely difficult (8.5 percent), despite this being the least costly solution for continuing higher education. On the other hand, only 13.2 percent of secondary school students' parents thought it would be difficult and 5.4 percent extremely difficult (Daigaku Keiei Seisaku Kenkyū Sentā 2007: 18, 52). The differing viewpoints of parents and children is highly interesting since it illustrates that young people hold a significantly more pessimistic – and no doubt more realistic – view of society and the future than their parents, for whom university education only becomes financially problematic if it takes place far from the family home.

Be that as it may, financial considerations weigh heavily for both groups in the decision to continue studying. Although virtually all secondary school students (97.9 percent) see their parents' financial support as necessary or indispensable to continuing their studies, 88.5 percent believe it will be insufficient and that they will need to supplement it with personal income, notably via part-time work

44   Christian Galan

(*arubaito*), while 52.7 percent believe they will need to apply for a grant from the student financial aid system (which is in fact a loan that must be repaid after graduation), or for some other kind of loan or scholarship (38.6 percent) (Daigaku Keiei Seisaku Kenkyū Sentā 2007: 28).

Among the parents questioned, 96.5 percent believed that "even with a university degree, there was no guarantee of a [stable] future" and 95.7 percent thought "university tuition fees should not increase any further". Furthermore, 82.4 percent desired "an increase in the number of places at national universities" (which are the least expensive), and 74.5 percent rejected the idea that it was "normal during a period of financial difficulty [for the country] that families and students pay more" (Daigaku Keiei Seisaku Kenkyū Sentā 2007: 66).

This study further illustrates how money has become the main factor either facilitating or blocking students' enrolment at university, as well as the enormous gap that exists in this area based on family income: while 60.7 percent of secondary school students' families with an annual income of more than ten million yen (approximately 88,000 €) considered sending their children to university, only 44.6 percent of families whose income was between four and six million yen (between 35,200 € and 52,800 €) did so, and only 33.9 percent of those earning less than four million yen (35,200 €) (Daigaku Keiei Seisaku Kenkyū Sentā 2007: 80). During their first year at university, 7.7 percent of these same secondary school students felt that it was "financially difficult to continue studying" and 59.2 percent were "anxious about their future after graduation". Moreover, no less than 9.7 percent wanted "to quit [their current] university" (Daigaku Keiei Seisaku Kenkyū Sentā 2007: 109).

A second survey was carried out in 2012 (MEXT 2013b), with the same objectives and on the same type of population, and the results were even more worrying. I will focus solely on the conclusions here. Compared to the 2007 study, the new survey found that (1) household income still plays an important role in the decision to continue studying (or not) at a private university; (2) that a family's income level now also influences the decision to continue studying (or not) at a national or public university, which was never the case previously; and (3) that the income level of families also affected the decisions made by the most gifted students. Over a period of five years, the gulf in terms of equal access to higher education has widened considerably between high-income families and those with low to middle incomes.

It is no coincidence, then, that the aforementioned MEXT study from 2012 highlights the importance of financial considerations in students' decision to drop out. In 2012, 20.4 percent of students who had dropped out before graduating, and 15.5 percent of those who had temporarily stopped attending classes, did so for financial reasons, whereas only 14 percent and 15.4 percent (respectively) did so eight years earlier in 2007. On a similar note, in 2012 there were 11,361 "tuition delinquents", representing 0.4 percent of all students. Although this figure had not changed from 2007, it illustrates above all a preference among Japanese students for abandoning their studies rather than defaulting on payments. In fact, as the *Japan Times* wrote in an editorial, "The number of students who paid tuition late also increased to over 10,000, according to universities, though the exact numbers were surely under-reported" (Japan Times 2014). In addition, there are the debts caused by a failure to repay student loans, which in 2014 "had reached 92.5 billion yen (0.85 billion US$)" (Kakuchi 2014), and the fact that, still in 2014, almost three-quarters of all universities saw a rise in requests for financial assistance, scholarships, tuition exemption and split payments.

It goes without saying that the current young generation is not the first to see disparity, injustice or discrimination on financial grounds. However, it is without doubt the first since the 1960s to be so aware of these issues and, for many, to have experienced them either directly or vicariously through friends and acquaintances (which also explains the previously discussed divergence in viewpoints among secondary school students and their parents). They have discovered these financial difficulties in concrete ways, consciously experienced them, and assimilated them as a recurrent source of stress and doubt, whereas the majority of parents still believe (or want to believe) in the continued existence of the previous model in which they grew up.

Today, students and parents from lower-income families can no longer even rely on national or public universities as a means of advancing to higher education. The entrance exams constitute one kind of hurdle, but students encounter others, even before they reach this stage. As we saw, the most prestigious national universities – which are also the cheapest – continue to recruit almost all of their students via competitive exams. For parents, having their child apply to national or public universities with limited intakes means paying for extra classes or preparatory courses, which can be extremely costly and therefore unaffordable for lower-income families.

Outlook

Until the early 1990s, the path that young Japanese people had to tread was clear and simple, having been mapped out for them by their parents and society. It had been explained to them from their earliest years, and they were conditioned to accept it. In addition to being clear and simple, it was reassuring. Students would be classified into those who went to university and those who did not, with the former enjoying a higher social rank and the possibility of aspiring to a better material life. The efforts they devoted to the task – which would also serve to illustrate their capacity for such effort – would be beneficial not only to them but to their future employers and to society at large. Though the system was neither entirely fair nor entirely egalitarian, it was seen as being just that – fair and egalitarian. Presented as reflecting a choice made by society, in reality this system met the immediate needs of the economy and the need for social control, but all accepted it.

The system gradually began to collapse in the 1990s when Japan's economy went into decline and stagnation, and this despite the fact that at least for a while, adults continued to espouse the same views. The promise of job security, a smooth career arc, and a comfortable family life was no longer credible, let alone

46   *Christian Galan*

respected. With anybody able to enroll at university, attending university lost its meaning, or at least, it ceased to have the same meaning as before. In particular, it no longer guaranteed a job. For businesses, young graduates no longer offered the same guarantee of being competent and resilient workers.

Only the most prestigious universities continued to maintain the status quo, for young people and businesses alike. However, entering these universities became even more difficult than before, since they were now the only place where academic competition continued to exist, and places were extremely limited. Even worse, Japan's youth discovered – no doubt before their parents – that they lived in a socially stratified society and that, even among the middle-class, some could no longer afford such a future. From being a generation divided into (at least) two, between those who went to university and those who did not, the new generations of young Japanese are now divided into (at least) three, between those who do not go to university, those who do but who attend one with a low to medium academic focus, and those who attend the most prestigious institutions in the top 30 or top 50.

And yet for previous generations – or more specifically, *generation units* or *generations as actuality*, to borrow the terms employed by Karl Mannheim, becoming an adult meant successfully completing one's studies, obtaining a job (the most qualified position possible, with the best salary possible), getting married and having children. Achieving all of the above, *and in this order*, ensured that society considered you an adult. In other words, you had to demonstrate your personal abilities, your professional responsibilities, and your family responsibilities. An adult was someone society recognized as being responsible – for themselves, for their family, and for others.

The objectives pursued by previous generations – harmony, equality, security – are no longer attainable for the present generation of young people. In contrast to previous generations, only a minority of young people today can achieve these objectives, and most of this group was either born into privilege or is well endowed in social and cultural capital. Those who lack such attributes face mounting difficulties – the objectives have become pipe dreams. If a degree no longer guarantees young people a stable job, it also becomes more difficult to get married and have children – and thus to make the transition to adulthood.

The temptation for young people is to take the easy way out and withdraw – from education, from work, from home, from society and from adulthood and responsibilities. They prefer to withdraw than to be regarded as "less competent adults", "less complete adults"; in other words, "not really adults".

Japanese adults and politicians complain that young people have stopped studying, have no aspirations for the future, no desire to progress in school or society, and that they are losing traditional Japanese values or the traditional Japanese spirit. Faced with the growing number of dropouts, *hikikomori, furitā* and NEET, they attempt to curb the phenomenon out of fear for their pensions and the country's economic future. However, adults and politicians are no doubt mistaken in their assessment of the situation. The four phenomena presented here (universal access to higher education, evolution of the admissions system and resulting dichotomization of universities, failure of degrees to provide automatic access to a secure and well-paid professional life, and poverty or low parental income as a barrier to tertiary education) act as generation-making mechanisms both for the current young generation and for those to come. There will be no going back to the situation enjoyed by past generations. While the majority of young people today seem to have understood this, the same cannot be said of their predecessors (meaning their parents and adults in general).

The concept of "collective disillusionment", developed by Pierre Bourdieu (1984: 144) almost 40 years ago to describe France, may prove highly pertinent and effective in analyzing the Japanese situation and predicting how it is likely to evolve. If we replace the words "secondary education" by "higher education" in the quote below, what follows could be considered a fairly accurate description of the current reality for young Japanese people with regards to tertiary education, diplomas and their entry into the world of work. This is particularly true if we recall that the subtitle added by Saitō Tamaki (1998) to his pioneering book *Shakaiteki hikikomori* ("social withdrawal") is *owaranai shishunki* ("adolescence without end"). Leaving school and university to join society, leaving home to go out into the world, leaving childhood and adolescence behind to become adults – such acts are not beyond the young generation, they simply do not see the point. They no longer share their parents' dream, because for many, this dream is out of their reach. To quote Bourdieu:

> The greatest losers in this struggle are those whose diplomas have the least relative value in the hierarchy of diplomas and are most devalued. In some cases, the qualification-holder finds he has no other way to defend the value of his qualification than to refuse to sell his labor power at the price offered; the decision to remain unemployed is then equivalent to a one-man strike [. . .].
>
> Newcomers to secondary education [tertiary education in the case of Japan, CG] are led, by the mere fact of having access to it, to expect it to give them what it gave others at a time when they themselves were still excluded from it. In an earlier period and for other classes, these aspirations were perfectly realistic, since they corresponded to objective probabilities, but they are often quickly deflated by the verdicts of the scholastic market or the labor market [. . .].
>
> The collective disillusionment which results from the structural mismatch between aspirations and real probabilities, between the social identity the school system seems to promise, or the one it offers on a temporary basis, and the social identity that the labor market in fact offers is the source of the disaffection towards work, that *refusal of social finitude*, which generates all the refusals and negations of the adolescent counter-culture.
>
> (Bourdieu 1984: 143–144)

"Collective disillusionment": the term aptly describes the despondency felt by Japan's youth today. Looking at the facts presented here, the ultimate question

48 *Christian Galan*

may not be why young people are like this, why they feel like this and act like this, but why this comes as such a surprise to adults, politicians, and maybe even to us.

Notes

1 The number was approximately 2,491,000 in 1966.
2 Private universities (*shiritsu daigaku*) are essentially privately funded, in contrast to national and public universities (*kokuritsu daigaku* and *kōritsu daigaku*, respectively), which receive public money. In the case of national universities, this funding is provided by the government; in the case of public universities, by local authorities.
3 There are two types of university in Japan, four-year universities (*daigaku*) and two-year junior colleges (*tanki daigaku*). The latter are gradually disappearing due to plummeting enrollment numbers as students desert them in favour of four-year courses.
4 In 1989, this figure stood at just 29.8% (109,395 out of 366,668 admissions) (Mukogawa Women's University 2014).
5 These specialised post-secondary schools form part of Japan's tertiary education system.
6 "A rising share of tertiary graduates is experiencing a change in employment in the first three years of their working lives – from 28% (1987) to 35% (2001). (In the decade of 1993–2003 the share changing jobs in first year after university graduation rose from 9.4 to 15.3%)." (Newby/OECD 2009: 66).
7 The exchange rate applied here is from early September 2016: € 1 = ±114 yen.

References

Bourdieu, Pierre (1984) *Distinction: A Social Critique of the Judgment of Taste*. Cambridge: Harvard University Press.
Cabinet Office, Government of Japan (2014) *Jūhassai jinkō to kōtō kyōiku kikan e no shingakuritsu nado no sui'i* [Changes in the Population of 18-Year Olds and Rates of Progression to Higher Education]. Online available at: www8.cao.go.jp/cstp/tyousakai/kihon5/1kai/siryo6-2-7.pdf (accessed 2 September 2016).
Daigaku Chūtaisha no Shūshoku Shien Saito (2016) *Daigakubetsu no daigaku chūtairitsu no keikō* [Trends in Dropout Rates by University]. Online available at: http://大学中退就職.com/column/university-dropout-rate.html (accessed 2 September 2016).
Daigaku Keiei Seisaku Kenkyū Sentā (2007) *Daigakusei chōsa* [Survey on University Students]. Online available at: http://ump.p.u-tokyo.ac.jp/crump/resource/crumphsts.pdf (accessed 1 December 2017).
Galan, Christian (2010) Out of This World, in This World, or Both? The Japanese School at the Threshold. In: *Language Life in Japan. Transformations and Prospects*. Patrick Heinrich and Christian Galan (eds.), 77–93. London: Routledge.
——— (2014) Dete iku ka tomaru ka, soshite "ikani" – "hikikomori" o rikai suru tame no yotsu no tegakari [Staying In or Going Out, and How? Four Possible Keys to Understanding hikikomori]. In: *"Hikikomori" ni nani o miru ka – gurōbaruka suru sekai to koritsu suru kojin*. Suzuki Kunifumi et al. (eds.), 115–141. Tokyo: Seidosha.
Ide, Sōhei (2014) Daigaku ni okeru taigaku/hikikomori/futōkō [Dropouts, *Hikikomori* and Absenteeism at University]. *Synodos. Academic Journalism*. Online available at: http://synodos.jp/society/7731/2 (accessed 2 September 2016).
Ishiguro, Fujiyo (2012) Shidaisei no hachinin ni hitori ga chūtaisha ni natte ita!? Daigaku kara umareru "kakusa shakai nippon" no osorubeki jittai [One in Eight Students at Private Universities Is Now a Dropout!? How Universities Risk Making Japan an Unequal

From youth to non-adulthood in Japan 49

Society]. *Diamond Online*. Online available at: http://diamond.jp/articles/-/23780 (accessed 2 September 2016).

Japan Times (2014) Poorer Students Dropping Out (editorial). *Japan Times* (4 October). Online available at: www.japantimes.co.jp/opinion/2014/10/04/editorials/poorer-stu dents-dropping/#.VjU7yaTf2To (accessed 2 September 2016).

Japanese Ministry of Health, Labour and Welfare (2007) *Heisei jūkyūnen kokumin seikatsu kiso chōsa no gaikyō* [Outline of the 2007 Comprehensive Survey of Citizens' Living Conditions]. Online available at: www.mhlw.go.jp/toukei/saikin/hw/k-tyosa/ktyosa07/2-1.html (accessed 2 September 2016).

Kakuchi, Suvendrini (2014) Record Numbers Drop Out Facing Financial Problems. *University World News* (25 October). Online available at: www.universityworldnews.com/article.php?story=20141025084313992 (accessed 2 September 2016).

Maita, Toshihiko (2014) Daigaku nyūshi kyūwari wa gōkaku no jidai – nankankō wa shiretsu na kyōsō mo [The Era of 90-Percent Acceptance Rates at University: Fierce Competition at Struggling Institutions Too]. *Nikkei duaru*. Online available at: http://dual.nikkei.co.jp/article.aspx?id=2768 (accessed 2 September 2016).

——— (2015) Daisotsusha no shūshokuritsu no chōki sui'i [Long-Term Changes in Graduate Employment Rates]. *Dēta essei* (blog). Online available at: http://tmaita77.blogs pot.fr/2015/04/blog-post_4.html (accessed 2 September 2016).

MEXT (2004) *Kokuritsu – kōritsu – shiritsu daigaku no jugyōryō oyobi nyūgakuryō no sui'i* [Changes to Tuition and Admission Fees at National, Public and Private Institutions]. Online available at: www.mext.go.jp/b_menu/shingi/chukyo/chukyo4/005/gijiroku/011201/011201e1.htm (accessed 2 September 2016).

——— (2006) *OECD Thematic Review of Tertiary Education, Country Background Report for Japan*. Online available at: www.oecd.org/education/skills-beyond-school/37052438.pdf (accessed 2 September 2016).

——— (2008) *Sotsugyōshasū, shūshokushasū oyobi shūshokuritsu nado no sui'i* [daigaku (gakubu)] [Changes in Number of Graduates and Employed Persons, and in Employment Rates (by University and Department)]. Online available at: www.mext.go.jp/b_menu/toukei/001/08072901/003/sanzu11.pdf (accessed 2 September 2016).

——— (2013a) *Daigaku nyūgakusha sentaku, daigaku kyōiku no genjō* [Current State of University Education and the Selection of New Students]. Online available at: www.kantei.go.jp/jp/singi/kyouikusaisei/dai11/sankou2.pdf (accessed 16 September 2016).

——— (2013b) *Daigaku shingaku to gakuhi futan kōzō ni kansuru kenkyū* [Research on Progression to Higher Education and the Burden of Tuition Fees]. Online available at: www.mext.go.jp/b_menu/shingi/chousa/koutou/057/gijiroku/__icsFiles/afield file/2013/07/08/1337608_02.pdf (accessed 16 September 2016).

——— (2014a) *Gakusei no chūto taigaku ya kyūgaku nado no jōkyō ni tsuite* [Examination of University Students Abandoning or Temporarily Interrupting Their Studies]. Online available at: www.mext.go.jp/b_menu/houdou/26/10/__icsFiles/afield file/2014/10/08/1352425_01.pdf (accessed 2 September 2016).

——— (2014b) *Gakusei e no keizaiteki shien no arikata ni tsuite* [Information on the Types of Financial Assistance Available to Students]. Online available at: www.mext.go.jp/b_menu/shingi/chousa/koutou/057/gaiyou/1352044.htm (accessed 2 September 2016).

——— (2015a) *Heisei nijūnananendo gakkō kihon chōsa (sokuhochi) no kōhyō ni tsuite* [Discussion of the Publication of Initial Findings from the 2015 School Survey]. Online available at: www.mext.go.jp/component/b_menu/houdou/__icsFiles/afield file/2015/12/25/1365647_01.pdf (accessed 2 September 2016).

50 *Christian Galan*

————— (2015b) *Heisei nijūnananendo kokukōshiritsu daigaku-tanki daigaku nyūgakusha senbatsu jisshi jōkyō no gaiyō* [Overview of Selection Methods for New Students at National, Public and Private Universities and Junior Colleges in 2015]. Online available at: www.mext.go.jp/b_menu/houdou/27/10/1362966.htm (accessed 2 September 2016).

————— (2015c) *Heisei nijūnananendo kokukōshiritsu daigaku nyūgakusha senbatsu jisshi jōkyō no gaiyō* [Methods for Selecting New Students at National, Public and Private Universities and Junior Colleges in 2015]. Online available at: www.mext.go.jp/b_menu/houdou/27/10/__icsFiles/afieldfile/2015/10/20/1362966_01.pdf (accessed 2 September 2016).

Mukogawa Women's University (2014) *Daigaku nyūgakusha no suisenritsu no sui'i* [Changes in Rate of Students Accepted at University by Recommendation]. Online available at: www.mukogawa-u.ac.jp/~kyoken/data/07.pdf (accessed 2 September 2016).

Nakajima, Hiromi (2014) Daigakusei no chūtairitsu jūpāsento to futōkō [Absentee Students and the 10% Dropout Rate]. *Taijin enjo gaku magajin* 17. Online available at: www.humanservices.jp/magazine/vol17/8.pdf (accessed 2 September 2016).

Newby, Howard, David Breneman, Thomas Johanson and Peter Maasen (2009) *OECD Reviews of Tertiary Education*. Paris: OECD. Online available at: www.oecd.org/edu/skills-beyond-school/42280329.pdf (accessed 2 September 2016).

Saitō, Tamaki (1998) *Shakaiteki hikikomori – owaranai shishunki* [Social Withdrawal: Adolescence Without End]. Tokyo: PHP Shinsho. (Published in English in 2012 as: *Hikikomori: Adolescence Without End*. Minneapolis: University of Minnesota Press).

4 Youth sexuality under the spotlight in a super-aged society with too few children

Beverley Anne Yamamoto

Introduction

This chapter is concerned with the issue of youth sexuality in an era of well-below replacement fertility and hyper-aging. Despite its huge and very visible sex industry and highly sexualized media output, as a nation Japan seems rather uncomfortable with the issue of sexuality. It is generally not regarded as an appropriate subject for serious public discussion, academic research, or for educational instruction. While international research and human rights documents suggests that sexuality could well be viewed as a potentially healthy and enjoyable area of life (WHO 2006; Lindau and Gavrilova 2010; Smith, Frankel and Yarnell 1997), in Japan deeply rooted taboos and negative attitudes remain strong (Asayama 1977: 577; Yonemoto 1997: 18). This impacts the discourse around youth sexuality and constrains young people's access to sexuality education. Given this situation, young people are often accessing information about sex and sexual relationships from pornographic material, magazines, manga, blogs, or other social media forms. It is suggested that this may mean that young people engage in "abnormal sex" based on these media presentations, that later result in revulsion or antipathy (Sugiura 2011: 64–65).

The taboo around sex means that sex education is not well developed in Japan, and attempts by schools to offer a more comprehensive approach have been fraught with difficulties. A nationalist backlash against what was represented as "excessive" or "radical" sex education arose in the 1990s, but became more coordinated from 2002 (see Asai et al. 2003; Murase 2005). This backlash squeezed further what was already a very limited curriculum of sex education. The movement was able to exert sufficient pressure to secure restrictions on the language use in the classroom and led to a decrease in taught content. Those protesting "excessive" sex education do not regard schools as an appropriate space for such teaching and regard very basic abstinence education as the only appropriate form of instruction (Tashiro, Ushitora and Watanabe 2011).

On the other hand, there has also been a vocal and dedicated group of liberal academics, health care professionals, and educators who have tried to expand teaching around sexuality, with the more obvious names here being Kitamura Kunio, Director of Japan Family Planning Association, Kōno Miyako, a gynaecologist

52 Beverley Anne Yamamoto

with her own clinic in Hiroshima, and Murase Yukihiro, former academic and current Chairperson of The Council for Education and Study on Human Sexuality. As with those involved in the backlash movement, these advocates are from a generation who were born during or just after the baby boom following the end of the Asia Pacific War. Their vision of sexuality education is comprehensive, upholding teaching about the value of life, human rights, and youth empowerment. Yet this Shōwa-born generation holds values around sexuality that are arguably different from that of the Heisei youth of today. Few view youth sexuality in a wholly positive light, but take a pragmatic approach that if young people are clearly sexually active, then it is necessary to protect them against the risks of unplanned pregnancy, sexually transmitted infections (STIs), and HIV. Trying to identify the distinguishing features of the sexual values and behaviors of the Heisei youth relative to that of the generation who are able to shape the wider discourse around sexuality is one aim of this chapter.

This chapter, then, explores the sexuality of young people of the Heisei era, the millennials. It asks whether there is a generational divide around sexual interest, values, and behavior between those who have the power to create the discourse in this domain and young people themselves, whose voices have been given little authority to date. It highlights some of the ways that youth sexual behaviors may be regarded as different from that of previous, post-war generations. In particular, the chapter looks at recent concern about the rise of a generation who are reported to have little interest in sex. The epitome of this representation of youth sexuality is that of the herbivore male (*sōshoku danshi*) who is depicted as having little interest in matters of the flesh, namely sex. He is contrasted with the carnivore males (*nikushoku danshi*) of the Shōwa generation, who are presented as virile and even predatory. The latter part of this chapter offers emic views on sexuality voiced by young people. This is achieved first by looking at texts generated from a class I have taught to first-year university students for the past 10 years on "Thinking about sexuality". These texts are in the form of comments and reports based on thoughts about sex education in Japan. Next, an emic voice is presented on the basis of specific feedback offered verbally and in written form by four young people involved in health advocacy and sexual health counseling in Tokyo. This emic perspective is far from comprehensive, but it offers a counter narrative of youth resilience and creativity.

Through this exploration of Shōwa gatekeeper voices on youth sexuality with that of a small group of Heisei youth, I hope to identify some of the distinct generation-making mechanisms in the domain of sexuality that are in operation in low fertility and hyper-aging Japan.

Sexual behavior across generations

This section considers the quite dramatic changes that have occurred in self-reported youth sexual behavior over the past 40 years. By drawing on data from regular, nationwide surveys of youth sexual behavior carried out by The Japan Association for Sex Education (*Nihon seikyōiku kyōkai*, abbreviated to JASE) since 1975, we can gain a good overview of this changed landscape (JASE 1975, 2013, 2016).

The JASE Surveys on The Sexual Behavior of Youth show that between 1974 and the most recent survey, 2011, there was a dramatic increase in high school and university students reporting experience of sexual intercourse (Figure 4.1). The change in reported behavior was particularly marked for young women. Whereas in 1974 only 5.5 percent of female high school students and 11 percent of female university students reported experience of sexual intercourse, this rose to a peak of 30.3 percent and 62.2 percent respectively in 2005. While the upward trend is not as dramatic for young men, the percentage of male high school students reporting experience of sexual intercourse more than doubled between 1974 and 2005, from 10.2 percent to 26.6 percent and rose from 23.1 percent to 61.3 percent for male university students.

The remarkable shift in reported experience of sexual intercourse of young people across these surveys reflects the very changed trajectory of young people's lives, one that was characterized by increased independence, affluence and gender equality from the 1980s through into the 1990s (see Yamamoto 2009). It is also said to reflect an ideology of individualism where sex is a matter of individual choice (Kato 2010: 73) and a loosening of constraints on women where losing one's virginity is a "rite of passage" for young women (Sugiura 2011: 64).

In contrast to the dramatic increase in young people reporting experience of sexual intercourse from 1974 to 2005, in recent years much attention has been given to the sharp decline in young people reporting experience of sexual intercourse between the 2005 and 2011 surveys. Similar declines have been noted

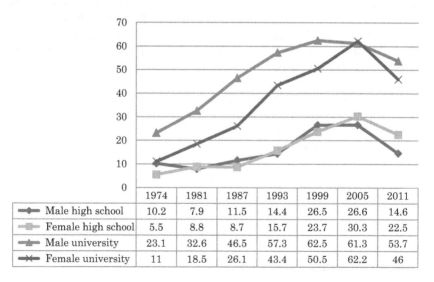

Figure 4.1 Percentage of students reporting experience of sexual intercourse, 1974–2011
Source: JASE (2013: 24)

54 *Beverley Anne Yamamoto*

in other surveys that measure sexual activity among young people. The dip in the number of young people reporting experience of sexual intercourse between 2005 and 2011 in the JASE survey has fed concerns, if not panic, about the possible "sexual lethargy" of young people, especially that of young men. While this is an issue that will be dealt with more substantively when we address the discourse around "herbivore" males, if we look only at high school level, male sexual behavior does appear somewhat lethargic when compared to that of their female counterparts. Nevertheless, the picture changes at university level. Figure 4.1 reveals that the recent decline in high school students reporting experience of sexual intercourse is far more marked for males than females. Already in 2005, more female than male students were reporting experience of sexual intercourse both at high school and university levels. In the 2011 survey the gap had further widened between male and female reporting of sexual experience at high school level (14.4 percent for males and 22.5 percent for females). Nevertheless, there was a sharper decrease for female than for male students at university level. In 2005 slightly more females than males reported experience of sexual intercourse (62.2 percent and 61.3 percent, respectively), but in 2011 the female figure had fallen to 46 percent, whereas for males it had only dropped to 53.7 percent).

Given that the data only tells us whether respondents have ever experienced sexual intercourse, we are left to speculate on the disparity between male and female high school students in reports of sexual intercourse. It could be that sexually active female high school students are having or have had sex with older males rather than with young men in their own age cohort. Certainly we know that on average young women marry men two years their senior (Beppu 2010: 11). Just as possible is that a smaller pool of sexually active high school male students are having sexual intercourse with multiple partners from a larger pool of less promiscuous female students. There is support for both these explanations in the literature (Genda and Kawakami 2006; Kitamura 2011). Whatever the explanation, the so-called "sexual revolution" in Japan has clearly been more dramatic for young women than young men (Sato and Iwasawa 2015). This suggests not just a change in sexual norms, but gender norms as well.

While there was a dip in the number of young people reporting that they had experience of sexual intercourse between 2005 and 2011 in the JASE surveys that sparked widespread angst, we should not overlook that well over four times as many female high school and university students reported experience of sexual intercourse in 2011 compared to 1974. While the increase is not as dramatic for males, over 53 percent of men in university report experience of sexual intercourse compared to 23.1 percent in 1974. Thus, we should not be too quick to represent the millennials as "sexless" and young men as "herbivores" in comparison to their fathers and grandfathers. At the same time, Figure 4.1 does reveal an interesting shift.

Changed meanings around sexuality

By the end of the 1990s, well over half of all university students surveyed by JASE reported experience of sexual intercourse. With the average age of marriage

Youth sexuality under the spotlight 55

in the late 20s for women and early 30s for men by this time, it is reasonable to assume that much if not most of the upward trend in young people reporting experience of sexual intercourse represents a rise in premarital or perhaps more accurately non-marital intercourse.

JASE and other surveys confirm that by the 1990s, the majority of young people were accepting of premarital sexual intercourse. This is in sharp contrast to earlier generations. The National Fertility Surveys show that even by 1992 the number of 18–24-year-olds reporting that they were accepting of premarital intercourse was as high as 78 percent for men and 73 percent for women. This figure rose even higher to 84 percent and 82 percent respectively by 2005 (Sato and Iwasawa 2015: 137–138). Retherford, Ogawa and Matsura also note an across the board change in values relating to premarital sex that began in the 1980s, but resulted in a sharp shift in behavior among young people in the 1990s (Retherford, Ogawa and Matsura 2001: 89). There is agreement that during this period there was a "normative transformation of premarital sex from deviant behavior to acceptable behavior" (Sato and Iwasawa 2015: 142). With marriage increasingly delayed, it appears that sexual encounters for Heisei youth are no longer linked to the promise or prospect of marriage or even a more intimate relationship.

Whereas previously, sexual relations had been regarded as a way of cementing a relationship, research suggest that it was now happening quite early on in relationship, if not at the start. "For young people today, a sexual relationship is not the goal of a romantic relationship, but rather a gateway to it" (Sato and Iwasawa 2015: 144). The main evidence for this conclusion is that despite a sharp rise in young people reporting experience of sexual intercourse, the proportion who are either married or in a romantic relationship has declined sharply. This points to the casual nature of sexual relationships among young people today (Sato and Iwasawa 2015: 144).

The National Surveys on Family Planning offer some insights into sexual activity of single women through questions on current use of contraception. This suggests a close relationship between male friendship and sexual intimacy. Between the 1990 and 1998 surveys, the percentage of single women aged 16 and over reporting they were currently using contraception rose from 38 to 53 percent. Given that not all sexually active women will be using contraception, these figures reflect a minimum percentage of single women who were sexually active at the time of the surveys[1] (see Retherford, Ogawa and Matsura 2001). Retherford, Ogawa and Matsura note that in the 1998 National Surveys on Family Planning, 55 percent of all single women responded that they had at least one male friend, leading them to conclude that most women with a male friend were having sexual intercourse. The number of single women reporting current use of contraception had risen to 57 percent in the 2000 round of the National Survey on Family Planning (Retherford, Ogawa and Matsura 2001: 88).

The intimate association between having a male friend and being sexually active is also voiced by popular essayist Suigiura Yumiko. Talking about single women in their 20s who she interviewed, she argues that [hetero]sexual relationships for women are largely grown out of a friendship with a male friend. She argues that

56 *Beverley Anne Yamamoto*

the move to sexual intimacy is in the form of an extension of feelings of friendship (*yūjō enchō*). As such, a sexual encounter may mark the move from friendship to one of "sex friends", hence it acting as a "gateway" to romantic intimacy (Sugiura 2011: 108). In the context of the rise of women going to co-ed four year universities rather than all-women (gender segregated) junior colleges, it became easier in the 1990s for single women to strike up friendships with males (Suigiura 2011: 108). Yet at the same time that college-age men and women found themselves more likely to be in the same classroom, further education gave women more independence over who and if they dated (Kato 2010: 72).

Sugiura also suggests that with women's greater independence and sense of individualism, single women do not feel it is necessary to become friends with or move to sexual intimacy with men they are not attracted to. There are perceived dangers to intimacy, especially regarding loss of independence, so only if there is a strong attraction will they take the risk. She also points to pragmatism among women who entered their teens in the years after the economic bubble burst. With fewer men able to support a family wage, she argues that women are no longer waiting for a knight in shining armor to rush them away on a white horse (Suigiura 2011: 64–65). She argues that women are also no longer limited to a passive role in sexual relationships and are more likely to express sexual desire if they find a man attractive (Suigiura 2011: 64).

Sugiura's conclusions support those of Genda and Kawakami (2006) who argue, based on an analysis of the Japan General Social Surveys, that there has been a polarization of male sexual activity based on their attractiveness to women. Men in high status positions have high levels of sexual activity even if they are working long hours. Long hours have been regarded as depressing sexual desire. Nevertheless, for men in insecure positions or unemployed, sexual activity was low. They conclude that "being out of work diminished the meaning of sexual behavior" (Genda and Kawakami 2006: 80). This suggests that an unemployed or underemployed male may internalize his own lack of attractiveness and not even search out a relationship. Certainly, Kato notes that over the lost decades of the 1990s and early 2000s, there was a "decline in economically attractive men" (Kato 2010: 77). While the high school and university years may be a period of greater sexual activity, this appears to tail off by the 30s and 40s with some men being "winners" in the sexual attractiveness game and others emerging as "losers".

A generational shift?

The generation whose behavior was reported on in the 1975 JASE survey would have been born in the mid- to late-1950s and are today around retirement age. As a generation, they married earlier, and their transition to adulthood was more predictable and more highly gendered. This generation played a significant role in and enjoyed the fruits of the period of economic growth and prosperity that lasted through to the 1990s. For this generation, education was framed as a time of restraint, and evidence of early sexual onset was regarded as deviant, especially for female students. The restraints placed on women were stronger and their behavior more heavily supervised (see, e.g., Matsumoto 1985: 171; Arahori 1990: 625). This suggests a profound generation gap.

Even those with relatively liberal views from this generation can express quite negative views about teenage sexual experimentation. For example, despite alarm over the percentage of youth saying they have no interest in sex, many adult commentators on youth sexuality find it hard to move away from the default discourse that has dominated the literature for nearly three decades, even those calling for comprehensive sexuality education. Ishiwata Chieko, in her paper on "Sexual health education for school children in Japan: Timing and contents", which appeared in the *Japan Medical Association Journal* in 2011, outlines a comprehensive program of sexuality education proposed by the School Health Committee of the Japan Medical Association. The proposal is impressive, yet the author begins the paper by making a highly negative case for the need for a better program of sex education:

> People tend to think that sexual behavior between two people not legally married is nothing special. This means that accurate knowledge about sexuality is increasingly essential to ensure a more meaningful life. There would be almost no sexual problems if people refrain from sexual activity before marriage or until they can be fully responsible for their own actions. However, in reality this is not the case.
>
> (Ishiwata 2011: 155)

The idea that there is an age when it is possible to be "fully responsible" for your actions and that this happens sometime after you reach the age of majority is commonly echoed in adult-generated discourses around youth sexuality, but no evidence is provided to back up such claims. There is a marked tendency in the literature for those of an older generation to construct the teen years as an extension of childhood when it comes to sexuality, rather than a transitional stage before adulthood where sexual experimentation may be healthy and positive. This is seen frequently at academic meetings when presenters refer to sexually active teenagers as *kodomo* ("children"). This has resulted in a lack of distinction about the background to and risks associated with sexual intercourse for young people. Discursively constructed as "children", there is no space for a discourse of sexual pleasure to emerge (Fine 1988). Likewise, efforts to expand sex education have been dogged by the idea that it is better not to wake sleeping children (*nerareru ko o samasu*), suggesting that young people are not only infantilized in some adult discourses, but also de-sexualized. This is evident in recent MEXT directives that prohibit any teaching relating to sexual intercourse or contraception at elementary school (6–12 years) level, perhaps understandably, but while these subjects can be taught at junior high school level (12–15 years), the phrase "sexual intercourse" (*seikō*) must be replaced with imprecise vocabulary, "sexual contact" (*seiteki sesshoku*), even when teaching about STIs, HIV, and unplanned pregnancy (Ishiwata 2011: 158). While the huge generational gap between the

58   *Beverley Anne Yamamoto*

gatekeepers of discourses around youth sexuality is recognized, even the most liberal adult speakers articulate values that are very different from the young people their policies and ideas target.

Concerns about sexless youth

In this section I would like to move on to explore the more recent discursive landscape, which has been characterized by concerns about "sex-phobic youth", often conflated as "herbivore men", who are seen to be contributing to Japan's demographic woes. There is also concern that "herbivore" men will not have the strength to support a growing elderly population, as they do not have the drive of "meat-eating" men.

Herbivore men

Mariko Fukusawa, a popular media communist, coined the phrase *sōshoku danshi* ("herbivore male" or "grass eating man") in 2006 to indicate males who were not driven by a desire for sex or money, but instead were concerned about their looks and being frugal. They were depicted as gentle and somewhat effeminate. The idea gained significant coverage in the media as columnists lamented the perceived loss of assertive, competitive, and hard masculinity. In 2009, the phrase *sōshoku danshi* was nominated as one of ten top buzzwords for that year (Morioka 2013). Morioka Masahiro credits the sudden popularity of the term, especially in the media, with the way the idea of the herbivore male matched the more feminine sensitive male figure that people were seeing in daily life (Morioka 2013).

Kon Issho, in his popular book entitled *Ubawareta seiyoku* (*Stolen Sexual Desire*), focusing on the herbivore male, laments young men who not only lack drive but have no strong desire to strike up a romantic relationship even if they have an opportunity for a relationship with someone of "the opposite sex" (Kon 2009: 3). He claims that while on the one hand the herbivore male has little desire, on the other any desire he does feel is experienced as something gross (*kimochi warui*) and so is to be avoided (Kon 2009: 25). This is in contrast to the carnivore male who "does not hesitate to ask [for sex]" and even if he is rather inexperienced in the beginning, "acquires strategies and accumulates know-how and experience of negotiating" with women. The carnivore male "takes for granted that 'sex is a negotiation'" (Kon 2009: 24). Kon suggests that for herbivore men even the desire to ejaculate is feared as a loss of control of self. He then speculates further by claiming that for the herbivore male to then "transfer this to a desire for sexual intercourse without being able to establish whether this is a legitimate desire (*seitō na seiyoku*) or not leads him to flounder before he has even made a move" (Kon 2009: 104).

While Kon and many others discussing the herbivore male are doing little more than speculating, within this discourse we witness attempts to reinforce a heteronormative and highly gendered understanding of what sex is and how it should take place. Morioka suggests that those most concerned about the rise of herbivore men are middle-aged and older men.

For men in middle-age and older, the herbivorization of young men seems to be seen as something truly deplorable. I think this feeling of disapprobation on the part of older men comes in two varieties. One type is simply a feeling of regret and sadness that young men have lost their "manliness". They deplore the fact that young men have lost their masculinity and become effeminate, and that as a result they will be unable to support Japan's economic growth going forward and the country will succumb to international competition. When it comes to family life they suspect that in the future men will be shamefully henpecked and dominated by their wives.

(Morioka 2013)

Morioka carries on to suggest that the herbivore male could be welcomed for being a more gentle and peace-loving male, which could result in a society with less propensity for violence (Morioka 2013). Kon argues that the herbivore male is a product of a peaceful society where men do not have to fight to survive. Under such circumstances their sexual desire is weak. He argues that, in contrast, Japan's peaceful society since the war has created circumstances where women are able to express their sexual desire more easily, suggesting a mismatch between young men and women in contemporary Japan (Kon 2009: 37).

While both authors, in keeping with much of the discourse around the herbivorization of Japanese males, are highly speculative and often reinforce heteronormative assumptions (Kon more than Morioka), they differ in their interpretation of the trend they describe. Yet, at the same time, they agree that young men today are characterized by a low level of sexual desire beyond auto-eroticism, and may be conflicted even by the latter. Let us now look at some of the evidence that has added fuel to this speculation.

The rise of a generation who "dislike sex"

The Japan Family Planning Association's (JFPA) biannual Surveys of Male and Female Lifestyle and Attitudes: The Sexual Attitudes and Behavior of Japanese People provides a data source that records the "evolution" of sexlessness among the population generally (JFPA 2016). This traces the rise of sexlessness among Japanese couples over the past 15 years. The latest data (2016) shows a steady increase in couples reporting that they are sexless since the first survey in 2002 (see Figure 4.2). This data has been reported widely in the Japanese and western media, and has helped to constitute Japan as a "sexless nation" (Sechiyama 2014).

Kitamura Kunio, who has led this research, has specifically drawn attention to what he presents as a generation of young people who have little interest in sex. In the latest JFPA survey, singles with an experience of sexual activity were asked whether they had had sex (sexual intercourse) over the past month. Only 37 percent answered positively to this question, and 57.9 percent reported that they had been sexless over the past month. This is perhaps not surprising as for singles a critical impediment is lack of a partner. For singles, "not having a partner"

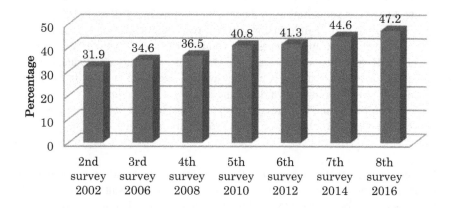

Figure 4.2 Trends towards sexlessness among Japanese couples, 2002–2016
Source: JFPA (2016)

was given by 68.8 percent of respondents as a reason they could not be positive (*sekkyokuteki*) about sex (JFPA 2016).

Data from the JFPA surveys goes further to support the idea that many young people are not only failing to engage in any sexual activity, but that they have no interest in sex. Figure 4.3 shows that depending on age group and gender, between 10 and 50 percent of young people in the survey reported they were not interested in sex or were averse to sex. The figures for women at each age range are notably much higher than they are for men. This is in contrast to data presented earlier that shows young women more likely to report experience of sexual intercourse than young men. There has been little exploration of why the figure is so high for women.

In his popular book, *Sekkusu kirai na wakamonotachi* (*Young People who Hate Sex*), Kitamura Kunio devoted all but a few pages of the book to discussing male youth and their apparent lack of interest in having sexual relationships. Female sexuality is not touched upon until page 111. Kitamura suggests that young men are turning their backs on three-dimensional sexuality (person-to-person) and instead engaging in two-dimensional, masturbationary encounters through digital media and manga. This viewpoint has gained currency in the media. He suggests that many young men do not feel they have the economic resources for dating and/ or they are not confident in their ability to attract women. Within the context of a gendered discourse of youth sexuality, female sexuality is being represented as largely passive. Kitamura speculates that if young women are reporting that they dislike or lack interest in sex, the cause must be the poor skills or performance of young men. Nevertheless, no evidence is presented in the book to back up this idea (Kitamura 2011). What I would like to do now is move on to provide space for an emic perspective on youth sexuality.

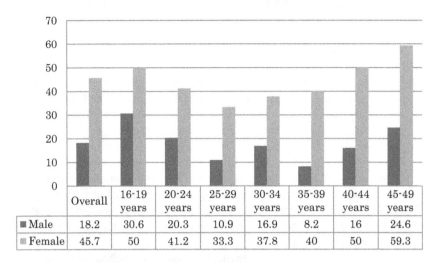

Figure 4.3 Percentage of men and women reporting no interest in or dislike of sex by age group, 2016

Source: JFPA (2016)

The voices of young people on sex education

Without wanting to over-emphasize the influence of sex education in its highly marginalized positioning in the Japanese curriculum, I would like to argue that it functions as a regulatory mechanism within a broader, highly conservative discourse that denies young people a space as "legitimately sexual" and does so in highly "constraining gendered and heteronormative ways" (Allen and Carmody 2012: 458). In the context of below-replacement fertility, this regulatory mechanism may be having unanticipated effects with young people ending up regarding sexual behavior us "dangerous, dirty, risky and/or murky".[2]

I have been delivering a lecture on sexuality to first-year undergraduate students at Osaka University as part of the course "Women's studies, men's studies: Thinking about discrimination" for the past ten years. As an elective assignment, I have had students write reflectively about their associations with the word "sex", and their experiences of sex education. I also asked them to imagine what school-based sex education should look like if the aim were to convey a sex-positive message. They were also asked to give their opinion on "sexless youth". While this is a highly selected voice of youth, over the past ten years there has been incredible consistency in the way my students have talked about sex and sex education. Their surprise at the idea that sex could be healthy and the consistency with which certain words appeared to describe how sex was constructed through sex education, such as scary (*kowai*), dirty (*kitanai*), impure (*yogore*), dangerous (*kiken*), and taboo (*tabū*), runs through most of the reports I have received over the past decade.

62 *Beverley Anne Yamamoto*

Drawing on reports submitted in the 2016 academic year, I would like to cite some representative views. All translations of the original Japanese are my own.

> While at junior high and high school, due to the policy of those in charge I received much more in-depth sex education than took place at other schools (we even learned how to use a condom while at junior high school). However, because the content was treated negatively the image I gained of sex was "scary". As this way of thinking about sex was so profoundly instilled in me I never thought I might want to embrace a more positive image, but for those students who have yet to have any sex education I would really like them to be given more positive contents. When it comes to the causes of young people having no interest in sex, I think the compression of time is one reason. In other words, we are expected to be efficient with everything and work time has increased so time to spend on sex is just not there and we are too tired to get into that kind of mood anyway. I think this is probably the main cause.
>
> (Female, first year in the School of Engineering)

The above passage is impressive for its insights, and in different ways I have heard young people articulate ideas about sexuality education and sexlessness in similar ways.

> Up until now I have naturally thought about sex negatively with the view that it is dirty, and shameful. However, Japanese sex education is only from the perspective of biology and medicine and although there are many things I would like to know about sex it is hard to ask because talking about sex is taboo. In addition, the very important topic of "consent" is not covered at all. I think that the fact that there are problems around sex and sex crimes can be put down to this kind of sex education. I would like us to start thinking about sexuality as something healthy.
>
> (Female, first year student in the School of Letters)

Consent was one issue that we discussed in class. Despite Japan having an age of sexual consent that is lower than most other developed countries, age 13, the issue of consent is not covered in schools. Indeed, legal issues around sexuality are not covered in sex education.

Students express surprise that they have been given space to think and discuss sexuality, as the following student's comment makes clear.

> In Japan, when you have sex education students breath a heavy sigh and the atmosphere that is created makes you feel that there is something embarrassing about the whole thing. For me too, I feel strongly that this was how I was made to feel. As it is always necessary to attune yourself to the opinion of others I have never had the opportunity to express positive views up until

now. I think that today's lecture allowed me to think more about sex than I ever had in my life before.

(Male, first year student in the School of Engineering Science)

The comments I have received over the years suggest that the young internalize a negative image of sex and have few resources to develop a more positive image. This does not necessary stop young people from engaging in sexual relationships as the JASE data presented earlier makes clear, but it may affect how they think about such relationships and the way in which they value it. It is important not to lay the blame solely on sex education, but to understand how sexuality is represented in wider society. As one student astutely noted:

I think the reason why we cannot be open about sex has less to do with sex education and more to do with the negative way in which sex is dealt with generally in Japanese society. I don't know if this is good or not, but I think this way of thinking may have speeded up the trend towards very low fertility (*shōshika*).

(Male, first year student in the School of Engineering Science)

Some of the ideas expressed by the students echoe Kon's writing about herbivore men who may feel sexual desire is something "gross" (Kon 2009: 25). While the Heisei generation may have different values around sex, the tendency to view it negatively may be a point of commonality with older generations.

Youth as opinion leaders around sexuality and their discourse of resilience

When planning to write this chapter, I spoke with a group of four young people, two male and two female, who are active around reproductive and sexual health/rights issues in Tokyo, in March 2016. Two gave me permission to use their names. Both are organization leaders. One is Yanagida Masayoshi, President of Link-R,[3] a Japanese NGO providing sexual and reproductive health/rights related services to youth in Japan. He is also a member of the World Association of Sexual Health (WAS) Youth Initiatives Committee and a former member of U-COM, a youth committee established by the Japan Family Planning Association. Born in 1983, he is not quite a member of Heisei youth, but a key member of the youth movement on sexual and reproductive health.

The other youth leader is Horisawa Mio, a university student training to be a *yogo*, or nurse teacher. Horisawa is leader of the Adolescent Health Committee[4] (Shishunki Hoken I'inkai), a volunteer group with links to Link-R made up largely of students studying health, medicine or health education. She has been involved with organizing the annual LGBT Seijinshiki@Saitama (LGBT coming

64 *Beverley Anne Yamamoto*

of age at Saitama) activities. The other two interviewees are active in this group. One is a nurse and the other a university student. Horisawa and her group seek to make up for the gaps in school-based sex education to ensure that young people not only have correct knowledge, but also like themselves and feel empowered.

When asked whether young people felt pressured to marry and have children given the very low birthrate, the consensus was that these seemed quite a distant issue for most young people that they spoke to. For many, they thought, the focus was on successfully becoming a *shakaijin*, or a full contributing member of society, which was largely measured through *shūshoku*, or getting employment. This was seen to be the case whether the young person was male or female. With anxieties about the future, it was seen as difficult to commit to a relationship in the present. Having a relationship was not a priority even under the weight of societal expectations to produce the next generation.

Echoing Sugiura noted above, these four activist young people noted that the gendered pathways to adulthood that dominated in the past, where a man was expected to work and be the economic provider and the woman the homemaker and mother raising children, seemed to have less resonance in their lives. Getting steady employment was seen as the main worry and unless that part of the transition to adulthood was successfully negotiated, then getting a partner and starting a family was something far in the distance. Even more casual dating seemed to be off the agenda. Issues around economic instability mentioned as important by writers such as Genda and Kawakami (2006) and the complexity of negotiating a successful transition to adulthood noted by Ishida (2013) and Kato (2011), among others, were reflected in the understandings of these young people.

Psychological reasons were also forwarded for any reluctance of young people to date or enter sexual relationships. One member of the youth group, a nurse, suggested that many young people raised in families where they are the only child or only have one sibling are not used to sharing or being physically close to others. She noted that some young people find it difficult to be physically close to others. The idea of embracing the sweaty body or smell of another person is repugnant, she felt. In a society where many young people wear masks in order to protect themselves from the "germs" of others, physical intimacy may be difficult.

Rather than accept the current status quo, theses four young leaders have been working as advocates and opinion leaders around reproductive and sexual health/rights. They are offering drop-in counseling sessions at different locations in Tokyo, conducting workshops and lectures on sexuality, and taking part in youth-adult think tanks and projects to raise awareness around sexuality. Asked the importance of their activities around sexuality and reproductive health/rights for them personally, and for other youth and wider society, Yanagida and Horisawa offered the following explanations:

> For me personally, when I was 19 years old, I decided to work on promoting sexual health issues and solving adolescent's concerns. So, I decided I will continue this work whatever happens. For other youth, I want to provide places and opportunities for young people to ask advice about their sexual problems. For wider society, if adults see that young people are *genki* (healthy and energetic) adults also become *genki*. If adults are *genki*, then young people will

Youth sexuality under the spotlight 65

be *genki*. As a result of this cycle, communities and wider society will also be active and healthy. Whether young people are socially, economically and politically strong or weak, as they become adults they have a role to play in society. To be able to do this it is necessary to learn life skills so that that the older generation can hand over the baton to the younger generation.

(Yanagida, 19 September 2017)

Yanagida offers an inclusive vision where everyone can contribute to society whether strong or weak. He also articulates a very strong interest in the promotion of youth sexual health.

Horisawa's response was in many ways more pragmatic. She sees it as one aspect of her future career as a nursing teacher. However, her vision is of herself as a teacher who acts as a facilitator to help young people to think about their sexual and reproductive health/rights. Horisawa states:

I don't want to be the kind of nursing teacher that is tied to her own experiences and values relating to sex. I want [my students] to be able to think deeply about their own life plan based on their own thinking about reproductive health and rights.

(Horisawa, 19 September 2017)

She hopes to make a difference to young people by passing on knowledge about sexuality when topics relating to sex and relationships come up. She can introduce her own youth activities and this she thinks will make it easier for them "to ask her questions without hesitation". As a result of this, Horisawa hopes to contribute to wider society by helping to decrease the number of unwanted pregnancies and sexually transmitted infections. She also hopes that her role in sexual counseling and LGBT activities will be "a model for students to take part in activities about sexual issues" (Horisawa, 18 September 2017).

When asked about the challenges they face in their activities, Yanagida talked about economic constraints and having to deal with social prejudice. Economically, it is hard to raise funds to support their activities. On the other hand, they come face-to-face with deep-rooted taboos around sexuality.

As we are involved in sex education it is thought that we are going to awaken young people to sex and they will be promiscuous. Young women will take the pill and then will be sexually promiscuous, etc. As a result of this kind of mistaken thinking and prejudice (social values) there are many cases when we just can't move things ahead.

(Yanagida, 18 September 2017)

Horisawa notes that it is difficult to get young people involved in the activities and that there is a trust issue when you are dealing with sexual issues.

One problem is that the number of members of our organization is small. People are happy to take part in events, but it is hard to get them to be active in

66 *Beverley Anne Yamamoto*

the organization. There is also the problem that when you introduce yourself as an organization involved in activities around sex then people are suspicious. I think it is good to hold events that are a little removed from the subject of sex that students will think of as fun and interesting.

(Horisawa, 19 September 2017)

These young people's activities are a clear demonstration of their resilience. While on the one hand, wider society is concerned that young men are not interested in sex, on the other, youth who are attempting to change the conditions in which young people understand and experience the sexual face tough barriers that make it difficult to bring about change.

Outlook

This chapter has explored youth sexuality in low fertility and hyper-aging Japan. We have focused both on survey data and popular discursive accounts of youth sexuality to do this. On the one hand, survey data points to a dramatic shift in values and behavior between the mid-1970s and the mid-1990s, in which sexual intercourse became an accepted and relatively normal (normative) part of young adulthood. Yet the data also suggests that many young people are not sustaining sexual activity into adulthood, when fewer and fewer men or women report having an intimate or even friendship relationship with the "opposite sex". On the other, sex education remains limited and efforts made to engage young people on sexual issues generate criticisms that they are being sexualized.

While adult society resists recognizing young people as legitimate sexual beings, it also desires men to be carnivore males with strong sexual desire and the motivation to pursue women for sexual intimacy. The discourse around herbivore men reproduces stereotypical ideas around gender and sexuality. It seems to be tied to notions of manhood that belong in an earlier age. While logically, recent concerns about sexlessness should create a space for thinking about sex in a more positive way, this is not generally happening. On the one hand, the young people whose voices come through clearly in this chapter are engaging in a positive way with sexual health and rights, and active around LGBT issues. On the other, adult gatekeepers still frame intimacy in terms of men pursuing sex with women, who in turn are positioned as "the opposite sex".

Notes

1 It is reasonable to assume that those currently using contraception are either engaged in a sexual relationship or expect to be in the near future for the minority who might be using an oral contraceptive or IUD. The male condom remains overwhelmingly the most commonly used form of contraception in Japan even today.
2 These are words that have frequently been offered by students in my classes to describe their immediate association with the word "sex".
3 Link-R website in English Online available at: www.link-r.org/english
4 The website is only in Japanese Online available at: http://hoken.link-r.org/

References

Allen, Louisa and Moira Carmody (2012) Pleasure Has No Passport: Revisiting the Potential of Pleasure in Sexuality Education. *Sex Education* 12(4): 455–468.

Arahori, Kenji (1990) Shishunki ninshin no toriatsukai – ishi no tachiba kara. [Dealing with Adolescent Pregnancy: From the Perspective of the Doctor]. *Shūsanki igaku* 20(5): 625–628.

Asai, Haruo, Kunio Kimura, Noriko Hashimoto and Yukihiro Murase (eds.) (2003) *Jendā furii sei-kyōiku Bashing* [Bashing of Gender-Free Education]. Tokyo: Ōtsuki Shoten.

Asayama, Shinichi (1977) Current Status of Sex Research and Sex Education in Japan. In: *Progress in Sexology: Selected Proceedings from the International Congress of Sexology*. Robert Gemme and Connie Christine Wheller (eds.), 577–581. Boston: Springer.

Beppu, Motomi (2010) Analysis of Marriage Divorce and Transition to Adulthood: Marital Status Life Tables, 1930–2005. In: *The Changing Transition to Adulthood in Japan: Current Demographic Research and Policy Implications*. National Institute of Population and Social Security Research (ed.), 3–32. Tokyo: National Institute of Population and Social Security Research.

Fine, Michelle (1988) Sexuality, Schooling, and Adolescent Females: The Missing Discourse of Desire. *Harvard Educational Review* 58(1): 29–54.

Genda, Yuji and Atsushi Kawakami (2006) Seigyō no nikyokuka to seikōdō [Job Polarization and Sexual Behavior]. *Nihon rōdō kenkyū zasshi* 556: 92–105.

Ishida, Hiroshi (2013) Transition to Adulthood Among Japanese Youths. *The ANNALS of the American Academy of Political and Social Science* 646(1): 86–106.

Ishiwata, Chieko (2011) Sexual Health Education for School Children in Japan: The Timing and Contents. *Japan Medical Association Journal* 54(3): 155–160.

JASE (=Japan Association for Sex Education) (1975) *Seishōnen no seikōdō – wagakuni no kōkōsei, daigakusei ni kansuru chōsa hōkoku* [The Sexual Behaviour of Japanese Youth. A Report on the Study of Japanese High School and University Students in Japan]. Tokyo: Shōgakukan.

——— (2013) *Seishōnen no seikōdō – wagakuni no kōkōsei, daigakusei ni kansuru chōsa hōkoku* [The Sexual Behaviour of Japanese Youth: A Report on the Study of Japanese High School and University Students in Japan]. Tokyo: Shōgakukan.

——— (2016) *Nihon seikyōiku kyōkai (JASE) ni tsuite* [About the Japan Association for Sex Education (JASE)]. Online available at: www.jase.faje.or.jp/about_jase/index.html (accessed 16 July 2016).

JFPA (=Japan Family Planning Association) (2016) *Dai-8-kai danjo no seikatsu to ishiki ni kansuru chōsa – nihonjin no sei'ishiki seikōdō* [Report on the 8th Survey of Male and Female Lifestyle and Attitudes: The Sexual Attitudes and Behaviour of Japanese People]. CD ROM.

Kato, Akihiko (2010) The Mechanism Underlying Very Low Fertility in Japan: The Trend toward Later and Less Marriage, the Rising Divorce Rate, and Declining Marital Fertility. In: *The Changing Transition to Adulthood in Japan: Current Demographic Research and Policy Implications*. National Institute of Population and Social Security Research (ed.), 139–156. Tokyo: National Institute of Population and Social Security Research.

——— (2011) Mikonka mekanizumu [The Mechanism of Increasing Singlehood]. In: *Shōshika no gen'in toshite no seijin ikō no henka ni kansuru jinkōgaku-teki kenkyū – dai 3 hōkōsho*. National Institute of Population and Social Security Research (ed.), 5–39. Tokyo: National Institute of Population and Social Security Research.

Kitamura, Kunio (2011) *Sekkusu kirai na wakamonotachi* [Youth Who Hate Sex]. Tokyo: Mediafakutori Shinsho.

68 Beverley Anne Yamamoto

Kon, Issho (2009) *Ubawareta seiyoku* (Stolen Sexual Desire). Tokyo: Maikomi Shinsho.

Lindau, Stacy Tessler and Natalia Gavrilova (2010) Sex, Health, and Years of Sexually Active Life Gained due to Good Health: Evidence from two US Population Based Cross Sectional Surveys of Aging. *BMJ* 340: c810. Online available at: www.bmj.com/content/340/bmj.c810 (accessed 31 August 2017).

Matsumoto, Sei'ichi (1985) Health Needs of Adolescents and Sex Education. In: *Basic Readings on Population and Family Planning in Japan.* Minoru Muramatsu and Tameyoshi Katagiri (eds.), 156–178. Tokyo: Japanese Organization for International Co-operation in Family Planning.

Morioka, Masahiro (2013) *Kanjinai otoko* [Man Who Do Not Feel]. Tokyo: Chikuma Shobō.

Murase, Yukihiro (2005) The Backlash Against Sex Education and HIV/AIDS Issues. *Women Asia 21 Voices from Japan* 14(4): 55–58.

Retherford, Robert, Naohiro Ogawa and Rikiya Matsura (2001) Late Marriage and Less Marriage in Japan. *Population and Development Review* 27(1): 65–102.

Sato, Ryozaburō and Miho Iwasawa (2015) The Sexual Behaviour of Adolescents and Young Adults in Japan. In: *Low Fertility and Reproductive Health in East Asia.* Naohiro Ogawa and Iqbal Shah (eds.), 137–159. London: Springer.

Sechiyama, Kaku (2014) Japan, the Sexless Nation. *Tokyo Business Today* (19 December). Online available at: http://toyokeizai.net/articles/-/56360 (accessed 30 August 2017).

Smith, G. Davey, Stephen Frankel and John Yarnell (1997) Sex and Death. Are they Related? Findings from the Caerphilly Cohort Study. *BMJ* 315: 1641–1644.

Sugiura, Yumiko (2011) *20-dai josei ga sekkusu shiteinai – joseitachi wa naze dansei ni mitomerarenai?* [Why Do Women in Their 20s Not Have Sex: Why Are These Women Not Desirable to Men?] Tokyo: Kakokawa Shoten.

Tashiro, Mieko, Kaori Ushitora and Daisuke Watanabe (2011) The Actual Situation of Sexuality Education in Japan and its Problems: Fact-finding for Teachers Interested in Sexuality Education. *Journal of Saitama University Faculty of Education* 60(1): 9–22.

WHO = World Health Organization (2006) *Defining Sexual Health: Report of a Technical Consultation on Sexual Health* (28–31 January 2002). Geneva: World Health Organization.

Yamamoto, Beverley Anne (2009) A Window on Trends and Shifting Interpretations of Youth Sexual Behaviour: The Japan Association for Sex Education's "Wakamono no Hakusho" Reports 1975 to 2006. *Social Science Japan Journal* 12(2): 277–284.

Yonemoto, Shohei (1997) AIDS Policy in Japan: Integration within Structured Paternalism. *Journal of Acquired Immune Deficiency Syndromes and Human Retrovirology* 14: 17–21.

5 Raising children and the emergence of new fatherhood in a super-aging society

Masako Ishii-Kuntz

Introduction

In Japan, some major demographic changes over the past decades such as social aging, delay in first marriage, decline in fertility, and an increase in women's labor force participation have necessitated adjustments in the parental sharing of childcare. For example, although the Japanese overall population has been rapidly aging, we have witnessed a decrease in the number of three-generational households. This means that for many young Japanese families, grandparents can no longer be considered as a main support for childcare at home. A rise in female labor force participation also makes it necessary to reevaluate and improve both formal and informal support systems for childcare, with the latter including fathers' involvement in childrearing. These recent demographic changes, along with the shortage of daycare centers and other childcare facilities, and the father-friendly revisions of the childcare leave law all point to the direction of increased paternal involvement in childcare. The emergence of "new fatherhood" since the mid-2000s, therefore, can be seen as a result of these changes and demands.

In this chapter, I discuss the new generation of fathers called *ikumen* ("child caring dads") in contemporary Japan. To accomplish this objective, I will first explain how demographic changes and family policies and laws have contributed to the rise of *ikumen*. Second, I will summarize research findings on fatherhood in Japan. I will also discuss the effects of social aging on the emergence of new fatherhood. Finally, I will explain how the post-bubble generation of Japanese men has adopted this new fatherhood and the sharing of childcare responsibilities with their spouses.

Demographic changes and family policies/laws

Social aging: current state and future outlook

According to the Cabinet Office (2017), only 4.9 percent of the total population was older than the age 65 in 1950, but this percentage increased dramatically to 26.7 percent in 2015. It is projected that by 2055, almost 40 percent of the entire population or one in 2.5 Japanese will be over the age of 65. Additionally, the

70 *Masako Ishii-Kuntz*

population ratio of over-65-year-olds and those between 15 and 64 was 1:11.2 (one elderly person for every 11.2 younger people) in 1960, but it dropped to 1:3.3 in 2005 and 1:2.3 in 2015, and it is predicted to fall down to 1:1.3 by 2055 (Cabinet Office 2017). Despite the increase of the aged population in Japan, the proportion of extended households has been decreasing over the past few decades from 19.2 percent of the total households in 1970 to 6.6 percent in 2013 (Ministry of Health, Labour and Welfare 2013). This implies that although their parents may be living in a close proximity, younger fathers and mothers are less likely to be able to depend on their own parents to care for their children. This also means that many younger parents today are faced with a challenge of coordinating who cares for their children while they are at work and when children are sick. This, in turn, leads to a redefinition of the roles for the younger generation in terms of what it means to be a man or a woman, a father or a mother.

Delay in first marriage, increase in never-marrieds, and declining fertility

The decline in birthrates is caused not only by the cost of raising children in Japan but also by the delay of the first marriage and the increase of ever-single individuals. According to the 2015 Japanese National Fertility Survey, 43.3 percent and 41.9 percent of single men and women, respectively, cited "not having sufficient amount of money" as the most serious obstacle against marriage (National Institute of Population and Social Security Research 2016). Considering other reasons such as not possessing a residence to live after marriage and job-related demands, the lack of financial resources seems to be a major reason for the delay in first marriage. This is consistent with the personal economic decline experienced among those born in the Heisei period. In addition, the same survey found that among the singles, 69.5 percent of men and 59.1 percent of women have no intimate partners, and that 30.2 percent and 25.9 percent of men and women, respectively, do not wish to have such partners, perhaps reflecting the emergence of a "relationless" Japanese society.

Marriage may not always be a prerequisite for having a baby in other countries. However, marriage is often considered as a necessity for having a baby in Japan (Osawa and Komamura 1994). This is evident by the smaller proportion of babies born out of wedlock in Japan (2.1 percent in 2008) compared to those in other countries (e.g., France 52.6 percent, Sweden 54.7 percent, US 40.6 percent, and Italy 17.7 percent). This low number of children born outside of marriage in Japan may be attributed to the discriminatory Civil Law which states that these children are not fully entitled to their fathers' inheritance, and the negative images given against single or unwed mothers and their children in Japanese society. Thus, the delay in marriage and an increase of never-marrieds are likely to reduce the fertility rate in Japan (Tachibanaki and Kimura 2008; Yamae 2013).

The average age of the first marriage was 26.9 for men and 24.2 for women in 1970, but these ages increased to 31.1 and 29.4 for men and women, respectively, in 2015 (Ministry of Health, Labour and Welfare 2016). Additionally, the number of men and women who have never been married at the age of 50 increased between 2010 and 2015 from 20.1 percent to 23.3 percent for men and 10.6 percent to 14.1 percent for women. These data also reveal that the delay in marriage and the increase in never-marrieds are particularly evident for Japanese men.

Japan's birthrate has steadily declined from the mid-1970s, and in 1989, Japan experienced the so-called "1.57 shock" with women having the average of 1.57 babies that year which was lower than the birthrate of 1.58 recorded in 1966, the year of the "Fire Horse" which is associated with disasters. In 2005, Japan's lowest fertility rate of 1.26 was reported, but it slightly increased to 1.45 in 2015.

Rise in mothers' labor force participation

Another demographic change affecting parental roles is an increase of employed mothers. When Japanese women's labor force participation rate is illustrated according to age, it shows a characteristic M-shaped pattern, with the early 20s and late 40s forming the two peaks of the letter "M" and a dip in between (30s and early 40s). However, a growing number of women in the 25–29 and 30–34 age groups are remaining in the workforce in recent years, resulting in the acceleration of the bottom of this M-shaped curve. For example, approximately 43 percent of women in their late 20s and early 30s were employed in 1975, but this figure went up to 75 percent in 2014 (Cabinet Office 2015). Citing the reasons for this increase, the White Paper on Women's Labor (Ministry of Health, Labour and Welfare 2002) concludes that, besides the growing number of women receiving higher education and not marrying, the changing trend may be explained by the increasing willingness (or necessity) of women to work and raise a family at the same time.

It should also be noted that despite an increase of working women, many of them are non-regular employees (e.g., part-time workers and temporary dispatched workers) instead of regular, full-time employees. In 2014, these non-regular workers constituted 56.7 percent of all female employees. According to the Labor Force Survey (Ministry of Internal Affairs and Communications 2017), 17.1 percent of women reported "childcare demand" as the main reason to be employed part-time. With respect to the relationship between women's employment and the sharing of household labor, their husbands' participation in housework and childcare was found to encourage women's full-time employment (Fujino 2002).

Social aging, decrease in three-generational households, decline in fertility caused partly by delayed marriage, and the rise of women's participation in labor force are all related to how younger Japanese parents today raise their children. For much of Japanese history, families maintained the patriarchal-hierarchal system with an emphasis on highly gendered relationships of a husband as a breadwinner and a wife as a caregiver. These demographic changes, however, necessitate the change and adjustment of the traditional familial roles pointing to the direction of more equally shared childrearing and housework between husbands and wives.

72   *Masako Ishii-Kuntz*

Family policies and laws

There are two types of support for younger Japanese parents today: one is a formal support provided by the government policies, laws, and programs and the other is an informal support given by family members, relatives and friends. In this section, I will review the formal support system for Japanese parents raising younger children, including the Childcare Leave Law, daycare facilities, and other family support programs, all of which have been receiving great attention by parents who are most likely to be part of the post-bubble generation.

In 1999, the Japanese government enacted the Basic Law for a Gender-equal Society, which lays down the basic principle related to the formation of gender-equal society, and clarifies the respective duties of the state, local governments, and citizens. This law clearly states that both women and men can equally participate in many activities, including paid work and family care, without resorting back to the traditional gender roles. In 2000, the Basic Plan for a Gender-equal Society was drawn up to further promote gender equality in Japan. The third phase of this plan emphasizes the importance of changing men's lives, such as reducing their long work hours and increasing their involvement in childcare. It also promotes men and women to take childcare leave from work.

Partly in response to the "1.57 shock" in 1989 and with the assumption that the husbands' participation in childcare would encourage women to have more babies, the Childcare Leave Law was revised in 1992 allowing fathers, for the first time, to take the leave from work. Although this revision was considered "progressive" at the time, men still had to clear many hurdles to actually take such a leave. These problems included the lack of financial compensation and health insurance coverage during the leave as well as harassment by and lack of understanding of their bosses and coworkers (Ishii-Kuntz 2013a).

After several minor revisions over the past decades, the government decided to strengthen the "father-friendliness" aspect of the law by introducing the following three major revisions in the 2010 Child and Elder Care Leave Law.

- Men whose wives are full-time homemakers can take the leave. (Prior to this, only men whose wives were employed could take the leave.)
- If fathers take the first childcare leave during their wives' maternity leave, they can re-take the leave after the maternity leave ends. (Prior to this, men could take the leave only once during the 12-month period after the birth of the baby.)
- If both mothers and fathers take childcare leave, then they can extend the leave up to 14 months. This is called "Papa Mama Childcare Plus". (Prior to this, whether it is a father or a mother, they could only take up to 12 months childcare leave.)

As shown in Figure 5.1, 1.38 percent of working fathers took childcare leave in 2010, and it was almost doubled to 2.63 percent in 2011, after the law was revised. It should also be noted that 2.65 percent in 2015 was the highest record since the

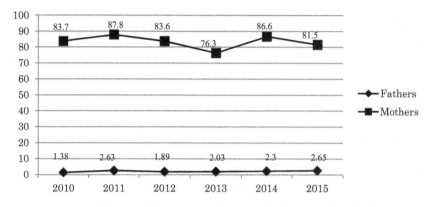

Figure 5.1 Percentage of fathers and mothers taking childcare leave, 2010–2015
Source: Adapted from Ministry of Health, Labour and Welfare, figure compiled by the author

law made it possible for fathers to take the leave in 1992. However, the table also shows that whereas the majority (about 76–88 percent) of working mothers took childcare leave between 2010 and 2015, only a very small proportion of fathers took such a leave.

This gender gap is also clearly seen with regard to the length of childcare leave taken by mothers and fathers. For mothers, the most frequently reported length of childcare leave was ten to 12 months with 32.4 percent of them taking a leave of this length, whereas for fathers, only 0.4 percent took ten to 12 months leave (Ministry of Health, Labour and Welfare 2010). In contrast, most fathers (81.3 percent) were taking childcare leave of less than a month. Of these fathers, 17.3 percent took a "two to four week" leave, 28.9 percent took a "five day to less than two week" leave, and 35.1 percent took a "less than five day" leave. Atsumi (2010) coined the term *nanchatte ikukyu* ("just kidding childcare leave") to refer to these men who were taking extremely short childcare leave. This type of short childcare leave is usually taken because the company is under a lot of pressure from the government to create a gender-equal work environment (Ishii-Kuntz 2013a), thus male employees taking even a short childcare leave can be seen as the company making efforts toward gender-equality.

Shortage of daycare centers

The 2006 white paper on the national lifestyle entitled *Perceptions and Lifestyle of the Child-Rearing Generation* used the term "the socialization of childrearing" as "the process by which the whole of society becomes involved (in childrearing) rather than treating the issue as strictly the responsibility of families" (Cabinet Office 2005: 28). It further expresses the concern over the child-rearing

74   *Masako Ishii-Kuntz*

generation shouldering an excessive burden of pension funding, taxes, and social security. Apparently, what is behind this recommendation is to achieve a speedy recovery in the fertility rate. However, despite the government's concerted efforts for the whole society to get involved in childcare, the goal still seems far away as exemplified by the problem of the shortage of daycare centers. This problem is evident by the persistent number of children on the waiting list to enter daycare centers that provide care for 0 to 6-year-old preschoolers. According to the Ministry of Health, Labour and Welfare (2017), although there is a wide local variation, more than 20,000 children have been waitlisted annually since 2010.

This problem caught the public attention by one mother's online rant in February 2016. Entitled *Hoikuen ochita. Nihon shine*!! ("Didn't get a slot in daycare. Drop dead, Japan!!"), this anonymous mother described her continuing struggle with the daycare center shortage and asserted that the failure to address the problem belies the vow by Prime Minister Abe to promote women's active engagement in the society. Several dozen people inspired by the blog, mostly women, held a rally in front of the Diet building to call for an increase in the number of daycare centers. Others began an online campaign on the petition site demanding a systemic overhaul (Japan Times 2016).

In addition to the complexities involved in the paperwork to apply for a daycare center (Omagari 2014), several other factors are cited as the reasons why this problem remains in spite of the low childbirth rate in Japan. First, due to the prolonged economic recession, there has been an increase of dual-earner couples but the supply of daycare centers has not caught up with the demand for such centers. In fact, the number of dual-earner households has steadily increased since 1980 and finally exceeded to that of single-earner households in 1997, and in 2014, approximately 60 percent of all the married couple households were dual-earner families (Prime Minister's Office 2015). Second, the shortage of daycare centers is particularly evident in larger cities because of the ever-increasing inbound migration into cities that provide many job opportunities. At the same time, however, these cities are experiencing difficulties to build additional daycare facilities because of the oppositions by the neighbors in many communities. These are the people living near the proposed sites of daycare facilities, and most of them express their concerns over the elevated noise level caused by children attending daycare centers. Third, the shortage of daycare center staff has been a major problem. Recently, the Abe administration announced the increase in salary for these daycare center staffs. However, in addition to lower pay scale, stressful working environment and overwork may also be the reasons why there are few applicants who want to work at daycare centers.

Other family support programs

The government's effort for the socialization of child-rearing can be seen in two family support programs, the Family Support Center and Childcare Giver (*hoiku mama*) program. The Family Support Center was first established in 2005 with a funding support from the Ministry of Health, Labour and Welfare. Both the

Raising children and new fatherhood 75

recipients and the providers of childcare are registered at each center, then the advisor coordinates by matching the parents with preschool or school-age children with those who want to provide care for them. These paid childcare givers provide all kinds of assistance for parents such as taking children to daycare center or school, picking them up after school, and caring for them when they are sick. The length of care time can be flexible depending on the needs of parents and the availability of care providers. As of 2015, there are 490,000 members listed as recipients of support whereas 130,000 members are listed as care providers, thus the demand-supply imbalance still exists.

The origin of the childcare giver program dates back to the late 1940s when they were called "foster parent for the day". In the 1960s and 1970s, the name was changed to "family welfare agent". Today, these are mostly women who provide care in their homes for children under the age of three whose parent(s) is employed, and who could not enter the daycare centers. In 2010, the new certification system began, which made this position "official". The childcare givers could be certified if they were daycare and kindergarten teachers, nurses, midwives, or public health nurses. With the loosening of the standard, those without these credentials can now become childcare givers after completing some set amount of training.

Emergence of new fatherhood: summary of research findings

Fathers' involvement in childrearing: past and present

In recent decades, the demand for Japanese fathers' participation in childcare has been increasing not only among their wives but also by the government and private companies. This does not mean, however, that Japanese fathers have never been involved in raising their children in the past. By analyzing the diaries of lower-ranked samurai in the Edo period (1603–1868), Ōta (1994) found that fathers in this period were actively involved in educating and disciplining their sons although the physical care was given by mothers and maids. Between Meiji and pre-WW II eras, Japanese salaryman families adopted what became "traditional" gender roles in which fathers became breadwinners, and mothers assumed family care giving role (Muta 1996). Under this family system, "authoritarian" fathers were feared by their children at the same level as earthquakes, thunder, and fires. Japanese men's devotion to work has contributed, in a larger context, to Japan's postwar "economic miracle" (Vogel 1979). At the same time, it has also resulted in limited involvement of fathers with their families (Ishii-Kuntz 1992).

It was not until the 1990s when the Japanese began paying more attention to fathers' roles and diverse types of fatherhood (Ishii-Kuntz 2013a). The increasing attention over the roles of fathers in the early 1990s can be attributed to the so-called "1.57 shock" of 1989. The low fertility rate of 1989 marked the beginning of the governmental efforts to establish family-friendly laws and policies, including the campaigns for the increased paternal involvement. The diversity

76　*Masako Ishii-Kuntz*

in fatherhood was also debated in the 1990s. On one hand, a strong presence of fathers as authoritarian figures is desired, as Hayashi (1996) wrote in his book *Fusei no fukken (Restoration of Paternity)*. On the other hand, several books about involved fathers were written by men who took childcare leave, and who went on daily one-hour "strikes" to take their children to daycare centers (Otoko mo Onna mo Ikuji Jikan o Renrakukai 1995; Tajiri 1990).

What contributed to the increasing attention to fatherhood in the 1990s were the decline in fertility and the subsequent government campaigns promoting paternal involvement, fatherhood research in developmental psychology, the introduction of men and masculinity studies to the Japanese academia and general public, research on mothers' childcare stress and anxiety in family sociology, and the emergence of men's and fatherhood movements.

First, in response to the sharp decline in fertility since the 1970s and with the assumption that fathers' participation in childcare would encourage Japanese women to have more babies, Japanese government formulated several plans to reduce childcare demands for younger parents (mothers, in particular). One such effort is the 1992 revision of the Childcare Leave Law that allowed men to take the leave. Eventually, the Japanese government conducted several nationwide campaigns to increase both the awareness and the level of fathers' involvement in childcare. The first such campaign was carried out in 1999 by the Ministry of Welfare with the poster caption of "A man who doesn't raise his children can't be called a father." This caption was considered "sensational" at the time but a poster picture of a long-haired choreographer called "Sam" wearing a somewhat feminized white shirt did not look anything like a typical Japanese salaryman. Nevertheless, the campaign contributed to raise the awareness of the general public on the importance of paternal involvement (Ishii-Kuntz 2013a).

Second, the increased attention on fatherhood can be attributed to research in developmental psychology that found various positive effects of paternal involvement on child development (e.g., Kashiwagi 1993; Makino, Nakano and Kashiwagi 1996). These pioneering studies on fatherhood contributed to an increase in research attention on fathers' child caring roles at home.

Third, the field of men's studies was introduced to Japan by Itō (1995) in the 1990s. Itō argued that the problems Japanese women faced were a central concern in Japan in the 1970s and 1980s, but the 1990s should be the era to solve the problems that men were experiencing. These problems included men's inability and struggle to escape from the hegemonic masculine ideals. It was thus considered necessary to change the traditional gender ideology that emphasized men's breadwinning and women's care giving roles. The emergence of men's studies in 1990s contributed to cast a doubt on the hegemonic salaryman masculinity in Japan.

Fourth, many reports of maternal stress and anxiety, a few of which resulted in the killing and abusing of children in the 1980s, prompted research attention on mothers' childcare stress and anxiety. Makino's (1982) series of studies on these topics highlighted the importance of supportive networks for mothers as well as their husbands' participation in childcare and housework to improve mother's psychological wellbeing.

Raising children and new fatherhood 77

Finally, in response to the needs of men and women, a good number of men's support groups and NPOs were established in the 1990s. The roots of these groups date back to the 1978 formation of *Otoko no Kosodate o Kangaeru-kai* ("Association to Think about Fathers' Participation in Childcare"). The establishment of *Otoko mo Onna mo Ikuji Jikan o Renraku-kai* ("Network of Men and Women for Childcare Hours") in 1980 also contributed to the rise of men's movement groups in the 1990s. One such group was *Men's Lib Kenkyūkai* (Study Group on Men's Liberation) that was founded in 1991. With a wide range of men's activities such as sponsoring forums and festivals, these men's groups presented the diverse images of Japanese fatherhood to the general public. Although this movement came to an end by the late 1990s, it greatly contributed to the creation of an *ikumen* culture in the 2000s (Ishii-Kuntz 2013a; Taga 2006).

New fatherhood: the ikumen *phenomenon*

Ikumen are those men who actively participate in the care of their children, and the term was coined by a group of fathers who were working for a major advertising company in Japan (Ishii-Kuntz 2013a). The phonetic resemblance of *ikumen* to *ikemen* ("handsome men") is no coincidence since the creators of the term wished to portray men's child caring in the 2000s as a "good-looking" and "fun" activity. This is in a stark contrast to the "embarrassing" image given to child-caring fathers back in the 1970s and 1980s. The emergence of these new child caring fathers in the 2000s can be attributed to the governmental efforts to promote fatherhood, research findings that confirmed the importance of paternal involvement on children and wives, and men's movement that created the foundation of supportive networks for child caring men and women.

The concept of *ikumen* has quickly spread throughout Japanese society. It can now be considered a "phenomenon". For example, the word, *ikumen*, was nominated as one of the Top-ten words in the 2010 Buzzword of the Year Contest. Additionally, the government started an *ikumen* project in 2010, the year that the Childcare Leave Law adopted extremely father-friendly revisions. The major objective of this project is to be a leader in promoting men's involvement in childcare by recruiting individual and corporate sponsors, disseminating useful information to encourage fathers' childcare, and sponsoring various events such as *ikumen* seminars and symposia throughout Japan. Furthermore, magazines and numerous books about *ikumen*, and cooking books for men have been published in the last decade. *Ikumen* also created a huge market industry in which men's baby care goods are sold. In addition, TV dramas and movies about *ikumen* have been produced and received high audience ratings. There are also many *ikumen* SNS communities and role models such as the heads of several wards (districts) in Tokyo, Prefectural Governors and celebrity men appearing on TV and giving talks at conferences throughout Japan. Finally, Fathering Japan, an NPO that offers many training courses for active paternal involvement and conduct surveys was established and recently celebrated their tenth anniversary. Unlike several men's groups in the 1990s, Fathering Japan has been quite

78   *Masako Ishii-Kuntz*

successful in recruiting members and lobbying the government for improving the family lives of men and women.

Ikumen *and their families*

The effects of active paternal involvement on families have been extensively researched within the past decade. Most of these studies focus on how fathers are influencing young children and their social and emotional developments (e.g., Ogata 1995). Other studies examined the effects of *ikumen* on their wives and themselves. In terms of the relationship between paternal involvement and children's development, Katō et al. (2002) found that fathers' daily caregiving and play with children were positively associated with children's emotional stability and sociability. For children between the ages of 10 and 15, more frequent interaction with their fathers was related to higher levels of friendliness toward their friends and other adults (Ishii-Kuntz 2004). Fathers' participation in childcare was also found to reduce childcare stress and anxiety among mothers, which, in turn, results in their more positive childrearing style (Ogata and Miyashita 2003). Additionally, having *ikumen* husbands was associated with a greater level of happiness on the side of the wives (Aoki 2011). Finally, fathers' childcare involvement also brings a sense of accomplishment and personal growth for fathers themselves (Ishii-Kuntz 2013b).

Social aging: a problem or opportunity for younger parents?

When it comes to raising children, social aging can be considered both as a problem and opportunity for younger parents. It is problematic because of the probability of a "double care" and the lack of assistance for childcare. Double care refers to being responsible for both childcare and care for elderly, i.e., one's parents or parents-in-law. The middle-aged generation has sometimes been called a "sandwich generation" because they are faced with the challenges of double care. The burden of double care has recently become a serious concern in Japanese society (Gender Equality Bureau Cabinet Office 2016). Several studies (Kuroda 2014; SONY Life Insurance 2015) found that approximately 8.2 percent of mothers with children not yet in college age experienced double care in the past, and 27.1 percent of people in their 30s are expected to be involved in double care within the next few years. It was also reported that men in their 40s and women in their 30s were most likely to be involved in double care with 36.1 percent and 37.4 percent, respectively. Additionally, it was found that 61.2 percent of men and 66.5 percent of women who are involved in double care have preschool-age children, and that the majority of these double caregivers reported high levels of stress.

There have always been middle-aged adults taking care of both their children and elderly parents at the same time. However, these people were most likely to be in their 50s or beyond. That is, when most of the former generations were having their babies in their 20s, their children became adults when they were still in their 40s. Thus, these parents in their 40s would have at least a decade until they

Raising children and new fatherhood 79

became responsible for taking care of their elderly parents. Due to delayed child-birth, the present-day parents have not concluded childrearing when their parents become frail and require their support. In this way, the experience of double care today sets the current generation apart from the previous generations.

Another problem that younger parents experience today may be indirectly related to social aging. That is, the decline in extended families implies that older people today wish to live a more independent lifestyle from their children compared to previous generations of older people (Cabinet Office 2006). Therefore, they prefer to continue working after retirement or seek their own recreational activities such as traveling, doing sports, or engaging in hobbies. According to the government's data (Cabinet Office 2015), Japanese elderly are much more likely to be employed after the age of 65 (29.6 percent overall, and 26.4 percent and 32.5 percent for men and women, respectively) than those in France (21.3 percent), Germany (23.8 percent), Italy (24.2 percent), Korea (14.6 percent), Sweden (14.5 percent) and the US (18.1 percent). This means that younger parents today cannot always rely on their own parents to provide help with childcare.

The demand of double care and the lack of assistance for childcare from one's parents are problematic for younger parents. At the same time, this also provides opportunities for younger parents to share child care responsibilities. That is, if grandparents cannot be counted on for care giving, then younger fathers and mothers must come up with an alternative planning of who cares for their children. Given the shortage of formal support such as daycare centers, one solution is for fathers to participate in childcare more frequently, thus increasing an opportunity for younger parents to engage in shared parenting or co-parenting. As previously stated, the benefits of fathers' active participation in childrearing are wide-ranging, from the positive effects on children's emotional and social development to reducing the wives' childcare stress and anxiety.

Social aging also provides opportunities for grandfathers in providing care for their grandchildren. For many years, grandmothers have been assisting their daughters and sons with childcare whenever necessary. However, in recent years, perhaps echoing the emergence of *ikumen*, a growing number of grandfathers have become willing to be involved in the care of their grandchildren, as expressed by the word *ikujii* ("grandchild caring grandpa"). Findings of *ikujii* research (Dentsu 2012) indicate that 91.1 percent of grandfathers enjoy spending time with their grandchildren and that almost 70 percent of them see their grandchildren more than once a month, and about 19 percent of these grandfathers are even frequently engaged in the care of their grandchildren.

Outlook

The main cause of the recent socio-demographic changes such as the delay in first marriage and the subsequent decline in fertility, and the increase in women's labor force participation described in this chapter, and elsewhere in this book, may be the personal economic hardship experienced by the post-bubble generation in Japan. It is the lack of financial resources that these younger generation

80 *Masako Ishii-Kuntz*

men and women today report as the number one reason for not getting married, which, in turn, causes the delay in having children. The increase in women's labor force participation can also be seen as a necessity for the post-bubble generation to maintain a decent level of living and quality of life. These "adjustments" along with the governmental campaigns contributed to the emergence of new fatherhood among those born after the economic bubble burst. In terms of family life, what sets the current young generation apart from their previous generations, is the ways that their family roles are redefined and redistributed to accommodate these socio-demographic changes.

First and foremost, co-parenting or shared parental roles have become more or less the norm since the mid-2000s with the rise of *ikumen*. Although men's participation in childcare still lags far behind that of women, the culture of involved fatherhood has become much more accepted among the younger generation compared to their counterparts of former young generations. This also implies that for women of the current young generation, labor force participation has become the norm rather than an exception. All of these phenomena indicate that in contrast to former generations of parents, a smaller number of young parents today are raising their children in homes with a breadwinning father and a homemaking mother.

Second, due to the collapse of the permanent employment system, which marks one of the largest generational breaks between the pre- and post-bubble generations, younger workers today are more likely to prioritize their family life over paid work compared to their older counterparts. Therefore, it is possible to consider the emergence of *ikumen* as a result of younger fathers' efforts to establish an identity as "family men".

Finally, Ishii-Kuntz (2016) found that factors encouraging men's childcare leave are father-friendly practices at work, fathering education, and the existence of role models such as senior coworkers who had taken childcare leave in the past. All of these factors did not exist for the generation of fathers before the burst of the bubble. It should also be noted that many men improved time management skills and increased their work productivity after taking the childcare leave (Ishii-Kuntz 2013a). This is in a stark contrast to the mostly negative experiences that the fathers of the pre-bubble generations had during their childcare leave. Additionally, younger wives today report some concerns over the income reduction during their husbands' childcare leave, but they generally appreciate their husbands' support for childcare. Again, these positive reactions from the side of the wives were almost unthinkable for child-caring men of the pre-bubble generations.

References

Aoki, Satoko (2011) Nyūyōji o motsu otto ya tsuma ni totte haigūsha ga ikuji no pātona de yokatta koto – jiyū kijutsu e no kaitō kara [Merits for Having a Spouse as a Childcare Partner for Husbands and Wives with Young Children: Responses to Open-ended Questions]. *Gakkō kyōikugaku kenkyū ronshū* 24: 101–110.

Raising children and new fatherhood 81

Atsumi, Naoki (2010) *Ikumen de ikō! Ikuji mo shigoto mo jūjitsu saseru ikikata* [Let's Ikumen! Lifestyle That Enables Childcare and Work]. Tokyo: Nihon Keizai Shimbun Shuppansha.

Cabinet Office (2005) Perceptions and Lifestyle of the Child-Rearing Generation.. Online available at: www5.cao.go.jp/seikatsu/whitepaper/h17/01_honpen/ (accessed 31 March 2017).

—— (2006) *Kawaru kōreishazō* [Changing Profile of the Elderly]. Online available at: www5.cao.go.jp/seikatsu/whitepaper/h18/01_honpen/html/06sh030102a.html#06sh03 0102b (accessed 22 September 2016).

—— (2015) *Danjo kyōdō sankaku hakusho* [Gender Equality White Paper]. Online available at: www.gender.go.jp/about_danjo/whitepaper/h27/zentai/ (accessed 31 March 2017).

—— (2017) *Kōreika no jōkyō* [State of Aging]. Online available at: www8.cao.go.jp/ kourei/whitepaper/w-2016/html/gaiyou/s1_1.html (accessed 30 April 2017).

Dentsu (2012) *Iku G chōsa* [Research on Child-Caring Grandfathers]. Online available at: www.dentsu.co.jp/news/release/pdf-cms/2012084-0731.pdf#search=%27 (accessed 15 October 2016).

Fujino, Atsuko (2002) Kakei ni okeru shusshō kōdō to tsuma no shūgyō kōdō – otto no kaji ikuji sanka to tsuma no kachikan no eikyō [Fertility Behavior and Labor Supply of Married Women in Japan: The Impact of a Husband's Participation in Household Work and a Wife's Family Values]. *Jinkōgaku* 31: 11–35.

Gender Equality Bureau Cabinet Office (2016) *Ikuji to kaigo no daburukea no jittai ni kansuru chōsa hōkokusho* [Research Report on Double Care of Child and Elder Care]. Online available at: www.gender.go.jp/research/kenkyu/wcare_research.html (accessed 5 January 2017).

Hayashi, Michiyoshi (1996) *Fusei no fukken* [Restoration of Paternity]. Tokyo: Chūō Kōron Shinsho.

Ishii-Kuntz, Masako (1992) Are Japanese Families Fatherless? *Sociology and Sociological Research* 76: 105–110.

—— (2004) Fathers' Involvement and School-Aged Children's Sociability: A Comparison Between Japan and the United States. *Japanese Journal of Family Sociology* 16: 83–93.

—— (2013a) *Ikumen genshō no shakaigaku – ikuji/kosodate sanka e no kibō o kanaeru tame ni* [Sociology of Child-Caring Men: In Search of Realizing Fathers' Involvement in Child-Rearing]. Kyōto: Minerva.

—— (2013b) Work Environment and Japanese Fathers' Involvement in Childcare. *Journal of Family Issues* 34: 250–269.

—— (ed.) (2016) *Factors Affecting Men's Involvement in Child Care: Findings from Interviews to Child Care Leave Takers*. Tokyo: Dai'ichi Seimei Zaidan.

Itō, Kimio (1995) Otoko no sei mo mata hitotsu dewa nai [There Is Also No Fault by Men]. In: *Danseigaku*. Teruko Inoue, Chizuko Ueno, Yumiko Ehara and Masako Amano (eds.), 77–108. Tokyo: Iwanami Shoten.

Japan Times (2016) *Angry Blog Post Sparks Movement for Improved Day Care*. Online available at: www.japantimes.co.jp/news/2016/03/07/national/angry-blog-post-sparks-movement-for-improved-day-care/#.WQ7GyBSBi-V (accessed 22 September 2016).

Kashiwagi, Keiko (ed.) (1993) *Chichioya no hattatsu shinrigaku – fusei no genzai to sono shūhen* [Developmental Psychology of Fathers: Current and Surrounding State of Paternity]. Tokyo: Kawashima Shoten.

82 Masako Ishii-Kuntz

Katō, Kuniko, Masako Ishii-Kuntz, Katsuko Makino and Michiko Tsuchiya (2002) Chichioya no ikuji kakawari oyobi hahaoya no ikuji fuan ga sansaiji no shakaisei ni oyobosu eikyō – shakaiteki haikei no kotonaru futatsu no kohōto hikaku kara [Fathers' Involvement in Childcare and Mothers' Childcare Anxiety and their Effects on Sociability of Three-year-olds. A Comparison of two Cohorts with Different Social Backgrounds]. *Hattatsu shinrigaku kenkyū* 13: 30–41.

Kuroda, Shoko (2014) Chūnen no nenreisō no hatarakikata – rōdō jikan to kaigo jikan no dōkō o chūshin ni [Work Style of the Middle-aged. Focusing on Work and Elder Care Hours]. *The Japan Institute for Labour Policy and Training* 653: 59–74.

Makino, Katsuko (1982) Nyūyōji o motsu hahaoya no seikatsu to ikuji fuan [Lives of Mothers of New-Borns and Toddlers and Their Childcare Anxiety]. *Katei kyōiku kenkyūjo kiyō* 3: 34–51.

Makino, Katsuko, Yoko Nakano and Keiko Kashiwagi (1996) *Kodomo no hattatsu to chichioya no yakuwari* [Child Development and Father's Roles]. Kyōto: Minerva.

Ministry of Health, Labour and Welfare (2002) *The White Paper on Women's Labor.* Online available at: www.mhlw.go.jp/houdou/2003/03/h0328-3.html (accessed 31 March 2017).

——— (2010) *Basic Survey on Gender Equality in Employment Management* Online available at: http://www.mhlw.go.jp/toukei/list/71-21.html (accessed 5 March 2018).

——— (2013) *Graphic Review of Japanese Household Comprehensive Survey of Living Conditions.* Online available at: www.mhlw.go.jp/toukei/list/dl/20-21-h25. pdf#search=%27 (accessed 1 March 2017).

——— (2016) *Population Statistics.* Online available at: www.mhlw.go.jp/toukei/saikin/ hw/jinkou/geppo/nengai15/dl/gaikyou27.pdf#search=%27 (accessed 30 April 2017).

——— (2017) *Hoikusho taiki jidōsū no sui'i* [Changes in Number of Children Waitlisted to Enter Daycare Center]. Online available at: www.ritsumei.ac.jp/~satokei/sociallaw/ waitingchildren.html (accessed 30 April 2017).

Ministry of Internal Affairs and Communications (2017) *Labor Force Survey 2016.* Online available at: www.stat.go.jp/data/roudou/sokuhou/nen/dt/pdf/index1.pdf#search=%27 (accessed 1 February 2017).

Muta, Kazue (1996) Meijiki sōgō zasshi ni miru kazokuzou – "kazoku" no tōjō to sono paradokusu [Family Portrait Seen in General Magazine in Meiji: The Appearance of the Family and Its Paradox]. In: *Senryaku to shite no kazoku – kinsei nihon no kokumin kokka keisei to josei.* Muta Kazue (ed.), 51–77. Tokyo: Shin'yosha.

National Institute of Population and Social Security Research (2016) *The Fifteenth Japanese National Fertility Survey in 2015: Marriage Process and Fertility of Married Couples Attitudes Toward Marriage and Family Among Japanese Singles.* Online available at: www.ipss.go.jp/ps-doukou/e/doukou15/Nfs15_points_eng.pdf (accessed 11 June 2017).

Ogata, Kazuo (1995) Chichioya no ikuji to yōji no shakai seikatsu nōryoku – tomobataraki katei to sengyō shufu katei no hikaku [Fathers' Childcare and Social Ability of Young Children. A Comparison between Double- and Single-earner Households]. *Kyōiku shinri kenkyū* 43: 335–342.

Ogata, Kazuo and Kazuhiro Miyashita (2003) Hahaoya no yōiku kōdō ni oyobosu yōin no kentō – chichioya no kyōryokuteki kakawari ni motozuku fūfu kankei, hahaoya no sutoresu o chūshin ni shite [Factors Affecting Mothers' Childcare Activity: Focusing on Couple's Relationship and Mothers' Stress and Fathers' Cooperative Involvement. *Chiba University Department of Education Research Journal* 50: 5–15.

Raising children and new fatherhood 83

Omagari, Mika (2014) New Household Work by Dual-Earner Couples. Case of the Application Procedure to Nursery Schools. *Ningen bunka sōsei kagaku ronsō* 17: 247–255.

Osawa, Machiko and Kōhei Komamura (1994) *Kekkon no keizaigaku – bankonka no yoin* [Economics of Marriage: Causes of Delayed Marriage]. In: *Gendai kazoku to shakai hoshō*. Shakai Hoshō Kenkūyjo (ed.), 37–54. Tokyo: Tokyo University Press.

Ōta, Motoko (1994) *Edo no oyako – chichioya ga kodomo o sodateta jidai* [Parents and Children in Edo Period: Era of Fathers Raising Children]. Tokyo: Chūō Kōronsha.

Otoko mo Onna mo Ikujijikan o Renrakukai (ed.) (1995) *Ikuji de kaisha o yasumu yō na otoko tachi* [Men Taking a Leave for Childcare]. Tokyo: Yukkusha.

Prime Minister's Office (2015) *Tomobataraki tō setaisū no sui'i* [Changes of the Number of Households of Dual-Earner Couples]. Online available at: www.gender.go.jp/about_danjo/whitepaper/h27/zentai/html/zuhyo/zuhyo01-02-09.html (accessed 1 March 2017).

SONY Life Insurance (2015) Junko Yamashita and Naoko Souma (eds.), *Daburukea ni kansuru chōsa* [Research on Double Care]. Online available at: www.sonylife.co.jp/company/news/28/nr_170317.html (accessed 31 March 2017).

Tachibanaki, Toshiaki and Masako Kimura (2008) *Kazoku no keizaigaku* [Family Economics]. Tokyo: NTT Publications.

Taga, Futoshi (2006) *Otokorashisa no shakaigaku – yuragu otoko no raifu course* [Sociology of Masculinity: Life Course of Men in Transition]. Tokyo: Sekai Shisōsha.

Tajiri, Kenji (1990) *Tōsan wa jitensha ni note – otoko no ikujijikan suto tenmatsuki* [A Father Riding on a Bicycle: A Report about a Man Taking Childcare Hour Strike]. Tokyo: Yukkusha.

Vogel, Ezra F. (1979) *Japan as Number One: Lessons for America*. Cambridge: Harvard University Press.

Yamae, Shinji (2013) *Kazoku to shakai no keizai bunseki – nihon no shakai no henyō to seisakuteki taiō* [Economic Analysis of Families and Society: Changes in Japanese Society and Policy Response]. Tokyo: Tokyo University Press.

6 Struggling men in emasculated life-courses

Non-regular employment among young men

Jun Imai

An unsettling time for the young in Japan

Some young men in Japan, especially those who are in non-regular employment, are struggling today. The struggle is about becoming a full citizen male. This became difficult to achieve because non-regular employment does not provide for the security that comes along with the seniority-based wages and the various kinds of corporate welfare that have been the pillars of an exemplary life-course in Japan. For Japanese men, these resources are pegged to the cultural requirements for being a committed worker at the workplace and a breadwinner at home. Deprived of these opportunities and resources, the lives of non-regular employed men tend to be perceived as deviations and as being illegitimate. As an effect, they inevitably have to struggle for social recognition.

During the rapid economic growth, the segment of non-regular employment stood only at about 7 percent of total employment, but it began to increase after the oil crises in the early 1970s. By the end of the 1980s, it had reached 18 percent. At that time, this was not an issue for men. Most of the non-regular employed were married, middle-aged women. This started to change during the economic slowdown in the 1990s, especially after the deregulatory reforms of the labor market at the end of that decade. Today, non-regular employment amounts for some 40 percent of the total employment. For men, it stood just at about 7 percent in the mid-1980s, but it has risen to 20 percent today. Figure 6.1 shows that the expansion of non-regular employment for men happened across all age cohorts. At the same time, this figure also shows that the young age cohorts have been disproportionately more affected.

Given the structure of the Japanese labor market, where employers have strong preferences on hiring new graduates directly from schools for life-time employment, the failure of many young to seize such an opportunity can be expected to have important and long-lasting effects on their careers and lives. Such concern is not without ground. Tarōmaru (2009: 145) divides the young into several age cohorts (such as birth cohorts 1968, 1972, 1976, 1980 and 1984) and calculates the percentage of non-regular workers at some points of their life-stage (from the age of 20 to 40). Younger men tend to be in non-regular employment more likely than men in older cohorts. For instance, men born in 1968 show the lowest

Struggling men in emasculated life-courses 85

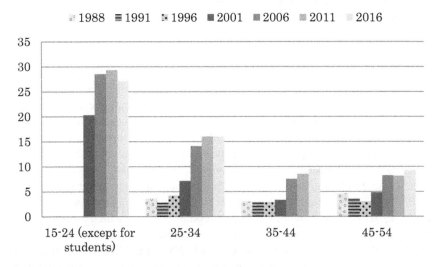

Figure 6.1 Percentage of non-regular employment among men by age
Source: Statistics Bureau Labor Force Survey, Time Series Data

percentage of non-regular employment at any points of their career, about 2 percent when they were 26 and about 7–8 percent when they turned late 30s. People born in the 1980s, on the other hand, have suffered from the changed conditions at the starting point of their career. More than 20 percent of them are in non-regular status when they are 20–25. This rate is decreasing the older they get, but their share among the non-regular employed is still significantly higher than that of other age cohorts.

One of the problems of the Japanese labor market is that once people are located in the non-regular segment, it is difficult to leave it and to become regularly employed (Tarōmaru 2009: 64–68; Lee and Shin 2009). The problem is not simply that the Japanese labor market has a dual structure, but that the life-courses are segmented into two tracks, a privileged one and a deprived one, with no channel to move between them.

This chapter examines whether the structural changes of the labor market since the 1990s triggered the formation of new sets of culture, especially of gender culture. It studies whether this resulted in the formulation of alternative ways of life for young people in non-regular employment. The culture is expected to be different from the existing gender order, represented by the hegemonic masculinity called "salarymen masculinity". This kind of masculinity has guided men to live smoothly along the institutional linkage of employment and welfare in Japan. Focusing particularly on young men in their 20s and 30s in full-time non-regular employment, this chapter reveals that many of them struggle to legitimatize and obtain recognition of their situation.

86   *Jun Imai*

Japan's employment-welfare regime and gender order

Salaryman masculinity

Becoming an adult man in Japan is strongly associated with a series of life events. Becoming a salaryman, that is, an economically independent individual who is ready to establish and take care of a family is such a crucial event. The cultural traits that these men need to obtain are called "salaryman masculinity" (Dasgupta 2013). It is the hegemonic masculinity in Japan. For men, this includes accepting the role as breadwinner, putting priority on company issues over individual issues, and maintaining a strong commitment to work assignments. A successful adherence to these norms gives men access to a privileged status under the umbrella of life-time employment, enabled by secure employment and corporate welfare measures. This allows them to maintain good prospects for their own lives, and the lives of their family. This hegemonic masculinity is defined as a social, historical, and cultural construct (Connell 1987, 2005; Itō 1996, 2003). It is a set of norms and attitudes pegged to the power and legitimacy over the control of resources and opportunities in society. It serves as a yardstick to hierarchically order other versions of masculinity and femininity. However, since hegemonic masculinity "is always constructed *in relation to* various subordinated masculinities as well as *in relation* to women" (Connell 1987: 183, emphasis mine), the boundaries of this gender order are also negotiable, and potentially contentious.

Salaryman masculinity as the hegemonic masculinity was constructed in relation with the structuration of resources and opportunities for regular employment in the post-war period.[1] Salaryman masculinity became the hegemon due to the expansion of a new middle-class during the rapid economic growth. "Salaryman" – regardless of white-collar or blue-collar differences – came to represent the standard of manhood in Japan then (Hidaka 2010; Taga 2011; Dasgupta 2013). Men acquired this culture through socialization effects on the family and school, school-to-work transition, workplace participation, and labor management practices (Taga 2001, 2006; Gordon 1993; Shire 1999). In particular, the Japanese labor management gives strong incentives to workers to learn and perform this salaryman masculinity. Secure employment and corporate welfare measures (which are better at large companies) function as incentives and they are supported by the social security system and tax policies of the state (Osawa 1993; Kimoto 1995; Shinkawa and Penpel 1996).[2]

Due to the linkage of employment and welfare, it is possible to say that hegemonic masculinity in Japan enjoys official recognition. It entails a strong social acknowledgment that such men and their lifestyles are "legitimate". As an effect of this, other ways of living, such as the lives of relatively independent and mobile workers, became portrayed as being irresponsible and unreliable (Miyashita 2003). Under this regime, homeless men are labeled as "failed men". It is for this reason that some homeless men avoid receiving welfare services. Doing so would entail for them a clear sign of stigma on their masculinity (Gill 2003; Mugikura

Struggling men in emasculated life-courses 87

2006). These examples reveal that the process of establishing and maintaining an order of masculinities (and femininities) is a dynamic process that involves legitimation and recognition. In Japan, the mobilization of many men for this kind of hegemonic masculinity – emphasized by the denial of alternatives – was so successful that the standardized life-course emerged as the only legitimate possibility under Japan's specific institutional arrangements (Shimazaki 2013).

Labor market changes and its consequences

The deregulatory reforms of the labor market from the mid-1990s onwards diversified and expanded non-regular employment (Imai 2011). The maximum of limited-term contracts was extended from one to five years. Furthermore, the range of occupation to which non-regular labor could be applied was also expanded. Initially, temporary dispatched work (*haken*) was developed in the 1980s for a limited number of occupations, but these limitations were basically abolished by the reforms of 1999 and 2004. Few areas of work remain unaffected by non-regular work today. It is beyond doubt that these reforms led to an increase of social inequality and of social exclusion as non-regular employees are often excluded from employment, health insurances, and the national pension system, although these are supposed to be universal services in Japan (Ogura 2008).

The deregulatory reforms of the labor market led to a diversification of life-courses. Since the institutionalization of life-courses is also a social and cultural project about the rights and duties attached to the status role at each life stage (Kohli 2009[1986]), the diversification of employment was accompanied by cultural re-negotiations about workplace commitment and male-breadwinner ideology. The expansion of non-regular employment among youth initially caused some moral panic. The rise of the term *freeter* is one of the major attempts, especially in the mass media (Goodman, Imoto and Toivonen 2012), to comprehend what was then hard to realize. At first, the term was used with a positive ring and an empowering connotation. Those in non-regular employment were seen as "free" workers, exempted from the many obligations given to regular employees. They were portrayed as organizing their lives in the way they wanted to. This view on *freeters* was strong until the late 1990s, when the labor-market situation turned particularly severe for the young. Although there had always been a sense of doubt about such a life, these doubts now moved to the fore. In the new millennium, the view dominates that there is no way to live a decent life without having regular employment, and without accepting the obligations that accompany it. This manifests, for instance, in a novel titled *Freeter, ie o kau* ("*A freeter buying a house*") that appeared first on the Internet in 2007, and was later turned into a book in 2009 and a TV drama in 2010. The title is satirical, emphasizing the impossibility for a not-fully-matured and non-independent man trying to do something only a fully-matured-man can do, i.e., buying a house.[3]

The emergence of this moral panic is a clear sign that there is an open social space where new meanings and norms may be created and realized. As a result,

88　*Jun Imai*

some anticipate that a second standard of life may emerge (e.g., Nakanishi 2009). This second standard for young, non-elite or non-regular workers would entail less commitment to work and (therefore) less rigidity about the gendered division of labor. It would nonetheless also enjoy social recognition. However, such a standard has not emerged yet. Rather, a number of empirical studies report exactly the contrary. The rigidity of the male breadwinner ideology – the very core of the hegemonic masculinity in Japan – is stronger among non-regularly employed men compared to those who are in regular employment (Meguro, Yazawa and Okamoto 2012; Inui 2015). This calls for an explanation.

A subordinated masculinity in the making?

In order to investigate the reasons for this seemingly puzzling finding, it is necessary to locate the situation of non-regular employees in relation to other aspects of the current gender order. So far, there exist some studies that reveal the values and attitudes of young men and women in non-regular employment in relation to their social class background (Kosugi 2002, 2003, 2005; Tarōmaru 2006). Although these works provide for important insights, they are essentially attribute-centered. It is not sufficient to explain the mechanisms of how non-regular employees shape their current values, attitudes, and the depth of their emotions. A relational perspective on "masculinity" and "gender order" argues that these are embedded in the institutional arrangement of employment and welfare. That is to say, they are shaped in relation to other sets of culture, performed by people in different contexts.[4]

Two decades have passed since the deregulatory reforms. The moral panic is over. Reality has set in. Especially after the Lehman crisis of 2008, "tent cities of jobless" became seen as a social problem. An unprecedented rise of social inequality and insecurity after the period of the rapid economic growth has become undeniable. A new masculinity is expected to be negotiated in this changed context. There is large agreement today that inequality and exclusion are rooted in the labor market, and that this is solidified under the non-changing citizenship norms (Imai 2015). It is necessary, especially today, to observe meso- and micro-level social interactions, where young men in non-regular employment interact with norms and attitudes presented by employers and regular workers. The latter typically take the current hegemonic masculinity for granted. We need to study how these young men strive for male legitimacy and recognition.

Notes on the empirical survey

Method

In order to investigate possible renegotiations of masculinity among young non-regularly employed men, I conducted surveys in five small and medium-size companies in the knowledge-intensive service sector in Sapporo, Japan. In order to take a distinctively relational perspective, I focused on the ways that the

Struggling men in emasculated life-courses   89

employing companies treat men in non-regular work. I studied how they adapted to and struggled in this situation with regard to their employers and their colleagues with regular employment status. The results enable us to observe how legitimacy and recognition are part and parcel of these interactions. Small and medium-size companies in this newly emerging industrial sector were chosen because they hire more non-regular employed men than other industrial sectors.

I interviewed employers and labor representatives in order to understand management practices, and conducted employee surveys and interviews with regular and non-regular workers. Investigating labor management practices is important to specify the positions and roles of non-regular workers at the workplaces. It clarifies labor conditions, expectations, and access to corporate welfare. From the employee surveys and interviews, information on job satisfaction, work attitude, gender values, and relations were collected.

Five companies participated in this research.[5] Questionnaire surveys and interviews were possible at four of them. The questionnaire was distributed to 526 workers, of whom 275 returned it. The number of valid responses was 272, resulting in a response rate of 51.7 percent. Among the questionnaire respondents, 23 accepted to be interviewed. 13 thereof were regular workers; ten were non-regular employees (seven thereof men). All non-regular employees in this sample worked full-time, and there is a strategic reason for this.[6] By collecting data on full-time non-regular employees, it becomes possible to observe direct influences of "status difference" between regular and non-regular employment by controlling working hours.

Sample overview

We have 272 people in our sample: 169 men, 102 women, and one with no gender information available. The percentage of non-regular workers is 23.7 percent. The average age for all is in the latter half of the 30s, 38.4 for regular and 35.3 for non-regular workers. Henceforth, those in their 20s and 30s will be called the "young", and those in their 40s and 50s, the "old" employees. As could be expected, the job tenure of regular workers is twice as long as that of non-regulars (13.1 years and 6.3 years, respectively). This already indicates that the lives of non-regulars are unstable.

Let's focus on men. For the young, the percentage of non-regular employment stands at 33 percent, that is, it is higher than the numbers shown in the introduction. This is probably due to the industry in which the survey was conducted. Among the regular men, the sample is divided between young and old in the proportions of 46.4 percent (30.7 percent are in their 30s) and 53.6 percent (42.5 percent are in their 40s). Among the non-regular men, 69 percent are young (19 percent and 50 percent in their 20s and their 30s, respectively). It is thus possible to see a concentration of non-regular employment among the young.[7]

Being a non-regular worker relates to a lower rate of marriage. Nearly half of the young workers with regular employment are married, as compared to less than one-third of the workers with non-regular status. However, we do not know

90   *Jun Imai*

whether non-regulars are not married because of their financial instability, or whether those who do not aspire to marry tend to be non-regular employees. It is, nevertheless, notable that one-third of the young non-regular men are married, with more than half of the non-regulars in their 40s being married (as compared to three-fourth among regulars in their 40s).

The changing structure of employment and life for young men

Experiences and perceptions of employment by young non-regular men

How does the changing labor market affect the lives of young workers? One of the most notable issues is the change of employment security. In this survey, I asked about the length of employment with the current employer. The average job tenure of regular workers was 13.1 years, and that of non-regular workers, 6.2 years. If we take a look at the young, the difference is smaller but significant. The length of employment is 8.7 years among the regular workers in their 30s, but that of non-regular workers in the same age category is 5.1 years. The tendency is clear. The difference in employment status is small at the early stage of the career but becomes larger at later stages. The careers of the non-regular workers tend to be fragmented as they accumulate a number of short employment experiences during their careers.

Our sample confirms that it is difficult to change employment from non-regular to regular. At one company, we find non-regular workers at lower-rank managerial positions, and some even work as supervisors. Non-regular workers in these ranks recognize that the content of their jobs is not different from that of regular workers. This notwithstanding, it is very difficult for them to change their status to regular workers. Almost all interviewees understand that the system of status transfer from temporary contracts to unlimited term contracts is only nominal. It does not result in a change of employment status.

The careers of non-regular workers are fragmented due to their short job tenure, and the career trajectories are segmented between regular and non-regular with almost impenetrable boundaries between the two. In addition, the careers of non-regular employment are associated with lower resources. From the survey, it is possible to summarize the salary distribution by age and employment status among men.

We can observe wide differences between regular and non-regular workers in both age groups. Among the young, the average salary of regular workers is about four million yen, while that of non-regular workers is about two million yen. Since there is a seniority curve for the wage system of regular workers, the difference grows bigger the older the employees get. Among the old employees, the average salary of regular workers is about six million yen, while that of non-regular workers is about three million yen. With relatively secure employment, the future level of wage (and of life) is predictable for regular workers. For non-regular workers,

Struggling men in emasculated life-courses 91

on the other hand, continuous efforts are required to maintain employment, and all the while their salary stays at a lower level. Access to welfare services such as corporate pension and retirement allowances also differs. In all companies of our sample, non-regular workers have limited access to these services. For instance, the welfare services of non-regular workers are outsourced, while specific and privileged corporate welfare is prepared for regular workers.

To sum up, our sample confirms the typical differences of attributes and employment conditions. A unique feature of our sample is that non-regular workers work at least as long as regular workers do, despite having lower wages and limited access to welfare schemes. Regardless of age, non-regular workers work longer per day than regular workers. Regular workers work ten hours and five minutes (10.08) per day, and non-regular workers work almost 11 hours (10.90). This tendency does not change for young men. Some of them work extremely long hours, as much as 15 hours per day. This finding undermines the dominant view that regular workers work longer.

We have seen that there are great differences between regular and non-regular workers in terms of the employment security, career experiences, wages and working time. How do workers perceive this situation? Towards this end, the survey investigated "work attitude" and "job satisfaction". With regard to "work attitude", I asked how important were "concerns on unemployment", the "level of wage" and the "promotion prospects" for them. "Job satisfaction" inquired about the level of satisfaction about the "actual wages", "job contents", the "arrangement of holidays", "work time", and the "overall evaluation" workers get at their workplaces (not just from employers but also from their colleagues).

Again, the difference of employment status matters. This is obviously an effect of the wide differences in the work conditions between regular and non-regular workers. The level of wage is seen to be most important for workers, followed by a concern of unemployment (regardless of the employment status). The biggest difference between regular and non-regular employees shows in their promotion prospects. Non-regular workers, especially the young ones, emphasize its importance far more than the regular workers. This indicates that they recognize the importance of having future prospects. In terms of the job satisfaction, it is therefore unsurprising to find that non-regular workers are far less satisfied with all aspects of their work lives. This manifests with regard to their wages, job assignments, working time arrangement, and the evaluation they get at the workplace. Among the young, the conflict between the employment status and the working time is by far the largest. Considering their long working hours, low salaries, and the lack of promotion prospects, it is unsurprising to find that young non-regular workers are frustrated about their situation.

Adaptations and three ways to deal with the situation

It is important to recall here that the situation and the choices of non-regular workers have never received positive social recognition. It has never been thought of as a legitimate life under Japan's employment-welfare regime. As Shimazaki

92   *Jun Imai*

(2013) points out, there is only one "official life-course" for men (and women) in Japanese society. It is in this sense that young non-regularly employed men live an "emasculated" life-course. However, their situation does not face a strong negation. For instance, a non-regular man in his mid-20s had a teaching diploma, but he could not obtain a teaching job. He felt uneasy about how his parents looked at him, although they did not criticize him explicitly. His parents did not directly show concern or anxiety, and they seemed to respect the life-course of their son. However, he says that "it [the parents' attitude, JI] hurts me somehow (*chotto kizu tsuku*)", knowing that the situation cannot be easily legitimated, and recognizing that his parents are aware of this.

The assessment of work for non-regular workers is primarily defined in relation to their employers and to the work of regular workers. It is common to hear in interviews of regular workers that the situation of non-regular workers "is their choice". On first sight, this may suggest a kind of silent respect for non-regular workers. It is only a respect on the surface, though. Everybody interviewed knows that non-regular work status for most is not a choice at all and that their employment status may lead directly to a life of poverty and hopelessness. It is probably no exaggeration to say that 20 years of experience of the expansion, and the entrenchment of inequality has taught people how to be indifferent towards those trapped in the lower stratum. It does not cause emotional conflict among regular employees. We can observe a societal divide. The comment "it is their choice" is a declaration by regular workers to not want to talk about the very apparent inequality and exclusion in contemporary Japanese society that they are witnessing at work every day. A sense of solidarity is overruled by the desire to maintain their privileged situation. This can be seen as an act of symbolic violence (Bourdieu and Wacquant 1992). The attitudes shown by regular employees make men in non-regular status recognize their emasculated situations. The indifference on the side of the regular employees is also crucially legitimated in a society where a neoliberal ideology of "self-responsibility" prevails.

Regular workers think that they are entitled to be "on the safe side", but in order to do this, they need to emphasize that they are more "responsible" than non-regular workers with regard to various organizational matters. When asked about what exactly they are responsible for, they typically take time to come up with an answer. Eventually, they insist that there are important matters where regular and non-regular workers are assigned different tasks and responsibilities. Consider the following excerpt of an interview.

Excerpt 1

Q: What do you think is the difference between regular workers and non-regular workers?

A: Well . . . I think, we are responsible for the entire coordination of the work organization. . . . For instance, when there are not enough part-timers, we have to cover up.

Struggling men in emasculated life-courses 93

Q: But in this organization, even non-regular workers do the coordinating work of other non-regular workers as group leaders. What is the difference between you and a non-regular group leader?

A: Hm . . . well, I accept workplace transfer (*tenkin*), but they do not need to do so.

It is true that labor management is coordinated differently for regular and non-regular employees at their companies. Regularly employed workers believe that this justifies their privileges. In the past, when there were fewer non-regular workers, this sense of responsibility was not underlined or simply taken for granted. However, after the emergence and the expansion of non-regular employment, together with the increasing necessity to justify the differentiated treatment, this sense of responsibility has come to be foregrounded. It has become a key-rationale for confirming and legitimatizing the privileged treatment of regular workers.

Regular workers try to distance themselves from non-regular men by softly indicating that non-regular men are failing. This is the social environment that stigmatizes those of non-regular employment. It puts the masculinity of young men in non-regular status under pressure. The difficulty of being a man under a pressure that threatens to emasculate you is a not an issue that comes to the minds of regular workers. Under such everyday circumstances, non-regularly employed men need to search for a social space where they can prove – negotiate, define and perform – their masculinities in relation to others in order "to ensure emotional, psychological and social survival employing strategies to mask self-perceived weaknesses or vulnerability and to attain status and legitimacy" (de Viggiani 2012: 271). Hence, non-regular workers need to gain or claim recognition and legitimacy about their situation by themselves. If there is a strong negation against them, they can present themselves as a kind of "anti-hero". However, they are not exposed to such a kind of strong negation. Facing only "soft indications" that they are failing, they find an open social space in front of them that needs to be filled with meaning. There are three ways this can be done: (1) situate yourself in a moratorium, (2) claim social independence, or (3) push gender conservatism. Let us consider these three options in more detail.

"Moratorium" refers to a mode of thinking that the current situation is a preparation period or a temporary state of life on the way to achieve the "real self" in the future. By thinking in this way, non-regular workers are enabled to reduce the pressure and the threat of their current situation. For instance, one 30-year-old man argued that his non-regular work style was suitable to achieve his long-term goal, in his case, a job in the filming and image industry with which he had been remotely involved since he was in college. In this sense, he has not retreated from the masculine ideology by emphasizing an alternative occupational career. All the while, his main source of income has always been the non-regular job at one of our sample companies – a call center, where he is already a supervisor. However, when asked about his life in general, the first thing he said was "I am different from others", because he claimed to not being committed to a career at his current employer. By stressing this, he tried to locate himself outside the world of

94   *Jun Imai*

Japanese mainstream norms. For him, having a non-regular job is a temporary state in his life, and he sees himself as being on the way to becoming someone different. Of course, this does not mean that he enjoys the moratorium. Quite on the contrary, he feels a relatively strong anxiety about his future that could be described as a "nagging sense of insecurity" (Genda 2006). Getting older, he begins to recognize that everything, including his job and his thoughts on marriage and gender, remain to be "pending".

Excerpt 2

> Yes . . . I know I am undecided [by having postponed an important decision of his career, JI]. I always feel that I have to do what I have to do, but it is too busy to seriously think about it. I know I cannot continue like this much longer.

Feeling anxious about the future and due to the pressure of existing norms on him, he is also thinking about the possibility of obtaining a regular job or certifications such as administrative procedures, legal specialist, or social insurance labor consultant.

The second option to deal with the dilemma of masculinity in non-regular employment is to present oneself as somebody emphasizing a good work-life balance. Many non-regular men strongly emphasize the necessity or the advantages for them of being non-regular. They highlight the obligations of regular workers with regard to overtime and job transfer, both issues perceived to be hurting the work-life balance in unacceptable ways. Claiming the necessity to control working time in order to take care of their families and to spend more time with them could be legitimate. Moreover, the fact that individuals who want to make such choices need to live an insecure life could be seen as being unfair. It is interesting to find that some of them claim in this context that their situation is economically rational. They state, "considering the wage per an hour, the non-regular wage is better than that of regular workers". The emphasis on economic rationality serves as a means to present their situation as being smart, gainful, and therefore manly. However, given the information on wages and working hours, this view is not correct. Even if it were, a wage-per-hour benefit would not compensate the lack of security and prospects that come along with regular employment. Why then do they make such claims? One interpretation is that they want to emphasize differences from regular workers – they are less obedient to their employers. Another possibility is that they want to be seen on par with their employers. They can claim and earn as much as they need and want to work – regular workers do not have this choice. All in all, it boils down to a desire to claim that they are socially, if not economically, independent men.

The last possibility is that of gender conservatism. It manifests, in particular, among young men. The survey results show that age explains differences of gender attitude. It is surprising to see that young men agree with statistical significance more emphatically than older men to statements such as "what women

Struggling men in emasculated life-courses   95

really want is a family and children" (gender essentialism) and "it is an embarrassing for men to earn less than their wives" (strong breadwinner norm). Young men are also slightly more conservative on the statements such as "men should work outside, women should take care of family members at home" and "wives should make their husbands look good in front of others". The wide difference between young and old in terms of breadwinner ideology is especially remarkable as it indicates the strength of this preoccupation for those who are in an early stage or in the middle of their career and family formation. Non-regular workers are even more obsessed with breadwinner ideology than the regulars in the same (young) age cohort. This trend also manifested in the interviews. Even when their spouses were working, young non-regularly employed men tended to claim that it was pitiful if the spouses earned more and/or were promoted faster than them. At the same time, they accepted the importance of their spouses' income. Non-regulars also tended to agree with male supremacy at workplaces ("men should be promoted faster than women").

At first sight, this conservatism of young men, especially among those with non-regular status, is astonishing. It reveals their recognition of the "official norm" of Japanese society, and it shows that they have internalized it. The reasons for this may be their intention to overcome the lack of recognition, and legitimacy of their lives. For those of non-regular status, the official norms are oppressing. This oppression, whether they are conscious about it or not, pushes them into negotiations of gender. It is difficult for them to claim that they are successful men in this society. Their inferior position in the employment-welfare regime makes them gender conscious because one of the most effective strategies to highlight their masculinity is to claim it in relation to women. Male superiority over women is the cornerstone of the gender order (in any modern society). It is the last resort to confirm their identity as a man for them.

These three options are not mutually exclusive. They are actually able to coexist in one person at the same time. One man in our interviews eloquently reported how he is stigmatized and confused, and then used all three strategies to rationalize his situation. The person in question is employed at one of our sample companies with non-regular status. He is assigned to work as a solo researcher in this company. He is in his late 30s, has a graduate degree and is married to a woman who is a regular worker at the same company, with an even longer career there than him. He is a reflective person and has more than enough vocabulary to describe his situation. He knows how he should think about gender relations, showing very progressive answers in the questionnaire. He has a good relationship with his wife, but at the same time he is plagued by the idea that he does not and cannot perform as a breadwinner.

Excerpt 3

Q: [You are not a regular worker]. Is this because you don't want to be restricted by working time requirements by the company?

A: . . . Because I don't think I am capable [to work as a regular worker].

96 *Jun Imai*

Q: So, you think you are not capable, rather than you don't want to be . . .

A: At my company, regular people talk like . . . [mimicking their business talk such as greetings]. Then I feel like this is not possible. . . . I am incapable to be a regular worker, so I have no regret that I am not the one. . . . The company assigns me a great job that fits me well. . . . You know, if you think about the wage-per-hour, we are actually better off. Only thing we don't have is retirement allowance.

[. . .]

Q: You don't have security either, although it is not immediately a problem in your case because your wife provides it for you. Doesn't this bother you?

A: Yes, a little. Well, I am not conservative, but, well, I often think that it should be me [who plays the breadwinner role] . . . but since she is capable . . . hm . . . yes, I feel not really right. I know it is expected in the society, but it should be ok that I am not, but I . . .

This long vignette from two separate interviews with him reveals that he is trying to convince himself that he is ok to be a non-regular worker as he is not capable to play the roles expected from regular workers. He also uses the rhetoric of economic rationality, which sounds clichéd since he obviously does not really believe in it. At last, he confesses his confusion about gender. He thinks it should be completely fine that he and his wife have reverse roles in their family. However, he is puzzled and confused that he cannot obtain an adequate recognition, and that he himself still feels he should be the breadwinner.

In his confusion, he tries to set up a barrier of self-containment. The mismatch between his understanding about his situation and the lack of recognition from society makes him feel uncomfortable. It deprives him of a sense of legitimacy about his life – a sense of legitimacy that regular workers can take for granted. There rests a hidden stigma on him. Telling others "I'm not capable, and it's my choice" looks to be a clever but desperate effort to keep others out from rubbing his lower employment status in his face. It is a strategy to keep him out of a world of oppressive norms. In order to not acknowledge this stigma, he, like other non-regular men, may take up a pursuit of loneliness and avoid continuous relationships with others. The underlying principle is clear: "if you don't belong to society, society can't hurt you" (Sennett and Cobb 1973: 55).

Outlook

The deregulatory reforms of the labor market created and expanded non-regular employment statuses. Being employed as a non-regular worker is now an increasingly common experience in Japan, especially among those who entered the labor market after the bubble burst in 1991. Whether or not this epoch and the experiences that resulted from it formed a "generation" is the fundamental question raised in this volume. Let us consider some conclusions to this with regard to employment. Since non-regular employment can only provide inferior resources and opportunities when compared to regular employment, one could expect the rise of a new culture – especially a gender culture – that would make sense of these new circumstances. Such a culture could have been significantly different from the existing salaryman masculinity culture, in which men need to put priority on their lives at employing organizations and take responsibility for their families as breadwinners. Such a new culture does not exist, though.

When people first recognized the increasing number of young people in non-regular employment in the 1990s and 2000s, a new discursive space for a re-negotiation of life-courses could be observed. Some went as far as seeing *freeter* positively, claiming that such a life-course was a free choice for ensuring more freedom from the traditional obligations. However, while the deregulation of the labor market led to a diversification of labor supply for employers, it did not result in a diversification of possible and new legitimized life-courses for workers. After two decades, it seems clear that young people in non-regular employment cannot establish a life-course that is less constrained with regard to the norms of salary-man masculinity. Rather, young men in non-regular positions tend to show an even stronger aspiration to be a breadwinner, in addition to being frustrated and dissatisfied with their labor conditions.

In order to understand this seeming contradiction, it is important to recognize that young non-regular workers in Japan have to live an emasculated life-course. They experience the inferiority in everyday life *in relation to* their employers and their colleagues with regular status, who do not – like them – have to question the existing norms of citizenship. Although regular workers certainly need to fulfill the managerial requirements such as flexible overtime and inter-regional job transfer, they *know* that they have a privileged status. Regular workers use a kind of rhetoric that shows respect to the situations of non-regular workers on the surface. They do so by underlining that their situation is "their free choice", a commonplace form of symbolic violence at the workplace today. All the while, non-regular workers need to make sense of their lives. They need to justify them-selves also in relation to others. As exemplified by the interviews above, there are several conventional ways to do this; putting oneself in a moratorium, claim-ing social independence, or upholding gender conservatism. The existence of these strategies reveals the very fact that young men in non-regular employment feel trapped in emasculated life-courses that are stigmatizing them. Embodying breadwinner ideology more strongly than regular men reveals that the oppres-sion makes them follow the key element of the dominant ideology in order to gain legitimacy. They participate in their own suppression, a key characteristic of symbolic violence.

The struggle by young men with non-regular employment status can be under-stood as the making of a subordinated masculinity that supports the current gender order with salaryman masculinity as the hegemon. The structural reform of the labor market could have been a threat to the hegemonic status of this order as new categories of people were created, resulting – for the first time since the economic miracle – in the possibility of a gender culture with the potential to confront and replace the current order. However, two decades of labor market deregulation taught regular and non-regular workers alike that non-regular employment results

98 *Jun Imai*

in a lack of resources and opportunities that at times does not even allow for the support of the minimum standard of life. Under such circumstances, being in non-regular employment, especially for young men, turns out to be a threat to their identity and, with no viable alternatives in sight, they feel confused.

Does this mean no change at all? I argue that there exists a foundation for a future change, but that the dominant ideology is still too strong to allow for its present realization. The most important basis for this argument is that a new and unique awareness has emerged over the past two decades. Young men in non-regular employment today, whether they like it or not, need to distance themselves from the obligations of regular employment. In order to do so, they clearly *articulate* these obligations. This is something that the previous generations that entered labor markets from the 70s to the early 90s did not (need to) do. It was taken for granted then. The ideology of salaryman masculinity was unquestioned and at its height then. The emergence of a new awareness indicates that the dominant ideology is being doubted. In addition, the timing of the emergence of a new awareness is favorable for change. When the hegemonic masculinity emerged during the rapid economic growth period (the 1950s and 60s), all those who had an alternative gender culture were forced to give it up and to adapt. Today, we find a situation of ambivalence. On the one hand, young non-regular workers are threatened by symbolic violence if they do not secure regular employment. On the other hand, hegemonic masculinity is under pressure to change. Everyone is aware that things have changed, but everybody also pretends that nothing has changed. Pretending requires an awareness of the changed realities in Japan, and this awareness constitutes in itself an irreversible change in Japanese society.

Acknowledgment

This research was partially supported by a Grant-in-Aid for Scientific Research (C) of Ministry of Education, Culture, Sports, Science and Technology, Japan (Grant number: 2353064101). The project leader was Jun Imai and the project name was "New masculinity in knowledge-intensive service economy. Basic research on the change of the employment-welfare regime".

Notes

1 The term "masculinity" has the tendency of essentialism, implying that a set of culture is inherent to some segments of the male population. It is important to recognize that it is not inherent for men. It is more appropriate to understand that the major work ethic in a society is dominated by men and considered to be the culture of successful men. The other side of the same coin is the development of a discourse that emphasizes the difficulty for women to follow or internalize this culture, because it also seeks to prevent them from reaching privileged positions.
2 Elsewhere I call this set of rights and duties under Japan's employment-welfare nexus "company citizenship" (Imai 2011). Company citizenship is a type of industrial citizenship, in which workers (men) need to accept various flexibility requirements (obligations) by their employment company in order to have access to the rights such as privileged corporate welfare (Imai 2011; Jackson 2001; Marshall 1950[1991]). It is a

Struggling men in emasculated life-courses 99

"citizenship" norm partially because many of the corporate welfare measures are state supported.

3 During the first decade of the 21st century, the media exploited the opportunity of moral panic as it provided an ample space for imagination and public attention. In 2007, there was also a TV drama that featured non-regular employment. It was titled *Haken no hinkaku* (A Temporary Staff's Dignity) in which a young female temporary agency worker, in the formal sense an outsider to the organization, seeks self-interest at the workplace where she only has a few months of commitment. She does not accept the workplace obligations that others (regulars) accept, but, ironically, her self-centered behaviors unintentionally bring justice to the workplace, and she starts building up popularity and credibility among her co-workers.

4 A rare study that takes up this issue from a relational perspective is Cook (2013). She studies men in non-regular employment and reports that even when non-elite men seek alternative life-courses, they cannot ignore the opinion of their relatively conservative potential partners (women). Male breadwinner ideology shown by women is one of the major obstacles for those who seek something different than salaryman life.

5 Research was conducted in the period from July to October 2013, in Sapporo, Hokkaido, Japan.

6 The biggest characteristic of this sample is that the largest subcategory of non-regular employment is *keiyaku/shokutaku*. 88% of the total non-regular workers in this sample fall into this category. They are limited-term contract workers who may work part-time or full-time, often recognized as the category of workers who are mostly men, skilled, and independent. They are usually distinguished from *pāto/arubaito* who are mostly middle-aged women who seek supplemental income for their households or student helpers, although they are in a legal sense not so different from *keiyaku* workers.

7 It is often discussed that employment status is associated with educational background. Our sample is no exception. As for educational background, more than 60% of regular workers were college graduates while little less than 50% were college graduates among the non-regular workers.

References

Bourdieu, Pierre and Loic J. D. Wacquant (1992) *An Invitation to Reflexive Sociology.* Chicago: University of Chicago Press.

Connell, R. W. (1987) *Gender and Power: Society, the Person and Sexual Politics.* Stanford: Stanford University Press.

———. (2005) *Masculinities* (second edition). Berkeley: University of California Press.

Cook, Emma (2013) Expectations of Failure. Maturity and Masculinity for Freeters in Contemporary Japan. *Social Science Japan Journal* 16(1): 29–43.

Dasgupta, Romit (2013) *Re-Reading the Salaryman in Japan: Crafting Masculinities.* London: Routledge.

de Viggiani, Nick (2012) Trying to be Something You Are Not: Masculine Performances Within a Prison Setting. *Men and Masculinities* 15(3): 271–291

Genda, Yuji (2006) *Nagging Sense of Job Insecurity: The New Reality Facing Japanese Youth* (translated by Jean Connell Hoff). Tokyo: I-House Press.

Gill, Tom (2003) When Pillars Evaporate: Structuring Masculinity on the Japanese Margins. In: *Men and Masculinities in Contemporary Japan: Dislocating the Salaryman Doxa.* James E. Roberson and Nobue Suzuki (eds.), 144–161. London: Routledge Curzon.

Goodman, Roger, Yuki Imoto and Tuukka Toivonen (2012) *A Sociology of Japanese Youth: From Returnees to NEETs.* London: Routledge.

100   *Jun Imai*

Gordon, Andrew (1993) Contests for the Workplace. In: *Postwar Japan as History*. Andrew Gordon (ed.), 373–394. Berkeley: University of California Press.

Hidaka, Tomoko (2010) *Salaryman Masculinity: Continuity and Change in Hegemonic Masculinity in Japan*. Leiden: Brill.

Imai, Jun (2011) The Limit of Equality by "Company Citizenship": Politics of Labor Market Segmentation in the Case of Regular and Non-Regular Employment in Japan. In: *Japan's New Inequality: Intersection of Employment Reforms and Welfare Arrangements*. Yoshimichi Sato and Jun Imai (eds.), 32–53. Melbourne: Trans Pacific Press.

—— (2015) Policy Responses to the Precarity of Non-Regular Employment in Japan: Path Dependence of the Negotiated Order of Inequality. In: *Policy Responses to Precarious Work in Asia*. Hisng-Huang Michael Hisao, Arne L. Kalleberg and Kevin Hewison (eds.), 49–80. Taipei: Institute of Sociology, Academia Sinica.

Inui, Akihiko (2015) Jakunen rōdō shijō no henyō wa dansei-sei o yurugaseteiruka – YCSJ chōsa fuantei shūrō-sō dansei no jirei kara [Does the Restructuring of the Youth Labor Market Transform Masculinity? Based on YCSJ Data of the Young Male Who Have a Precarious Trajectory]. *Kyōiku kagaku kenkyū* 29: 27–34.

Itō, Kimio (1996) *Danseigaku nyūmon* [Introduction to Men's Studies]. Tokyo: Sakuhinsha.

—— (2003) *Otokorashisa to iu shinwa* [The Myth About Masculinity]. Tokyo: NHK Shuppan Kyōkai.

Jackson, Gregory (2001) The Origins of Nonliberal Corporate Governance in German and Japan. In: *The Origins of Nonliberal Capitalism: Germany and Japan in Comparison*. Wolfgang Streeck and Kozo Yamamura (eds.), 121–170. Ithaca: Cornell University Press.

Kimoto, Kimiko (1995) *Kazoku jendā kigyō shakai – jendā apurōchi no mosaku* [Family, Gender, and Corporate Society: The Search for the Gender Approach]. Tokyo: Minerva Shobō.

Kohli, Martin (2009 [1986]) The World We Forgot: A Historical Review of the Life Course. In: *The Life Course Reader: Individuals and Societies Across Time*. Walter R. Heinz, Johannes Huinink and Ansgar Weymann (eds.), 64–90. Frankfurt am Main: Campus Verlag.

Kosugi, Reiko (ed.) (2002) *Jiyū no daishō/furītā – gendai wakamono no shūgyō ishiki to kōdō* [The Price of Freedom/Freeter: Work Attitude and Behavior of Contemporary Youth]. Tokyo: Nihon Rōdō Kenkyū Kikō.

—— (2003) *Furītā to iu ikikata* [Freeter as a Way of Life]. Tokyo: Keisō Shobō.

—— (2005) *Furītā to nīto* [Freeter and NEET]. Tokyo: Keisō Shobō.

Lee, Byoung-Hoon and Kwan-Yeong Shin (2009) *Job Mobility of Non-Regular Workers in the Segmented Labour Markets: Cross-National Comparison of South Korea and Japan*. Paper presented at the International Symposium on Globalization and East Asian Societies held at Jinan University, China, April.

Marshall, Thomas H. (1992 [1950]) Citizenship and Social Class. In: *Citizenship and Social Class*. Thomas H. Marshall and Tom Bottomore (eds.), 1–51. London: Pluto Press.

Meguro, Yoriko, Sumiko Yazawa and Hideo Okamoto (eds.) (2012) *Yuragu dansei no jendā ishiki – shigoto, kazoku, kaigo* [Uncertain Attitude of Gender Among Men: Work, Family and Care]. Tokyo: Shinyōsha.

Miyashita, Saori (2003) Sengo nihon no dansei jukuren rōdōsha-zō to sono hyōka [The Transfiguration and Evaluation of the Lifestyle of Male Skilled Workers in Postwar Japan]. In: *Shakai seisaku gakki-shi* (volume 9). Shakai Seisaku Gakkai (ed.), 203–223. Kyoto: Hōritsu Bunkasha.

Struggling men in emasculated life-courses 101

Mugikura, Tetsu (2006) Otokorashisa to hōmuresu [Manhood and Homelessness]. In: *Danseishi* (volume 3). Tsunehisa Abe, Sumio Obinata and Masako Amano (eds.), 92–123. Tokyo: Nihon Keizai Hyōronsha.

Nakanishi, Shintaro (2009) Hyōryūsha kara kōkaisha e – non erīto seinen no "rōdō seikatsu" keiken o yominaosu [From Drifter to Voyager: Re-Examining the Work/Life Experiences of Non-Elite Youth]. In: *Non erīto seinen no shakai kūkan*. Shintaro Nakanishi and Tomoki Takayama (eds.), 1–45. Tokyo: Otsuki Shoten.

Ogura, Kazuya (2008) Hi-seiki koyōsha no koyō/rōdō jōken to kōhei/kōsei [Employment/Labor Conditions of Non-Regular Employee and Fairness/Justice]. In: *Koyō ni okeru kōhei/kōsei*. Rengo Sōgō Seikatsu Kaihatsu Kenkyūjo (ed.), 79–105. Tokyo: Rengo Sōken.

Osawa, Mari (1993) *Kigyō chūshin shakai o koete* [Beyond Corporate-Centered Society]. Tokyo: Jiji Tsūshinsha.

Sennett, Richard and Jonathan Cobb (1973) *The Hidden Injuries of Class*. New York: Vintage Books.

Shimazaki, Naoko (2013) Jinsei no tayō-ka to raifukōsu – nihon ni okeru seido-ka, hyōjun-ka, kojin-ka [Diversification of Individual Lives and Life-Courses: Institutionalization, Standardization, Individualization in Japan]. In: *Raifukōsu sentaku no yukue – nihon to doitsu no shigoto, kazoku, sumai*. Maren Godzik, Hiromi Tanaka and Kristina Iwata-Weickgenannt (eds.), 2–22. Tokyo: Shinyōsha.

Shinkawa, Toshimitsu and T. J. Pempel (1996) Occupational Welfare and the Japanese Experience. In: *The Privatization of Social Policy? Occupational Welfare and the Welfare State in America, Scandinavia and Japan*. Michael Shalev (ed.), 280–326. Basingstoke: Macmillan Press.

Shire, Karen (1999) Socialization and Work in Japan: The Meaning of Adulthood for Men and Women in a Business Context. *International Journal of Japanese Sociology* 8: 77–92.

Statistics Bureau (2018) *Rōdōryoku chōsa* [Labor Force Survey]. Online available at: http://www.stat.go.jp/data/roudou/longtime/03roudou.html (accessed 12 April 2018).

Taga, Futoshi (2001) *Dansei no jendā keisei* [The Gender Formation of Men]. Tokyo: Tōyōkan Shuppan.

―――― (2006) *Otokorashisa no shakaigaku* [Sociology of Masculinity]. Tokyo: Sekai Shisōsha.

―――― (ed.) (2011) *Yuragu sararīman seikatsu – shigoto to katei no hazama de* [Uncertain Salaryman Life: Between Work and Life]. Kyoto: Minerva Shobō.

Tarōmaru, Hiroshi (ed.) (2006) *Furītā to nīto no shakaigaku* [Sociology of Freeter and NEET]. Tokyo: Sekai Shisōsha.

―――― (2009) *Jakunen hi-seiki koyō no shakaigaku – kaisō, jendā gurōbaruka* [Sociology of Youth in Non-Regular Employment: Class, Gender and Globalization]. Osaka: Osaka Daigaku Shuppan-kai.

7 The Fukushima event, or the birth of a politicized generation

Anne Gonon

The Fukushima nuclear disaster as an event

In Karl Mannheim's theory of generations, the emergence of a "generation unit" is an important aspect of his sociology of knowledge, providing insight into the process of generational renewal and social change (Mannheim 1998[1923]). This question of changing generations is closely linked to the notion of "event", an idea widely explored by historians and philosophers who view an event as the occurrence of something extraordinary, something that interrupts the everyday state of affairs (Bensa and Fassin 2002). When the nuclear reactor core one melted down at the Fukushima nuclear power plant on 11 March 2011, releasing millions of Becquerel of radioactivity into the atmosphere, the media called it "an accident". However, the simple combination of physical effects that had occurred can also bee seen as "an event". An event draws a clear line between "before" and "after". In the social shifts that follow an event, the essential question about the importance of life and law is cast anew. In his study on generations, Gérard Mauger (2013: 121) advances two hypotheses as the basis for analyzing events. Firstly, an event is something that is likely to have lasting effects on those who experience it, and, secondly, it has differential effects on people according to their age. Mauger identifies three types of crises that can significantly influence a generation: revolutions, wars, and political crises. I would argue that we could add nuclear disaster, which is a total crisis – not just ecological in scope, but also with profound social and political consequences (de Nateuil and Laville 2014). A nuclear disaster can be considered a "founding event" (*un événement fondateur*), the effects of which impact life-course events (Mauger 2013: 122).

One effect, in particular, sets the 2011 nuclear disaster apart from the types of disasters (e.g. earthquakes, floods, and typhoons) seen more frequently in Japan – the massive release of radioactive material forced residents of irradiated areas to leave their homes, with no idea whether or when they would be able to return. In other words, the residents of Fukushima Prefecture were suddenly consumed with the challenge of meeting their basic everyday needs, first in ill-equipped shelters and later in temporary housing, while also facing serious questions about their health and their future lives. Being plunged into a state of total uncertainty affected these people's very relation to life, and to political power. The authorities

The Fukushima event   103

were seen as incapable of ensuring the safety of the population, leading to a multitude of new phenomena in the public sphere. Mothers of Fukushima, concerned about the health of their children and protesting week after week in front of the Diet made a strong impression on the Japanese public. In a more local and less visible manner, the multiple lawsuits filed against TEPCO – the energy company that managed the nuclear power plant – and actions denouncing the limited support policy for affected families became a significant part of, and continue to punctuate, the lives of people in this region (Hino 2013). Individuals who had never before spoken in public gathered to make the voices of Fukushima's victims heard, sometimes with the support of non-profit organizations, many of which had been created immediately after the disaster. Life in the region changed drastically, but did this disaster constitute "an event" for young people? What did it mean for their generation, the age group most vulnerable to the insidious effects of exposure to radioactivity?

Of the many facets that impact youth, we shall examine one – the SEALDs youth movement. Studying the SEALDs (Students Emergency Action for Liberal Democracy) – created in 2015 and preceded by the SASPL (Students Against Secret Protection Law) movement – offers interesting insight into the generational effects of the Fukushima event. In forming these movements, young people thought of as apolitical stepped into the public sphere and became engaged in politics, just as older Japanese had done before them (Kikuchi 2015). A series of draft laws proposed by the Abe government on state secrecy and national security was serious enough to grab the attention of a large percentage of the population (Oishi 2016). That the younger generation would take to the streets in protest was not to be taken for granted and, in fact, it took many by surprise. This sudden appearance of youth in the public sphere can be explained by a combination of factors that emerged after the triple disaster, often referred to as the "Great East Japan Disaster" or simply the "Fukushima Disaster".

Was SEALDs a political awakening of youth?

Mannheim's idea that a generation simultaneously takes part in the same period of collective transformation is extremely relevant for the analysis of the Fukushima event. Mannheim asserts that the effects of an event may lead to a shift in the behaviors and values of young people, who are more malleable and receptive to new events than older people experiencing the exact same event. Mannheim also suggests that an event does not have the same effects on an entire age group, and that different members of an age cohort experience it differently (Mannheim 1998[1923]: 169). Indeed, when we look at young people's reactions to the Fukushima event, different behaviors can be seen between them. A nuclear disaster that obliterates the future of some youths (and not others) creates a divide within their generation, with those who experienced this disaster directly, and have directly suffered the consequences, and those who experienced the disaster from a safe distance, even if the images and first-person accounts affected them deeply.

104   *Anne Gonon*

In order to understand how certain young people reacted to the event, I will employ the notion of "generation units", defined as "groups within the same actual generation which work up the material of their common experiences in different specific ways" (Mannheim 1998[1923]: 184). From this perspective, the SEALDs movement can be seen as an example of how "groups may consciously experience and emphasize their character as generation units" (Mannheim 1998[1923]: 190). In the following section, I identify aspects of the dominant mode of generation that describe why the SEALDs movement had so little impact on the generation of Japanese youth overall.

The SEALDs movement

If we consider the term "generation" in the sense set forth by Mannheim and, in accordance with Arendt (1998), view political action as a "second birth", then the arrival of SEALDs is a manifestation, a form of generation, in two ways – firstly, with the appearance of youth in the public sphere, and, secondly, with "birth through action".

The members of the SEALDs movement shared similar sociological characteristics with their four young founders (Takahashi 2016; Shirafuji 2015).[1] They were well-educated, but generally not enrolled at elite national universities. They were students at universities in Tokyo such as Meiji Gakuin, in fields ranging from political science to art or design. Most SEALDs activists were between 18 and 24 years old, the age at which youth are most susceptible to change, i.e., to inflections in their behavior (Mauger 2013: 113). Many had atypical upbringings, such as schooling abroad or a difficult or unconventional family situation. One, for example, had a father heavily involved in helping homeless people. Fukushima was central in their process of becoming politically active – a number of them had protested outside the Diet in 2012, which is where they discovered the legitimacy of political protest. After this experience, Okuda Aki (born 1992) – often presented as the spokesperson of the movement in the media and even at the Diet – went abroad to visit different political youth movements (e.g., the Spanish Indigenous Movement and Occupy Wall Street in the United States). He returned from his travels convinced that the same form of expression needed to be adopted in Japan in order to oppose the new law on state secrecy. In 2013, he rallied his friends and created SASPL as a means of opposing a law they saw as concealing decisions on nuclear energy. The movement continued to grow, becoming SEALDs in May 2015. It criticized the legislation on national security, seen as a threat to the Japanese Constitution's principle of pacifism (SEALDs 2016). As SEALDs, the movement gained momentum, counting 500 members nationwide at its peak, with more than 4,000 young people turning out to participate in the protests it was organizing.

Although the movement became more structured over time, creating coordination when the need to do so arose, it refused to adopt a fixed structure, preferring to maintain its fluid and unpredictable way of operating, e.g., using Facebook or the messenger service Line for mobilization (SEALDs 2016). The movement changed over the following months, partly as intellectuals and politicians opposed to the politics of the Abe government were drawn to it. Furthermore, it developed new moral and intellectual ideas, going beyond the mere expression of anger or frustration that had first characterized its activities. The Upper House elections in July 2016 represented a chance for the opposition, especially because the Abe government was pushing for the revision of the Constitution, a highly sensitive issue in Japan. The SEALDs movement saw the forthcoming elections as an opportunity to take a different course of action. Moving beyond the minimalist chanting of a slogan over and over ("This is what democracy looks like"), the movement now chose a new repertoire of actions after engaging with Mizutani Takahisa, an experienced lawyer, and Nakano Koichi, a professor of political science at Sophia University and also a think tank consultant. This idea of learning from experts was in line with the direction the youth movement hoped to take, and with the new methods it planned to adopt henceforth. A think tank called ReDEMOS ("response to citizens") was created in December 2015 and designed as a platform that could be shared by candidates for the Upper House elections. This action emphasizes what was at stake for the movement and how their concept of politics was evolving. A series of short TV-style shows produced by ReDEMOS were posted on YouTube, illustrating SEALDs view of the elections as an opportunity to rethink politics and to reflect on the relation between politics and economy. Each theme was addressed in three 16-minute interviews of specialists, explaining the political agenda known as Abenomics (TV 1.1; 1.2; 1.3), the rationale for Japanese to invest their savings in stocks and the dangers of doing so (TV 2.1; 2.2; 2.3), and the system of political representation (TV 3.1 and 3.2).[2] Through this educational medium, SEALDs began exploring political issues in order to promote thought and dialogue on how to move Japan out of its economic and political deadlock. The choice of experts interviewed shows a clear intention of offering a critical perspective on Japanese society. Morihara Yasuhito and Hama Noriko, the two economists who participated in these videos, were staunchly opposed to the current politics of the Abe government, and the political scientist Miura Mari was critical of the Japanese political system for being dominated by elites. The interviews with them offered viewers some sort of crash course in economic politics, with academics outlining the changes implemented since 2013 and explaining the Abenomics goal of achieving renewed economic growth.

It is important to note here that the youths in the SEALDs movement did not engage in ideological debates. Rather, the young activists sought to understand how policies of justice would look, arguing in favor of a return to "classic" capitalist policies that would redistribute wealth within society. Most importantly to our discussion here, they thought that this kind of politics would only be possible if there was a generational shift in the political world, and one of their videos was actually titled "Why are politicians all old?"[3] However, the candidates supporting the ideas of the movement and its consulting think tank did not win the Upper House elections in July 2016, and SEALDs was dissolved shortly thereafter.

The slogan "Tell me what democracy looks like" undeniably united many groups across Japan who sought to connect local problems to broader issues over contested

106 *Anne Gonon*

topics such as the US military bases in Okinawa or the nuclear power plants in Fukushima. Combining their voices and their acts was, by nature, a political action (Takahashi 2016). By taking part in this movement, Japanese youths experienced the suffering or discomfort that comes along with standing up in front of people and developing ideas that were quite new to them – the same qualities that Arendt (1998) associates with entering the political realm. The young activists did not enter the conventional political arena. They introduced an idealized conception of politics into their own cultural universe, adopting a form of activism that some researchers consider to be a new social movement. The draft laws of the Abe government triggered responses from the young. Their choice of street protests – a mode of expression that acquired new legitimacy since Fukushima – is consistent with statistical surveys that show a trend of youth who want to work, act and take part in society, but who are at the same time critical of participating in conventional politics (Naikakufu 2013). Instead, young people chose their own forms of discourse as the voices of ordinary people talking about everyday life. As novices in these public practices, these young people saw self-education as an integral part of their actions. The interviews show that their activism and ethics were based on political ideas that they had studied in their university courses. The movement's activities were clearly and firmly rooted in the direct transmission of ideas between students and professors.

Forming their own relation to the Fukushima event

The appearance of a new generation is partly connected to the transformations of the mode of reproduction, which generally leads to an examination of these modes through family and schooling. Pierre Bourdieu (1998: 272–290) defines a mode of reproduction as a system of reproduction strategies adapted to the specific characteristics of the family heritage that is reproduced. The family mode of reproduction associated with family-owned farms, factories or businesses that are passed on (usually from father to son) is distinguished from the school-mediated mode of reproduction that is "characteristic of large bureaucratic companies whose capital is dispersed and [where] the academic title becomes a genuine entry pass" (Bourdieu 1998: 285). In the case at hand, we need to understand the transmission of cultural and educational capital in connection to the Fukushima event. In both the health-related issues driving the actions of parents of children affected by radiation, and in the actions by SEALDs with the support of academics, the Fukushima event can be seen as a break from the classic model of transmission usually observed in Japan between generations. The two categories of players, parents and youth, consciously and unconsciously broke with the standardized transmission process by exporting values into the public space. Health concerns by parents and political action by professors worked on a different register, but both types of action helped to create a way for youths to engage in civic life.

Reproduction as a key factor in parents' actions

In the decades before Fukushima, mass protests had all but disappeared from the social sphere in Japan. After the nuclear disaster, however, groups of people directly affected by radiation – ordinary people not thought of as political (mothers, farmers, teachers, etc.) – began protesting, determined to make their voices and concerns heard in front of the Diet. Anti-nuclear protesters joined them. The government's passivity prompted an outcry from those stressing the risks for the population in case the nuclear power plants were put back into operation. Protest were only the visible part of the deep social upheaval set off by the disaster. In Fukushima, where life (human life, animal life, plant life) was under threat or had been destroyed, a "moral community" emerged, made up of people in the same state of disorientation, sharing the same uncertainties and indecision, and criticizing the same representatives and authorities that refused to take responsibility for what had happened.

This moral community in Fukushima took shape around different repertoires of action, which everyone used in their own way and which gradually evolved over time. What stands out is the mobilization of women and local groups tackling concrete issues that urgently needed solutions. Support from Arnand Grover, UN Special Rapporteur on the right to health of the citizens in Fukushima, and prominent doctors, such as Professor Tsuda Hideo from Okayama University, who took a firm stance in calling for recognition of the dangers resulting from continued exposure to radiation, brought greater legitimacy to actions rooted in the concern for bare life itself. This made it easier for anxious parents and members of the community to participate, without a political party attaching radical thought or conventional political criticism to these actions. The concerns being publicly voiced were based on everyday life, and not on abstract political ideas. In fighting for the right to life and to health, the mothers of Fukushima, and also other adults, established the legitimacy of their protests and placed the practice of care for vulnerable people, a deeply private activity, at the forefront of public life.

Academics getting involved

Teachers generally transmit educational resources to their students, equipping them with the skills to think for themselves and to produce their own narratives, drawing on teachings in philosophy, political thought, and so on. Our analysis here will be limited to university students. In the case of the Fukushima event, the role of university professors involved a new aspect. A new form of knowledge transmission was made up of two components – public action and practical content. It seems that in some cases, university students (and sometimes secondary students, too) may have been the ones who initiated a change in the teaching mode in the classroom. They asked for information on authors whose work could help them meet their movement's objectives. Moreover, university professors did not confine themselves to the lecture hall. They, too, often took their discourse into the public sphere.

In addition to parents defending the principles of respect for biological life and concern for others, secondary school teachers and university professors defended political ideals. Their first major action was the creation of a "People's Tribunal on Fukushima", a public forum on the issue of responsibility for the

108 *Anne Gonon*

Fukushima disaster (Genpatsu Minshū Hōtei 2012). Modeled on the "Tribunal on the Vietnam War", organized by Bertrand Russell and Jean-Paul Sartre in the 1960s and 70s, the People's Tribunal on Fukushima sought to open up a discursive space on the question of responsibility for the nuclear disaster. It was initiated by three scholars and a jurist, all experts in political thought who had taken part in a similar tribunal on the issue of the so-called "comfort women" (actually, military sexual slavery) in 2000, or who had been involved in previous social movements. Putting their knowledge to use for the public, they formed a traveling tribunal that held sessions in ten Japanese cities from 2012 to 2014. The tribunal gave the floor to victims of the Fukushima nuclear disaster and other lesser-known accidents, as well as to citizens living close to other nuclear plants in Japan. The tribunal served to indict TEPCO and the Japanese authorities, but criticism about Japanese democracy in general also began to be voiced. Democracy was accused of being no more than a circle of experts and legislators who could not even ensure the most basic human rights – the right to life and the right to health. This type of debate was also taken up in classrooms and lecture halls.

When the government presented the draft law on state secrecy, these same intellectuals moved into more overt political arenas to fight the amendment of the Japanese Constitution. They formed groups such as the Article 96 Group, an initiative led by the prominent constitutional scholar Higuchi Yoichi that addressed the law on state secrecy promulgated in 2013. These jurists – "conservatives" in the sense of custodians of the Constitution – went outside the university arena in order to explain the content and dangers of this excessively complex draft law to the public. A voice of opposition born in academia was expressed beyond academic publications, that is, on the street, at public meetings, on social media, and sometimes in the national media as well. This lent a certain degree of legitimacy to the expression of opposition and the use of protests as a political tool. These forms of expression no longer appeared as outdated modes from the past. Moreover, the term "democracy" in its most basic sense, i.e., expressing one's views in the public sphere, was sure to resonate widely because this is how democracy was understood in the demands of many civil-society organizations that had long been working with local governments.

The youths who took part in anti-nuclear protests and who had been educated in ways that applied to the current state of affairs, learned that respect for life was not just a private affair, it was also a public matter. They understood that without concern for biological life, human life worth living would cease to exist. In order to express this view and to make themselves heard, entering the public sphere, with all the physical and moral demands that this implies, was the only possible response they could see. These actions were led by older Japanese, i.e., parents who mobilized to protect their children's health, professors engaged in the tribunal and the Article 96 Group. They brought new dimensions to the process of inter-generational transmission, reconciling the acts of protest with ideas and theories, and providing key tools needed to educate a generation of youths that were at odds with the world around them.

The Fukushima event   109

Is there a "SEALDs generation?"

It is too soon to say if and how history will remember the SEALDs movement. However, we can already advance several observations how the role of SEALDs in political debates has affected this generation of youth. Is it possible that a new form of civic engagement is emerging? Our first answer is no, based on the observation that the use of social media by SEALDs could have but ultimately did not incite keen and widespread interest in the group's action among young people. This leaves us with a number of questions. Does this mean that the movement's discourse on the concepts of democracy and political representation were not of interest to most young people, or did not reflect their real concerns? Does it mean that they could not relate to the SEALDs movement, and by extension, that the events surrounding the Fukushima disaster were somehow not strong enough to spark a level of anger and fear that would compel them to seriously question the impact of politics on their own lives and own their futures?

SEALDs under criticism

The SEALDs movement also came under criticism, and this criticism tells us a great deal about how its ideas were received. SEALDs was openly criticized in blogs and indirectly criticized in a number of books and articles. Those who challenged and engaged in controversies with its supporters were not other students (peers from the same age group), but rather older intellectuals. The two most outspoken opponents of the movement were Tanaka Hirokazu (born 1957), a blogger whose posts were published as a book in 2016, and Hemmi Yo (born 1944), another well-known author who also writes a popular blog.

Tanaka Hirokazu, widely known as Yoniumuhibi in his blog and Twitter account, writes in everyday terms about the ideas of political theorist Maruyama Masao. In 2016, he published a book entitled *The Truth About SEALDs*, a collection of posts about SEALDs that appeared on his blog from July 2015 onwards. Hemmi Yo is a journalist, essayist and poet who, in a blog post dated 16 September 2015, criticized SEALDs and the protests in front of the Diet. Both critics compare the movement with another event that shook post-war Japan – the protests against renewing the Japan-US Security Treaty in the 1960s. At the time, Maruyama Masao, Hidaka Rokurō and Tsurumi Shunsuke, to name only the most well-know figures, not only theorized the situation but were also active in a movement that sought to prevent the renewal of the treaty. Evoking this illustrious past, Tanaka suggests that, by contrast, the current debates lacked vigour and substance, especially those led by prominent intellectuals such as social historian Oguma Eiji. Tanaka claimed that such individuals were latching onto student actions in order to find a way of existing in the public sphere (Tanaka 2016: 72–77). The students involved in SEALDs are portrayed as manipulated and incapable of producing their own critical discourse on the political and social situation. For his part, Hemmi Yo derided the movement in a humorous text, railing against the absurdity of a situation in which "anti-military protesters ask the police to arrest

110   *Anne Gonon*

other protesters".[4] He saw this as a new form of fascism and offered his own twist on the SEALDs slogan: "What is democracy? This is fascism!"

Tanaka was generally infuriated with what he perceived as a manipulation of SEALDs by the communist party and the extreme left, which provided the movement with logistic support and knowledge about protest techniques. In his opinion, this devalued the members of SEALDs, reducing their action to a mere expression of the ambitions of intellectuals trying to establish their own legitimacy as politically engaged activists, usurping the movement in order to place themselves more prominently on the political stage. The SEALDs movement undeniably resonated with many adults, representing their hopes as much as those of many young Japanese. Moreover, like any other social movement, SEALDs was confronted with outside agendas looking to latch onto its energy and popularity. It is also true that the youths in the movement were somewhat naïve and gauche, and that a lack of political culture showed in their actions. This notwithstanding, the movement cannot be simply discounted, and the new possibilities that it tried to open up must be put into a larger perspective.

It is noteworthy that few of the posts by youths on the SEALDs blog convey a spirit of openness, or a desire to shatter conformism. The authors post critical messages ("this is fascism") rather than developed analyses, denouncing, for example, the trendiness of the movement, which came across to them as being self-righteous, or older authors who portrayed students demonstrating in the streets as being irresponsible and disturbing the social order rather than going to class (as "serious" university students are supposed to do). Critics seized on both the form and the substance, and the dissolution of the movement after the senatorial elections during the summer of 2016 may only have further reinforced their negative judgment on the SEALDs movement.

There have not yet been studies on how much or how little the SEALDs discourse impacted the vision of youths about their role in civic and political life, or on why the movement did not deeply resonate with many young people. Mannheim's concept of the generation unit as a group of young people participating in the same historical process (Mannheim 1998[1923]: 182) can help us examine what is vaguely referred to as "Japanese youth". Data from the White Paper on Youth give us a general idea about the living conditions and modes of thought of this segment of Japanese youth (ZDSKKR 2014).

Socioeconomic characteristics and attitudes of Japanese youth

SEALDs' fairly reformist discourse appears somewhat unusual for students who, for the most part, fit two socioeconomic profiles. (1) Youth either already active in the job market or enrolled at "second-tier universities", and (2) students at the top-ranked universities in the country, or at least in their region. For both groups, however, analyzing the generation status reveals two important factors they share and which may partly explain their lack of interest in SEALD's actions and discourse. Firstly, their low level of support for an anti-nuclear agenda, and, secondly, an economic situation that favors "the inheritors". As an effect, risks (professional,

The Fukushima event   111

health and safety risks, etc.) have become a determining factor in how young people organize their lives from secondary school onward (Tomoeda 2015).

As a general trend, polls of secondary and university students show that they support fairly conservative values. Post-university employment has improved since 2005, and each year, more than 80 percent of university graduates find a job right after graduation (Naikakufu 2013), even if their employment is often precarious and unsatisfactory. Students are more worried about their future quality of life than about unemployment (ZDSKKR 2014). In other words, their concern is not whether they will find a job, but whether they will find a job that is actually satisfactory. This has led to higher expectations regarding the role of university studies for their future life, compared to attitudes observed among students only ten years ago. 59 percent see school as a place to form friendships and university as a place to acquire qualifications and good references for their resume. University is perceived as the launch pad for one's career (Naikakufu 2013). In addition to their coursework, students are encouraged by their universities to complete internships at companies with which the university has partnerships. Focused on building their career, and often working part-time due to tight finances, students today seem less interested in taking part in clubs or in doing volunteer work. If they engage in these types of activities, it is primarily to help people in need. They seem to be more family-oriented and more attached to their close inner circle and their home. Convinced that their contribution has no influence on political decisions, they are little concerned with national affairs, or with Japan's role in the world (Naikakufu 2013). Instead, they bring their ideals and the knowledge acquired during their studies to a different sphere. Young people seem to increasingly transfer their interest in the world onto their job, and not onto politics or volunteer work. They expect companies to give them the opportunity to exercise their ideas on social and international issues. Companies displaying ethical and socially responsible stances are viewed positively by young people (Naikakufu 2013). Rather than being "conservatives" or "revolutionaries", the Japanese youth today can be called "reformists". They recognize the key role that companies play in economic development and accept the capitalist system in which they have grown up, but they also want to bring an ethical dimension to business.

Stances on politics and forms of civic engagement reflect class interests, and this pragmatism is at the very foundation of student behaviors. A poll of students at the University of Tokyo shows that their lack of interest in the SEALDs movement does not mean they are generally uninterested in political issues (Yamaguchi 2015). Rather, their concern in this area is taking a new form, or a form similar to that of their parents. According to political scientist Yamaguchi Jirō (2015), students at the University of Tokyo see education as an investment from which they expect to see a high return.[5] A poll of students at a smaller, private university showed the same results. Students' priorities are primarily economic. 38 percent think that groundwork for new economic growth needs to be laid, and 36 percent think that resolving financial problems is the top priority. Less than 10 percent of respondents place politics or the environment among their top concerns. They support no political party, or if they do, it is the party in power, the LDP, which is

112   Anne Gonon

perceived as keeping the society running smoothly. Moreover, the link between SEALDs, the communist party and the movement's opposition against the Abe government – regarded as simplistic by students – puts them off and makes them critical of SEALDs (Tanaka 2016). Such a perception of this situation has convinced these youths that the movement never had a chance of influencing politics or of reforming how democratic institutions operate. What is more, they do not see such changes as necessary in the first place.

Awareness of nuclear issues

One might have expected young people to respond to the Fukushima nuclear accident by taking a clear stance on nuclear energy and by opposing the continuation of the nuclear program by the Abe government. None of this happened. The anti-nuclear protests have a stronger appeal among older adults than among young people, and a 2013 poll of upper secondary students shows that most are actually strongly in favor of nuclear energy (Tomoeda 2015: 172–173). To understand this position, we need to look at various data. First, the risk of an earthquake seems much more real to them, because it is tangible. For 50 percent of the youth surveyed, the Fukushima nuclear accident did not lead them to question their values. The use of nuclear energy is still viewed as "a risk", rather than a "real danger" that has already caused an unprecedented environmental and public health disaster. Classifying it as "a risk" frames nuclear energy as something that can be foreseen and, therefore, as something that can be managed. This is a stance that reflects absolute faith in science to control risks of all kinds, including nuclear risk – a view which is very much in line with the official position and its approach to managing nuclear energy.

The effectiveness of this approach is illustrated by the many university students who were in secondary school at the time of the nuclear accident, and who took part in the Ministry of Education's programs to support the reconstruction process in Fukushima Prefecture. To pave the way for reconstruction, youths in the region have been involved in innovative projects that seek to improve the lives of local residents. For example, students from Fukushima University, in collaboration with the University of Aizu and a Fukushima Secondary School, have developed a robot that can perform operations in the nuclear power plant's other reactors, and they have been training personnel how to operate it. This project is part of the Fourth Science and Technology Basic Plan of Japan set up by the Ministry of Education (MEXT 2016). This type of initiative appeals to students. It is therefore not surprising to find that Fukushima University has registered an increase in applicants from outside the prefecture due to a desire to share the fate of the "victims". Thus, the Fukushima disaster has been a catalyst for youth action, but this action has, in fact, been guided by the government's policy to revitalize the region.

Understanding the connection between the Fukushima event and the general student population is complex. In order to support the victims of the triple disaster, secondary schools and universities began giving students the opportunity to

The Fukushima event 113

do volunteer work. Some institutions granted academic credits for these activities. At the same time, statistics show that youths are less involved than senior citizens in the non-profit sector (Naikakufu 2013). For the young people who volunteered after Fukushima, the event was an opportunity to discover solidarity. The experience was short-lived for some, but even so, the physical involvement was formative, bringing them into contact with people who had been through traumatic experiences. They learned how to work as part of a team, and their involvement gave them first-hand knowledge of a real social issue. Even now, volunteer groups of medical students, for example, travel to the region of Fukushima in order to provide medical and psychological support for local residents (Nara and Wakayama Medical Universities, August-September 2015), or to work with young people there such as in the case of a field trip by students from Sophia University to Idate in August 2015. The moral value placed on these volunteer actions is based on overlooking the hazards these young people are exposed to by spending time in the contaminated region. Unlike the SEALDs movement, which is the other form of youth action, these volunteer groups have accepted the government's (unfounded) claim that the risks are under control.

All in all, it seems unlikely that social criticism based on anti-nuclear attitudes will take root in Japan. Clearly, "young people today have to negotiate a set of risks that were largely unknown to their parents: this is true irrespective of social background or gender" (Furlong and Kartel 2007: 12). However, it seems that the risk-based discourse directs attention away from questions that would challenge the socioeconomic framework and the capitalist system. The thorough work of Miyamoto Michiko (2012), who takes a comprehensive approach in her research on the process of transition from youth to adulthood, shows no evidence of criticism on capitalist economic structures. Even in the case of SEALDs, which tried to unveil the connection between democracy and economic dysfunction, it stopped short of producing real criticism of the capitalist system, as is illustrated in the video interviews it produced together with ReDEMOS. All interviews are similar in their tone and their pragmatism, and they never call the existing system into question.

Outlook

Viewed from inside Japan, Fukushima seemed to be reabsorbed into ordinary life after the first few months of intense emotion. However, seven years later, we are beginning to see how this event has slowly changed the social and political landscape in Japan. By accentuating certain aspects of determined capitalism, such as cynicism, which prompted the least politically engaged citizens to take an interest in and to initiate debates in the public sphere, the Fukushima event opened the door to a multiplicity of new possibilities. Of the many facets of this phenomenon, we have examined one, the SEALDs youth movement, which seemed to express both the fear of young people seeing their world organized in a way that nuclear energy was deemed essential for its development, and of an interest in politics that provided a framework for organizing the political community.

114 *Anne Gonon*

In examining the transformations taking place in Japanese society, we arrive at the following ambiguous observations. Firstly, the radical engagement of youths on sensitive political issues stimulated activism among older age groups (such as older Liberal Democrats), re-engaging them and prompting them to reclaim values they themselves had fought for in their youth. Secondly, the authority exerted by academics, not only through their teaching, but also through taking risks in the public sphere, allowed young people to place their aspirations within a framework that allowed for general reflections. This gave them the resources to understand their own society and to question the legitimacy that ties them to the government, cultivating some sort of "realistic romanticism" with which to express their demands (Laugier and Ogien 2014). We can see some fluidity in the relationship to authority that seems to be wiping away the rigid lines between generations. This has allowed for a dialogue that seems more egalitarian, and at one point seems to even reverse generational hierarchies. At the same time, there is a new recognition of authority rooted in action – something that Hannah Arendt (1998) referred to as *vita activa*, active life.

By stripping the concepts of human life, reproduction and the future of their ordinary meanings, the Fukushima disaster brought these very notions to the forefront in Japanese society. Therefore, it is only natural that Fukushima destabilized the structure of social and inter-generational relationships. How can parents protect children whose health has been seriously compromised? How can young people live in a world that physically exposes them to the threat of nuclear disaster? The protests and actions undertaken since 2012 cry out these fears – fears that cannot be wiped out simply to suit the agenda of certain parties. Awareness about the threats to biological life contrasts starkly with attitudes of oblivion or denial that may offer a sense of solace, however false such a sense may actually be. This denial is the basis for the current government's reconstruction policy, not only for Fukushima Prefecture, but for the entire country.

To make sense of Fukushima, two main narratives are advanced – one of them, of fear and anger, tells us that Fukushima will never end. The other adopts terms such as "post-Fukushima", suggesting a "return to normal". The mode of reproduction for the generation of youth that SEALDs hoped to mobilize is caught between these two.

Notes

1 Some of this data are from personal interviews of three SEALDs members belonging to the Kansai group. The interviews were conducted in March 2016.
2 Online available at: www.youtube.com/channel/UCETJCfXO0TuvfQM8d2dzI5Q
3 Online available at: www.youtube.com/watch?v=wOOmlcPFIKc
4 Hemmi Yo, blog. Online at: http://togetter.com/li/880206
5 Tweet of 12 February 2015. Online at: http://pirori2ch.com/archives/1891813.html

References

Arendt, Hannah (1998) *The Human Condition* (second edition). Chicago: University of Chicago Press.

The Fukushima event 115

Bensa, Alban and Eric Fassin (2002) Les Sciences sociales face à l'événement [The Social Sciences Face the Event]. *Terrain – revue d'anthropologie* 38: 5–20.

Bourdieu, Pierre (1998) *The State Nobility: Elite Schools in the Field of Power.* Cambridge: Polity Press.

de Nanteuil, Mathieu and Jean-Louis Laville (2014) Crise du capitalisme et économie plurielle. Une perspective anthropologique [Crisis of Capitalism and Plural Economics: An Anthropological Perspective]. *L'option de confrontations Europe* 1(33): 69–78.

Furlong, Andy and Fred Kartmel (2007) *Young People and Social Change* (second edition). Maidenhead: Open University Press.

Genpatsu Minshu Hōtei (2012) *Fukushima jikō wa hanzai da – tōden, seifu no keiji sekinin o tou* [The Fukushima Incident Is a Crime: Questions on TEPCO and Governmental Responsibility] (4 volumes). Tokyo: San'ichi.

Hino, Kosuke (2013) *Fukushima genpatsu jikō ikkenmin kenkō kanri chōsa no yami* [The Fukushima Nuclear Plant Accident: Prefectural Health Management Survey]. Tokyo: Iwanami Shinsho.

Kikuchi, Fumihiko (2015) *Wakamono no jidai* [The Era of Youth]. Tokyo: Toransubyū.

Laugier, Sandra and Albert Ogien (2014) *Le Principe démocratie: Enquête sur les nouvelles formes du politique* [The Democracy Principle: Survey on New Forms of Politics]. Paris: La Découverte.

Mannheim, Karl (1998 [1923]) The Sociological Problem of Generations. In: *Essays on the Sociology of Language.* Paul Kecskemeti (ed.), 163–195. London: Routledge.

Mauger, Gérard (2013) "Modes de generation" des générations sociales ["Modes of Generation" of Social Generations]. *Sociologia Historica* 2(13): 111–130.

MEXT (2016) *Kagaku gijutsu kihon keikaku* [Basic Science and Technology Plan]. Online available at: http://www.mext.go.jp/a_menu/kagaku/kihon/main5_a4.htm (accessed 6 March 2018).

Miyamoto, Michiko (2012) Seijinki henō ikō moderu no tenkan to wakamono seisaku [Changes in the Model of Transition from Adolescence to Adulthood and Youth Policy]. *Journal of Population Problem* 68(2): 32–53.

Naikakufu (2013) *Heisei 25-nen wagakuni to shogaikoku no wakamono ni kansuru chōsa* [International Survey of Youth Attitude 2013]. Online available at: www8.cao.go.jp/youth/english/survey/2013/pdf_index.html (accessed 20 February 2017).

Nara Medical University Gakusei Saigai Borontia Basu (2015) *Fukkō shien katsudō – hōkokusho* [Reconstruction Aid: Activity Report]. Nara: Nara Medical University.

Oishi, Taru (2016) Abe seiken no fuchin o sayū suru kenpō kaisei [Influences of the Reform of Japanese Constitution on Abe Government's Future]. In: *Kore kara no nihon no ronten* [Main Issues for Japan's Future]. Nihon Keizai Shinbun (ed.), 234–245. Tokyo: Nihon Keizai Shinbun.

SEALDs (2016) *Minshu-shugi wa tomaranai* [All Liberals in Japan, Unite]. Tokyo: Kawade Shinsha.

Shirafuji, Hiroyuki (2015) SEALDs Intabyū – minshū-shugi-tte nanda? Jibun no kotoba de katarutte nanda? [SEALDs Interview. What Is Democracy? What Is Speaking in One's Own Words?] *Hōgaku Seminar* 9(728): 6–14.

Takahashi, Gen'ichirō and SEALDs (2016) *Minshūshugi-tte nanda?* [Tell Me What Democracy Looks Like?] Tokyo: Kawade Shobō.

Tanaka, Hirokazu (2016) *SEALDs no shinjitsu – SEALDs to shibakitai no bunseki to kaibō* [The Truth About SEALDs: Analysis and Autopsy of SEALDs and the Counter-Racist Collective Action]. Nishinomiya: Rokusaisha.

Tomoeda, Toshi (2015) *Risuku shakai o ikiru wakamonotachi – kōkōsei no ishiki chōsa kara* [Youth in the Risk Society: Study on the Attitudes of High School Students]. Osaka: Osaka Daigaku Shuppan.

Yamaguchi, Jirō (2015) *Tōdaisei ha naze demo ni sankashinai ka* [Why Tōdai Students Do Not Participate in Demonstration?]. Online available at: http://agora-web.jp/archives/1667817.html (accessed 7 March 2017).

ZDSKKR = Zenkoku Daigaku Seikatsu Kyōdō Kumiai Rengōkai (2014) *Dai-50-kai gakusei seikatsu jittai chōsa* [50th Survey of Student Life]. Online available at: www.univcoop.or.jp/press/life/report.html (accessed 22 February 2017).

Part II

Cultural and emotional reactions

8 "How average am I?" Youths in a super-aged society

Florian Coulmas

Introduction

When Italo Svevo wrote his celebrated *Senilità (As a Man Grows Older)*, he was 35, the age of the novel's protagonist, Emilio Brentani. That was in 1896/7. When Tanizaki Jun'ichiro wrote *Fūten rōjin nikki (Diary of a Mad Old Man)*, he *was* the mad old man Utsugi Tokusuke, of 75 years, madly yearning for his daughter in law, Satsuko, his youth long past. Svevo's Emilio lived in the waning years of the 19th century, while Tanizaki's Tokusuke inhabited the 20th century when it was well advanced and Japan was just a few years shy of entering the age of the aged society.

During the 60-odd years that lie between Emilio's and Tokunosuke's reflections about old age, Italy and Japan, as well as several other advanced countries such as Germany, registered rather impressive life expectancy gains (Kono 2008). A Japanese girl born in 1900 would live to be 44 years old on average, while her Italian peer had a slightly shorter life expectancy of 42.8 years. By 1960, their granddaughters had drawn level, having a life that was a full quarter of a century longer, 67 years (Table 8.1). Actually a bit more, for the gap between women and men was widening, while the aggregate figures cited in Table 8.2 represent the mean of both sexes.

Whether their life expectancy expanded because they bore fewer children is an interesting question. After all, childbirth is no child's play. However, complex processes such as life expectancy gains do not have a single cause. Reductions of infant mortality and the conquest of puerperal fever certainly contributed to the extension of life expectancy, but the relationship to fertility decline remains enigmatic. However that may be, over the decades of the 20th century, life expectancy gains and total fertility rate (TFR) drops show similar if inversely related tendencies – the older they became, the fewer children they had. In Japan, the birthrate dropped below the replacement level of a bit more than two children per woman in 1975, about the same time as in Italy and five years later than in (West-) Germany. It has stayed below the replacement level in all three countries ever since and in 2012 stood at 1.41 in Japan, and 1.40 in both Italy and Germany (Table 8.2).

120   *Florian Coulmas*

Table 8.1 Life expectancy in Italy, Japan, and Germany, 1900–2013

Life expectancy at birth	Italy	Japan	Germany
1900	42.8	44	48
1960	67.67	67	75
2013	82.9	84	82

Source: Data from Government of Japan, Therborn (2004), Statistisches Bundesamt

Table 8.2 Total fertility rates in Japan, Italy, and Germany

TFR, children per women	Japan	Italy	Germany
1900	5 (estimate)	4.4	4.8
1975	1.9	2.17	1.45
2000	1.36	1.26	1.38
2014	1.41	1.40	1.40

Source: Data from World Bank (http://data.worldbank.org/indicator/SP.DYN.TFRT.IN)

In the meantime, population aging progressed in all three countries. Japan has been a super-aged society (*chōkōrei shakai*) for some time, to be precise, since 2007 (Table 8.3). According to a standard definition by the World Health Organization and the UN, in an aged society 14 percent of the total population are 65 years old or older. Japan crossed this line in 1970. It became a super-aged society a generation later, in 2007, when the proportion of the 65-plus reached 21.1 percent.

This is a conventional measure and useful for population research, but it does not say very much about the social reality of this kind of society. It is worth noting in this connection that demographic aging occurred much faster in Japan than in other industrial countries and that, therefore, Japanese society and institutions had less time to adjust to the changing circumstances (Coulmas 2007).

Since 2007, Japan's seniors have added another 5 percent to their ranks, accounting for 26.4 percent of the total population, and as soon as 2030, almost a third of the population will be in that age cohort, 30.7 percent. What does this

Table 8.3 The super-aged society

	Population 65 years and older	Japan	Italy	Germany
Aged society	14%	1970		
Super-aged society	21.1%	2007	2015	2015
	26.4%	2015		
Projection	30.7%	2030		

Source: Data from Government of Japan, WHO

"How average am I?" 121

mean for everyday life, and what does it imply for being young in this society? To deal with this issue, I will address the following questions:

(1) What does it mean to be young?
(2) What does it mean to be young in a super-aged society?
(3) Can questions (1) and (2) be meaningfully separated from each other?

Contemplating these questions may pave the way for a more informed discussion of the topical question of this volume which, as it turns out, is less innocent than it appears at first glance; for in the context of demographic aging, age is not a constant and hence not a fixed variable. Because demographic aging instigates social change the young, for lack of experience, cannot fully understand, it is a source of anxiety that makes many youths seek comfort in conformity. This is the point I will argue in what follows.

What does it mean to be young?

"Young" is a fuzzy concept that defies a non-arbitrary definition. We can start by considering various classifications, as in Tables 8.4 and 8.5.

As soon as we try to put years to any of these boxes we run into difficulties, as there is wide variation across countries, societies and languages including much vagueness within a single language. Clear-cut boundaries between categories can only be set, not found out by observation. Definitions in terms of activities, licenses, duties, etc., are embedded into systems of social conventions and values and, therefore, variable across cultures. Being young is defined with reference to social, legal, religious, political, sexual, emotional, and intellectual contexts.

In many of these contexts, being young is construed as distinct from being a child. For instance, the age of consent is often understood as dividing children from youths, adolescents, or even adults. However, whereas in some countries consent is set at 12 years, e.g., Mexico, it is 18 in Iraq and California, among others. English common law had traditionally set the age of consent within the range of 10–12 years, but nowadays it is 16 in the UK. In our three focus countries, Japan, Italy, and Germany it is 13, 14, and 14, respectively (Table 8.6).

The age of consent is a legally defined lower limit, not an average. To most people age of consent is never an issue, as the data we have about age at first sex indicate (Table 8.7). It is much higher than the age of consent, in Japan more than six years, in Italy almost five years, and in Germany more than three years.

Comparing the age at first sex and the age at first marriage, an interesting gap of ten years in Japan, 11 years in Italy, and as many as 15 years in Germany appears. This gap is indicative of the almost complete uncoupling of sex and reproduction. This is further confirmed by statistics about frequency of sex, according to which – if they can be trusted – the Italians are twice as sexually active as the Japanese, with the Germans somewhere in between. Since the fertility rates of the three countries have been on a par for decades, we are led to the conclusion that

122   Florian Coulmas

Table 8.4 Life stages conceptualized in three languages

Japanese	Italian	German	English (UK)	UN
kodomo	*bambini*	*Kinder* legally: up to 14	children legally: up to 14	up to 18
Seinen one's children and those of one's generation are considered *seinen*, roughly, until they reach majority.	*giovane* the age that follows adolescence and precedes majority	*Jugend* persons between the ages of 13 and 21 years	youth adolescents	
wakamono	*adolescente*	*Jugendliche*	youths	
jakunensō	*giovane*	*Jugendliche*	the young	14–18 15–35
otona	*adulti*	*Erwachsene*	adults, grown-ups	
rōjin	*vecchi, anziani*	*Alte, Betagte*	old, elderly men/ women	

Table 8.5 Italian terms from a popular Italian website

Italian	Japanese	German
neonato	*shinseiji*	*Neugeborenes*
lattante	*nyūji*	*Säugling*
infanzia (prima, seconda, terza)	*yōnen*	*Kindheit*
adolescenza	*seinenki*	*Jugendzeit*
prima età adulta (22–39)		
seconda età adulta (40–59)		
terza . . .		
senilità, vecchiaia	*rōnen*	*Alter*

Source: Mypersonaltrainer (www.my-personaltrainer.it)

Table 8.6 Age of consent (the legal age to have sex) across selected countries

Age of consent	16	15	14	13
	Cyprus, Finland, Israel, Latvia, Luxembourg, Netherlands, Norway, Spain, UK	Czech Republic, Denmark, France, Thailand	Austria, China, **Germany,** **Italy,** Macau, Portugal	Cambodia, **Japan,** South Korea

having sex and having children are two different affairs – which, I hasten to add, they have been in the past to some extent, but only to some extent. Total birth control is a modern phenomenon, which is known to have contributed significantly to lowering the birthrate and hence to changing the family structure. To what extent

Table 8.7 First experiences and transitions

	Japan	Italy	Germany
Age at first sex	19.4[z]	18.9[z]	17.3[z]
Age at first marriage (f)	29.7 (2010)[x]	30.60 (2010)[x]	31.70 (2011)[x]
First childbirth	30.30[y]	30.0[y]	30.0[y]
% young adults (−35) living with parents	42.7	46.6	17.3

Source: [x] Quandl.com; [y] NationMaster; [z] Durex Network Research Unit 2009, Face of Global Sex report, 2005–2009, SSL International plc, Cambridge

simple and fool proof means of birth control can explain below-replacement level total fertility rates in western European countries and Japan is unclear as are the overall effects on interpersonal relations and the social fabric at large. Whether or not there is a causal relationship between reliable family planning and the advent of the super-aged society is yet to be found out, but we cannot fail to notice the temporal concurrence of both phenomena. In passing we may also note that the average age of first marriage has risen in the course of the 20th century more rapidly than the age of first childbirth, with the inevitable consequence that the number and ratio of children born out of wedlock has increased.

Returning to the question of what it means to be young, many other criteria can be listed. For instance, the license to kill people by becoming a soldier is not usually given to minors, but again the age of majority varies, as do other privileges, such as voting, drinking alcohol, driving, casino gambling, etc. Being young has been popularly defined by the absence of responsibility for one's actions, but when it comes to transgressing the law, the age of criminal responsibility, too, varies from one country to another. Going into details would be beyond the scope of this chapter, but the general point is clear. There is a lack of correspondence between biological age and the age deemed appropriate for various activities, obligations, rights, and permissions. Instead, it must be recognized that stages of the life cycle are determined socioculturally as much as biologically.

Intuitively we all know the difference between *kodomo* and *seinen, un bambino* and *un ragazzo*, a child and a young man or woman, but our intuition may not cover all relevant definitions. The *UN Convention on the Rights of the Child* defines a child as everyone under 18, presumably for a reason, such as establishing barriers against the exploitation and abuse of "children" including teenagers.

Yet another point to note is that the period of schooling and financial dependence on parents has been expanding steadily over the past half century and seems to continue to do so.

In Japan, some 43 percent of young adults up to 35 years live with their parents, and the rate of Italy's *mammoni* is even higher at 46.6 percent (Germany: 17.3 percent) (Table 8.8). Worldwide, there is a certain correlation between young adults living with their parents and child poverty. In addition to underlying economic reasons, tradition and culture also play a role, as in familistic societies the

124   *Florian Coulmas*

Table 8.8 Percentage of young adults living with their parents

	Japan	Italy	Germany
% young adults (−35) living with parents	42.7	46.6	17.3

Source: Eurostat, MLIT (www.mlit.go.jp/common/001081919.pdf)

incidence of inter-generational co-residence is higher than in more individualistic societies. However, although Japan is commonly considered to be a more collectivist, familistic society, Japanese social scientists have diagnosed this residence pattern as deviant and created new categories to describe various sub-groups of the young people concerned. Sociologist Masahiro Yamada (1999) coined the denigrating term "parasite singles" for young adults, mainly women, who continue to live at home, have few obligations, and spend the money they earn on luxury goods. By contrast, the single nobility (*dokushin kizoku*), are relatively well-to-do, postpone marriage, but live alone. The *hikikomori*, people suffering from social withdrawal, live at home, but are more pathological (Horiguchi 2012). Other labels for young people whose life-course differs markedly from that of their parents include *NEET* (not in education, employment or training), *otaku*, and *moratorium ningen* (those postponing necessary steps in their education or career).

   All of these phenomena point to an extension of the period of growing up that does not conform to expectations. Preparations for a self-sufficient and responsible adult life take more time nowadays than in former times, but in some respects the opposite can be observed. For instance, in Japan the age of majority has recently been lowered from 20 to 18 years. If majority is understood as the threshold to adulthood, the proportion of non-self-supporting adults has increased by this adjustment of the law. This can be considered an inconsistency in the social system, for the legally adult are not (yet) economically adult or mentally adult.

   The lowering of the majority age seems to contradict social tendencies which, as a result of the increasing complexity of our world and its technologies, have been extending youth and the period of "play" and schooling that is necessary for acquiring the skills needed in 21st century society. However, the majority age was lowered not primarily because young Japanese have become more mature, but for other reasons – which brings us to our next question.

What does it mean to be young in a super-aged society?

One of the reasons for lowering the majority age in Japan has to do with demographic aging, in the sense that in the super-aged society the younger cohorts are shrinking, while the older cohorts continue to grow, as does their relative influence in national and other elections. Thus, being young in an aging society means, among many other things, forming a decreasing share of the total population. To compensate for this trend, the Japanese Diet lowered the statutory age of adulthood by two years from 20 to 18 and with it the voting age, allowing an estimated additional 2.4 million people the right to vote in the 2016 Upper House election.

The short answer to the question, "What does it mean to be young in a super-aged society?" is, therefore: it depends. That this is not just begging the question becomes clear when we look at the median age over time. The median age is used to indicate the relative age of a society. It divides a population in such a way that 50 percent are older and 50 percent are younger than this age. Since the middle of the 20th century, the median age increased significantly across the industrialized world, most drastically in Japan where it more than doubled from 22.3 years in 1950 to 46.1 years in 2014 (Table 8.9).

Now, imagine what it meant to belong to the older half of the population in 1950 and what it means today. Returning to our model protagonists, Emilio and Tokusuke, both were and considered themselves old, although the latter counted more than double the years of the former. The example is a bit contrived, but it serves well to illustrate the population dynamics of the 20th century and what it actually means for the people concerned. When we read Italo Svevo's *Senilità* today, we have to remind ourselves that it was written 120 years ago, because, nowadays, no one would think of a man of 35 as old or even approaching old age. And while the 77-year-old author of Tanizaki's *Diary of a Mad Old Man* does not strike us as atypical today, there are many people that age who are active, professionally and otherwise, and not quite ready to submit to senile madness. In a word, old age isn't what it used to be, nor is youth.

On the basis of the median age, a society can be said to be young or old, but a young society is no more prone to be infantile or behave in a childish way than an old society is likely to be particularly wise or develop collective Alzheimer's disease, although we know that crime rates decrease with age and thus tend to be higher in low-median age countries (Table 8.10).

The figures in Table 8.10 show that violent crime is lower in countries with an old population, but they do not allow us to establish any causal relationships, for they also show that there is a conspicuous correlation with social wealth. Moreover, the two outliers, Luxembourg and India, suggest the influence of other variables. Japan seems to exemplify the correlation of high per capita income, high median age, and low crime rate ideal-typically, but again other factors that might have an influence such as culture and social control are disregarded. Care should therefore be taken when using the same terms, "young", "old", etc., indiscriminately for individual and collective bodies.

Table 8.9 Median age in selected countries and the world

Country	1950	2014	Rank (2014)
Japan	22.3	46.6	2
Italy	29	45.4	5
Germany	35	46.5	3
Monaco		51.1	1
World	23	29.7	

Source: UN Population Division

126   *Florian Coulmas*

Table 8.10 Wealth, age, and crime

Country	GNP per capita US$[a]	Median age[a]	Homicide per million people[b]
Rich and old			
Switzerland	54,800	41.6	6.6
Singapore	62,400	37.3	3.1
Iceland	40,700	34.9	3.1
Japan	37,100	44.9	3.9
Luxembourg	77,900	38.9	24.5
Poor and young			
South Africa	11,500	25.2	318
Honduras	4,800	22.0	913
Venezuela	13,600	26.1	450
Belize	8,800	20.9	418
India	4,000	25.5	34

Source: [a] UN Data for 2010, [b] Nation Master, data for 2011

Population aging is not like individual aging. An old social body is not like an old human body, which, perhaps, was once young and beautiful, matured, and then entered a phase of decay and degeneration that led to the inevitable end. For one thing, we do not know what a mature society is, and no society is known ever to die of old age. When societies (nations, peoples, ethnic groups) cease to exist it is because they are violently eliminated or because for one reason or another they stop reproducing themselves, and this, of course, is something that the young do or fail to do.

If "young" is defined, as is common among demographers, as being in reproductive age – 15–44 for women, as defined by the World Health Organization – then today's young do what only they can do and in the interest of sustaining their kind should do: reproduce. As we saw earlier, fertility in Japan, Italy, and Germany has been way below replacement level for decades. This is not just another cipher that demographers are interested in, for in human society having children is not only a long-term commitment, but a time-consuming activity during the period of their growth to maturity. The age of first childbirth in Japan is 30 on average, implying that being young up to the age of 30 does not involve spending time raising children. People in this age group spend their time otherwise. How?

As mentioned above, many of them still live with their parents. If living with one's parents beyond maturity is considered as lack of independence, it indicates a delayed transition to adulthood. Is this *because* these young people live in a super-aged society? This is a tricky question, as we don't have any data relating residence patterns with population aging. What is more, the super-aged society is not just super-aged. Present-day society is also a knowledge society, a consumer society, a postmodern society, a risk society, a neoliberal society, a (more) pluralistic society, etc. To what extent social aging influences behavior and lifestyle is very

"How average am I?" 127

hard to establish. We can observe people's behavior and learn about their opinions and attitudes by means of surveys and interviews. But how can we know that changing inter-generational residence patterns are driven by population aging? Do many young people live with their parents longer than those lived with theirs *because* of recent life expectancy gains? That would be difficult to prove.

We must be satisfied with observing what young people do and think and, on the basis of what we know of the super-aged society, formulate conjectures, or better, hypotheses about possible connections. What we know today is that the super-aged society has arrived for good and that the Old-Age Support Ratio, defined as the number of people of working age (20–64) relative to the number of people of retirement age (65+), has not yet reached its peak. In Japan, this ratio was 23 percent in 2010, but is expected to hover around 40 percent by 2060, depending on the fertility rate (Table 8.11).

Of these 40 percent, an increasing number of people will be very old, forming a society where celebrating one's 100th birthday is nothing out of the ordinary. Still, the number and proportion of dependent elderly will also grow, and someone will have to feed them and care for them. Not everyone will be still running strong at 105, as record breaker Miyazaki Hidekichi, but healthy life expectancy will go up and many people will stay active far beyond what is now retirement age.[1] Yet, the magnitude of the challenges associated with the process of social aging, which is not confined to a single country, can hardly be overestimated. Is this an aspect of the risk society? Perhaps so, for as Powel (2006: 118) has pointed out, an aging population poses a risk to the financial safety of western nation-states. And if we take a look at the global picture, it would appear that the young will be crowded out by the old (Figure 8.1).

The young will not only have to support the old, the latter will also cling to their jobs making it harder for the former to find employment. Such are the realities of the super-aged society. Not all young people may be aware of the situation or con-template the consequences for themselves, although the level of media attention in Japan is very high. However that may be, the circumstances in which they live inform their opinions and attitudes. The changing image of the once venerated elderly may be an indication of a generation conflict brewing under the surface. Politically, Japan is already a gerontocracy, being dominated by old men more

Table 8.11 Population projection for Japan until 2060 with medium, high, and low fertility

Millions	Year	Medium fertility	High fertility	Low fertility
Japan's total	2010	128,06	128,06	128,06
population	2060	86,74	94,6	79,97
Population aged	2010	29,48	29,48	29,48
65 and over	2060	= 23,0%	= 23,0%	= 23,0%
		34,64	34,64	34,64
		= 39,0%	**= 36,6%**	**= 43,3%**

Source: NIPSSR 2012

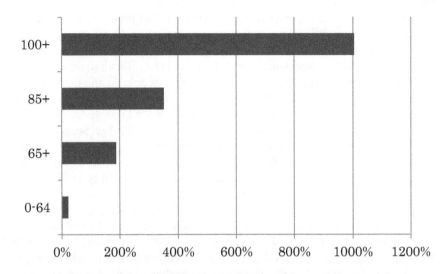

Figure 8.1 Percentage change in the world's population by age, 2010–2050

Source: Adapted from United Nations, *World Population Prospects: The 2010 Revision.* (http://esa.un.org/unpd/wpp)

than any other industrial democracy. And now the age of the "parasite silver" society has arrived, alternatively called *wakamono dorei no jidai* ("the age of youth slavery") where the law of the jungle applies. Manga author Yamano Sharin (2010) – well-known for his 2005 *Kenkanryū* ("Hate Korea") book – playfully turned the proverbial *jakuniku kyūshoku* ("eat or be eaten"), into *jakuniku rōshoku* ("the old eat the young"). In this book he topicalizes youth poverty, pinning the blame for it on the elderly whom to criticize, he says, is as much of a taboo as saying anything bad about the resident Koreans.

Can questions (1) and (2) be meaningfully separated from each other?

It is unlikely that all or even most young Japanese feel enslaved by the elderly. Yet, consciously or not, they are living with the various risks of social aging hanging over their heads. This leads me to a negative answer to my third question. No, the questions of what it means to be young and what it means to be young in an aging society cannot be meaningfully separated, because being young is always being young under certain circumstances. Being young today, in Japan and our other two reference countries means being young in a super-aging society. It means having few siblings, if any, and having parents who are older than parents on average were one or two generations ago; to be in education or training longer and start working to make a living later than one's parents and grandparents did;

"How average am I?" 129

and living in one's parents' home longer and getting married later than they did; among others.

What others, specifically? How do the young feel about being young in the aging society? I do not have any primary data, but there is plenty of secondary data to which we can refer, trying to answer this question. Within the framework of a bigger "Project 2030", NHK (2012) carried out a survey optimistically entitled "From the disconnected youth to a hopeful future". It was designed to gauge the wellbeing and attitudes of young people with special reference to the aging society.

Asked whether they were satisfied with their present life and the society, a clear majority said they were dissatisfied (see Table 8.12).

Mostly they were dissatisfied because of financial reasons and about conditions pertaining to work and study (see Table 8.13). How, according to this survey, what is their outlook on the future? Overwhelmingly uneasy. 82.2 percent say they have a sense of insecurity about the future (see Table 8.14). Employees in their 30s are worried about social security, believing that their pensions will worsen with rapid aging. Job satisfaction is low, 43 percent being dissatisfied with the work they are doing. Self-confidence is low, "rather yes" 30.9 percent, "rather no" or "no" 63 percent. 55.5 percent of the respondents feel lonely often or sometimes. Do they have hopeful expectations for 2030? "Yes" 44.4 percent, "no" 55.6 percent. The overall picture of Japanese society that emerges from this survey is rather glum.

Table 8.12 Satisfaction with present life and society

Rather satisfied	Rather dissatisfied	Dissatisfied
39.1%	39.9%	16.2%

Source: NHK 2012

Table 8.13 Dissatisfied with present life because of . . .

Cost of living, income	Work, study	Personal relations	Health	Other
58,6%	20.8%	8.6%	3.4%	8.7%

Source: NHK 2012

Table 8.14 Sense of insecurity about the future

Insecure	Not insecure	Don't know
82.2%	9.3%	8.4%

Source: NHK 2012

130   *Florian Coulmas*

How average am I?

The Japanese, young and old, never had a very optimistic outlook on life. That has been shown in opinion polls time and again. However, this is a time of rapid social change which evidently impregnates many youths with a "nagging sense of insecurity", to quote the title of Genda's 2006 book. To cope with this uneasiness, some take refuge in asking, "How average am I?", hence the title of a special issue of the Japanese monthly fashion magazine *CanCam* of October 2014. On the basis of a survey (N = 1000), it calculated the average values of bodily features such as height, weight, shoe size, length of eyelashes, etc., as well as lifestyle features, habits and life planning (group dating, how much time spent for makeup, number of sexual partners, ideal number of children, etc.). The survey questions are easy for young people to relate to. They are reported together with the results in the special issue which was sold together with a measuring tape as a marketing gimmick that not only allows readers to find out how average they are physically, but encourages them to do so. From the way the survey is presented, it transpires that being average rather than extraordinary is a desirable ideal.

In what is allegedly the age of "the new individualism in contemporary Japan" (Elliott, Katagiri and Sawai 2012), it may seem surprising that an influential popular magazine so strongly promotes being average as an ideal. However, considering the gloomy outlook on life revealed by the NHK survey and the uncertainties that population aging brings in its train, normality in the sense of not deviating too much from the average, being norm-conform and well-adjusted socially, may just offer some comfort and relief from the uncontrollable social forces to which the young are exposed. Regardless of whether they reflect on these developments and their consequences for themselves, hidden behind the frisky concern with being average in physical features, tastes, and habits may lie a more serious anxiety grounded in the pressure to conform, which, many recent assertions about the importance of creativity and individuality notwithstanding, may be rising for those who are young in the super-aging society of Japan.

Note

1 Born 22 September 1910, Miyazaki Hidekichi set a 100m world record in the over-100 age group at athletic games in Kōyto, 2015.

References

Coulmas, Florian (2007) *Population Decline and Ageing in Japan: The Social Consequences.* London: Routledge.

Elliott, Anthony, Masataka Katagiri and Atsushi Sawai (2012) The New Individualism in Contemporary Japan: Theoretical Avenues and the Japanese New Individualist Path. *Journal for the Theory of Social Behaviour* 42: 425–443.

Genda, Yuji (2006) *A Nagging Sense of Job Insecurity.* Tokyo: I-House Press.

"How average am I?" 131

Horiguchi, Sachiko (2012) Hikikomori: How Private Isolation Caught the Public Eye. In: *A Sociology of Japanese Youth: From Returnees to NEETS.* Roger Goodman, Yuki Imoto and Tuukka Toivonen (eds.), 122–137. London: Routledge.

Kono, Shigemi (2008) Demographic Comparisons with Other Countries with Emphasis on More Developed Regions. In: *The Demographic Challenge: A Handbook About Japan.* Florian Coulmas, Harald Conrad, Annette Schad-Seifert and Gabriele Vogt (eds.), 81–95. Leiden: Brill.

NHK (2012) *Shutoken supesharu purojekuto 2030. Tsunagaranai wakamonotachi kara kibō aru mirai e* [Tokyo Metropolitan Area Special Project 2030: From the Disconnected Youth to a Hopeful Future]. Online available at: www.nhk.or.jp/shutoken/2030/series1/index.html (accessed 22 February 2017).

NIPSSR (= National Institute of Population and Social Security Research) (2012) *Population Porjections for Japan 2011-2060.* Online available at: http://www.ipss.go.jp/site-ad/index_english/eisuikei/gh2401e.asp (accessed 7 March 2018).

Powell, Jason L. (2006) *Social Theory and Aging.* Lanham: Rowman & Littlefield.

Therborn, Göran (2004) *Between Sex and Power: Family in the World 1900–2000.* London: Routledge.

Yamada, Masahiro (1999) *Parasito shinguru no jidai* [The Age of Parasite Singles]. Tokyo: Chikuma Shobō.

Yamano, Sharin (2010) *"Wakamono dorei" jidai: "Jakuniku rōshoku" (parasaito shirubā) shakai no tōrai* [The Age of "Youth Slavery": The Arrival of the Society Where "The Old Eat the Young" (Silver Parasites)]. Tokyo: Shin'yūsha.

9 The structure of happiness

Why young Japanese might be happy after all

Carola Hommerich and Tim Tiefenbach

Introduction

Japan's youth is said to be dissolving (*yōkai suru wakamono*, Asano 2016). At least in the sense of a social category, it has become increasingly unclear who "the youth" is. Topics that used to be discussed as specific youth problems (so-called *wakamono basshingu*, youth bashing of, for example, parasite singles, *freeter*, *NEET*, *enjo kōsai*, or *hikikomori*) are now taken as structural or institutional problems or are being refuted as mere media panics (Asano 2016; Goodman, Imoto and Toivonen 2012).[1] The *freeter* or *NEET* of the late 1980s and early 1990s were first seen as an expression of the deteriorating work ethic of young entrants to the labor market. While working in non-regular employment, or not working at all, might indeed have been a lifestyle choice in the years of the bubble economy, the following economic downturn and its impact on the labor market quickly changed this, making non-regular employment more of a necessity than a choice. By the end of the zero years, the tone of the discourse on these young workers has changed, the dominant view now being that their weak labor market attachment is not a matter of choice, but rather caused by systemic problems and institutional restrictions of economic stagnation (Kotani 2017; Hommerich 2009). To accommodate the fact that the share of atypical employment is also increasing among older workers, the age ceiling for defining youth was continuously lifted (Toivonen 2012: 144). By now, it has become clear, that many issues surrounding youth are neither only the problem of a "lost generation", nor solely a "youth problem" anymore.

While it has become difficult to understand what exactly characterizes Japan's youth at the beginning of the 21st century, there is one point all researchers agree upon – the young generation is growing up in times of demographic and economic crisis and is affected by it more than other generations (Hommerich 2017: 72–73). The many uncertainties Japan's young adults are facing seem to be taking their toll. Various surveys indicate that the young feel highly anxious and vulnerable, and display higher stress levels than older generations (MHLW 2014). Their fragile mental health seems to be further demonstrated by increasing cases of social withdrawal, depression, and suicide among the younger generation. That these are not simply typical symptoms of a certain stage in the life-course becomes clear when comparing Japan's youth to its international peers – Japan's youth

The structure of happiness 133

has much lower self-esteem than young people from the US, the UK, France, Germany, Sweden, or Korea (Cabinet Office 2014). At the same time, they suffer from stronger anxieties with regard to finding employment, their current jobs, or the future in general.

It is at this point in time that the young sociologist Furuichi Noritoshi (2011) published his book *Zetsubō no kuni no kōfuku na wakamonotachi (The Happy Youth of a Desperate Country)* in which he presents data from a longitudinal government survey[2] that allow him to make the rather provocative claim that Japan's youth was happier than ever, despite all the negative aspects briefly mentioned above.[3] At the start of the 2010s, their life satisfaction is higher than that of all other age groups, and they are also more satisfied with their life than their peers were in the years of the economic boom of the 1970s (Figure 9.1). This rather unexpected result does not fit the discourse on the crisis-ridden youth maintained by older generations, and it subsequently caused quite a stir. A heated debate ensued on whether this should be taken as a valid result, and if so, how the high life satisfaction levels of the young could be explained (Asano 2016: 19–22).

Essentially, this data provides Japan's youth scholars with a new topic – the happiness of the young generation. Several scholars have tried to explain the mechanisms behind the apparent riddle of the positive life evaluation of the Japanese young generation (e.g., Chōsa Jōhō 2012; Fujimura, Asano and Habuchi 2016;

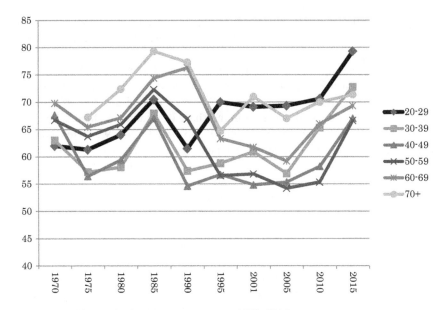

Figure 9.1 Life satisfaction across age groups, 1970–2015

Source: Assembled by the authors from the *Kokumin seikatsu ni kan suru yoron chōsa* (Public Opinion Survey on the Life of the People) carried out annually by the Cabinet Office (2015). Shares of respondents who answered "satisfied" or "rather satisfied" are shown.

134   Carola Hommerich and Tim Tiefenbach

Murata and Masaki 2013; Nakanishi 2012; Saito 2012). A conclusive answer, however, is yet to be found.

While we do not claim to be able to give a comprehensive answer ourselves, we hope to contribute at least another piece to the puzzle by analyzing some new data. To do so, we look at (1) which aspects of their lives Japan's youths are satisfied or dissatisfied with (as compared to other generations), and (2) which of these aspects they think of as important when considering their happiness. Under the assumption that happiness is not the same for everyone, we hypothesize that the "structure" of young people's happiness differs from that of older generations. What we call here "structure" includes not only the actual satisfaction with different life dimensions, but also the importance that is placed on them in the process of evaluation.

In the following, we first introduce Furuichi's account of the "happy youth" together with results of an empirical test of some of his assumptions. Then, after discussing the necessity to grasp happiness as a multidimensional concept, we use data of the Japanese National Survey on Lifestyle Preferences (NSLP) of the year 2010 to further analyze the structure of young Japanese's happiness in comparison to older age groups.[4]

Japan's "happy youth"

When Furuichi's book first came out in 2011, the government data it presented caused surprise (despite the data having been publicly available all along). Several years and waves of the same survey later, it has become clear that the upward trend in life satisfaction continues, with shares of satisfied 20–29-year-olds steadily increasing.[5]

Other longitudinal surveys provide similar results. For example, the five waves of the Survey on the Life and Attitudes of Middle and High School Students (*Chūgakusei, kōkōsei no seikatsu to ishiki chōsa*), carried out by public broadcaster NHK, shows a stark increase in the share of middle and high school students who state to be "very happy" from 1982 to 2012 (Figure 9.2). This indicates that the high subjective wellbeing of Japan's youth discussed by Furuichi and others is not a statistical artifact, but a somewhat robust finding, but the question remains how this phenomenon is to be interpreted.

For Furuichi (2011: 14), the high subjective wellbeing of his peers results from their experience of what he calls an "odd stability" (*kimyō na antei*). They evaluate their lives positively at a point in time at which they are still able to enjoy a relatively prosperous and carefree life, supported and protected by their parents. All the while, they see a rather bleak future hanging above their heads like the sword of Damocles, foreshadowing a not so distant time in which they will have to shoulder the expenses for care of an increasingly large share of elderly people, as well as for Japan's growing debt. Furuichi states that young Japanese are aware of this, and that they do experience anxieties and are dissatisfied with the society they live in – a seeming countertrend to their high subjective wellbeing also visible in various social surveys (Hommerich 2017: 73). However, instead of

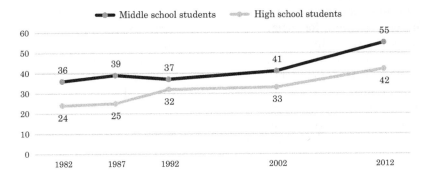

Figure 9.2 Happiness of middle and high school students, 1982–2012
Source: NHK Hōsō Bunka Kenkyūjo (2013: 171)
Note: Shares of respondents who state to be "very happy."

letting this "get to them", they are content to live in the here and now (*ima, koko*). Furuichi calls this attitude "consummatory" (Furuichi 2011: 104–105), which he uses as meaning "something close to self-satisfied" or "self-contained" (Furuichi 2011: 104–105), based on Toyoizumi (2010), who also draws on this term that originates back to Talcott Parsons in order to describe the attitude of Japanese youth.

The fact that they do not have positive expectations for the future, Furuichi assumes, results in higher levels of life satisfaction *in the present* – for the very reason that there is no positive reference point in the future. The comparatively small gap between aspirations and reality allows them to feel satisfied with their present lifestyle. His hypothesis that young Japanese's low hope for the future positively impacts their life satisfaction in the present, is supported by results from an empirical analysis of Hommerich (2017) using data from a nationwide survey from 2009. Two other claims made by Furuichi, however, do not find support in this analysis. While he states that young people's evaluation of their own "small world" is detached from the "big world", namely society in a more general sense, the data presented by Hommerich shows that feelings of not being a fully accepted part of society have a strong negative effect on the life satisfaction of 20–30-year-olds (Hommerich 2017: 86). As a matter of fact, being able to feel as part of society showed to have a stronger positive impact on the subjective wellbeing of the young generation as compared to that of older age groups.

The second point not supported is a claim very much emphasized by Furuichi also in a later publication, namely the importance of friends for young people's subjective wellbeing. According to Furuichi (2013), what especially counts for young people at the end of the two so-called "lost decades", the era of economic stagnation following the burst of the Japanese asset price bubble in 1991, is that they have friends (*nakama*) to rely on. Hommerich (2017: 86) tests this hypothesis, but finds no significant effect.

136 *Carola Hommerich and Tim Tiefenbach*

The results of Hommerich's examination may disqualify major parts of Furuichi's core argument. However, conclusions should not be rushed, as the function of friends for subjective wellbeing might very well be more complex than was possible to test for in the study quoted above. Regarding friends, for example, the variable used by Hommerich (2017) tries to capture the existence of friends who a respondent feels to be able "to rely on" and "trust in times of need". It does not capture whether he or she is satisfied with these friendships or whether she or he thinks that friends are important ingredients of their happiness in the first place. Depending on the way happiness is conceptualized, both aspects can be imagined as crucial. We will explain this in more detail in the next section.

Happiness as a multidimensional construct

That older generations cannot imagine the young to be genuinely happy might simply result from the fact that happiness "means different things for different people" (Frey and Stutzer 2002: 3). This implies that what is individually evaluated as "overall happiness" needs to be thought of as complex interplay of different topicalities that are weighted and judged against each other in the course of the evaluation. However, despite renowned happiness researchers admitting to the complexity of the task at hand, one-dimensional measurements of happiness remain most common (see e.g., Diener et al. 1985). Most researchers do not consider the fact that what an individual evaluates as overall happiness is an aggregate of his or her satisfaction with different life domains. Only few studies assume a multidimensional structure of happiness (e.g., Linley et al. 2009; Stewart et al. 2010), or investigate the relationship between subjective wellbeing and the satisfaction level with different life domains (Easterlin 2006; Loewe et al. 2014; van Praag, Frijters and Ferrer-i-Cabernell 2003).

Even if different life domains (e.g., family, friends, the local community or work) are taken into account, it is only the satisfaction with them that is considered as important for overall life evaluations. All studies implicitly assume that the importance ranking of these different life domains is the same across all individuals. It can, however, be imagined that a certain life domain is seen to be of essential importance by one individual, while another feels it to be only secondary. This would have implications for the comparability of general happiness levels. A recent study by Tiefenbach and Kohlbacher (2015a) shows that the way domain importance and domain satisfaction impact on individual happiness can differ. Some domains are correlated with higher or lower happiness, even if they are not explicitly considered as important by respondents (e.g., family). Other domains, on the other hand, only impact on happiness when they are also consciously considered as important for happiness by the respondents (e.g., finances). Going a step further, it can be envisioned that this interplay of satisfaction and importance differs among individuals depending on their individual circumstances, with certain patterns emerging depending on, for example, their socioeconomic status, the region they live in, or – as we discuss here – their generational location.

The structure of happiness   137

While a large array of variables can be imagined to play a role in determining the "structure" of happiness in this way, we focus here on a possible impact of generational location. Japan's young generation growing up or coming of age in the Heisei period has not experienced the affluent years of the bubble economy and the decades of economic growth leading up to it. Living their formative years in a socioeconomic context very different from their parents and grandparents, they can be expected to have a "common location in the social and historical process" (Mannheim 1998[1923]: 291), which distinguishes them from previous generations. Their specific generational location is most likely accompanied by different value patterns, which result in them placing importance on aspects of life that were not held equally important by older generations. We hereafter call this group the "Heisei generation". Thus, our general hypothesis to be tested here is as follows:

H1: Different generational locations result in different structures of happiness.

For more specific hypotheses on how these structures differ, we rely on the interpretations offered by Furuichi (as outlined above). He claims that friends (*nakama*) are of great importance, especially for the young generation's happiness, something that – so he implies – sets them apart from older generations. Therefore, we formulate our second hypothesis as follows:

H2: The Heisei generation places more importance on friends than older generations when evaluating their happiness.

While material interests play an important role in determining the happiness of generations who grew up in times of economic boom and material affluence, Furuichi explains that here money is less important for the Heisei generation. Instead of buying luxury brand goods, like clothes, accessories, or even expensive cars, the young generation is satisfied with simpler, less costly things. While this attitude is most likely born of necessity – simply because they have less money at their disposal than earlier generations – Furuichi indicates that the young have arranged themselves with this situation and are happy to wear low-priced (but still fashionable) clothes, and prefer a cozy and inexpensive "home party" to a fancy dinner at an expensive restaurant. This non-materialistic attitude, for Furuichi, also distinguishes them from older generations.

H3: The Heisei generation places less importance on their financial situation than older generations when evaluating their happiness.

Data and variables

To investigate these specific hypotheses, we use the data of the Japanese National Survey on Lifestyle Preferences of the year 2010, as the only government commissioned, publicly available dataset we are aware of that contains measures of

138   *Carola Hommerich and Tim Tiefenbach*

domain satisfaction as well as domain importance.[6] After its introduction in 1972, this cross-sectional survey has been commissioned annually since 1984 by the Japanese cabinet office. Since 2010, the focus has been placed on individual happiness and its determinants.[7] In the same year, the sample population of 4,000 persons was generated via a two-stage randomized stratified procedure, and includes men and women in Japan between 15–80 years of age. With a relatively high response rate (72.5 percent), we have 2,900 completed questionnaires available for analysis.

Our (dependent) variable of interest is the respondents' current happiness level. To measure this, respondents were asked to evaluate their current level of happiness from zero to ten on an 11-point scale, with zero meaning "very unhappy" and ten "very happy". The corresponding survey item reads: "How happy are you currently?" The mean level of happiness in the sample was 6.47 (SD = 2.02), which indicates that more than half of the respondents evaluate their wellbeing positively.

As we are interested in the structure of happiness regarding different life domains, our main explaining (independent) variables are domain importance and domain satisfaction of the following eight domains: financial situation, job situation (having a job or not, as well as job security), health condition, purpose in life (regarding work, hobbies, and social contribution, hereafter "*ikigai*"), family relations, friendship relations, social relations at work (hereafter "workplace"), and integration into the local community (hereafter "region"). We include these eight domains as respondents of the NSLP were asked to rate their satisfaction with them as well as indicate the importance placed on them when evaluating their happiness. While we use all eight domains to investigate differences in the structure of happiness across generations (H1), our focus lies on comparing the impact of satisfaction with and importance of happiness evaluation of friends (H2) and finances (H3) across age groups.

Domain importance was captured as a dummy variable, asking respondents: "When you evaluated your happiness feeling which of the following items did you consider important? Please check all relevant items." It is necessary to emphasize the precise wording of the question that explicitly asks respondents to evaluate the domains *in terms of their importance regarding the overall feeling of happiness*. Other surveys, i.e., the World Value Survey, ask respondents to "indicate how important it [the respective domain] is in your life". This is less precise and only loosely connected to happiness evaluations. This very specific connection of domain importance and happiness evaluation is what makes the NSLP so suitable for an analysis of the structure of happiness, based on not only satisfaction, but also importance of various domains of wellbeing.

Regarding domain satisfaction, the corresponding item reads "How satisfied are you with each of the following items? Please indicate on a scale from 'satisfied' to 'dissatisfied" the state which comes closest to your personal feelings." The respondents then indicated their level of satisfaction on a 5-point Likert scale.[8]

The structure of happiness 139

To compare the structure of happiness between different generations, respondents were grouped by age into four groups as follows:

a) *15–29 years*: Born between 1981 and 1995, this group represents what we previously described as the Heisei generation. This generation grows up and/ or comes of age in the Heisei period. It has not experienced years of economic affluence the way previous generations have. Instead, for this group, economic stagnation – which comes with the necessity for austerity – and a bleak labor market outlook pose everyday experiences.[9]

b) *30–44 years*: Born between 1966 and 1980, this generation grows up in times of economic boom and affluence. Younger members of this generation might also have experienced the economic ice age after the burst of bubble economy on entering the labor market at the beginning of the 1990s.

c) *45–64 years:* Born between 1946 and 1965, this generation grows up mainly in a time of economic boom and experiences upward mobility first hand.

d) *65–80 years:* Born between 1930 and 1945, this generation's formative years fall into the war as well as the immediate post-war years of economic hardship and endurance. When in their 20s and 30s, this generation created the economic miracle through hard work and a dedication to the company. In return, it experiences an overall positive trajectory of upward mobility over the life-course.

While our grouping strategy is based on the idea of generational location, we need to keep in mind that we cannot control for cohort effects with our cross-sectional data. Any differences we observe between the age groups may also be life-cycle effects. Despite this caveat, the results from our analysis are still meaningful, as they can help us understand whether and how happiness evaluations differ between age groups and, thereby, why it might be difficult for older age groups to comprehend how young Japanese at the beginning of the 21st century might evaluate themselves as happy, despite their comparatively bleak future outlook.

To account for the socio-demographic and socioeconomic context of the respondents, we included the following control variables: gender, family relations (cohabitation with spouse, number and age of children), employment status (including experiences of unemployment or occurrence of unemployment in the family), household income, and place of residence. Unfortunately, educational levels of the respondents were not assessed in the NSLP, so that we cannot control for a possible impact of education.

We test our hypotheses in two steps. First, we look at the mean satisfaction with different wellbeing domains and compare the mean importance placed on them across age groups. Then, we run OLS-regressions to find out which of our independent variables significantly impact the happiness levels of the different age groups and test whether we find specific differences.[10]

Descriptive results

The focus of our analysis lies not on whether happiness levels differ across age groups, but on *whether what contributes to happiness differs across age groups*. Before turning to our hypothesis test, we look at mean levels of happiness across age groups (Figure 9.3). We do not find the Heisei generation (15–29 year-olds) to be significantly happier than the other age groups. Overall, differences in mean happiness are small and not significant.

Regarding levels of satisfaction with different life domains, results are similar in that differences between the age groups are small and not significant (Figure 9.4 and Table 9.2 in the Appendix). For all age groups, satisfaction levels with family and friends were highest, while satisfaction with their financial situation was lowest, ranging around the middle category of the 5-point scale that indicates "neither satisfied, nor dissatisfied". Satisfaction with health showed the largest variation across age groups, being highest among the youngest respondents and decreasing with age – a rather unsurprising result.

The subjective importance of the same domains for happiness evaluation, however, showed differing patterns across age groups (Figure 9.5 and Table 9.2 in the Appendix). While "family" and "finances" were the most important domains for the three older age groups, it was "friends" that the highest share (60 percent) of the 15–29-year-olds thought of as important when evaluating their wellbeing, followed by "family" (54 percent) and – only then – "finances" (50 percent). Having a purpose in life (*ikigai*) was esteemed as important by 41 percent of the Heisei generation, a higher share than in the older age groups. The importance of health

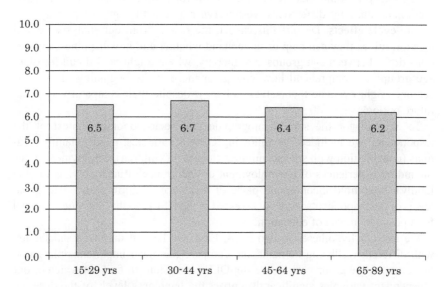

Figure 9.3 Mean levels of happiness by age group
Note: Overall mean = 6.47 (SD = 2.02).

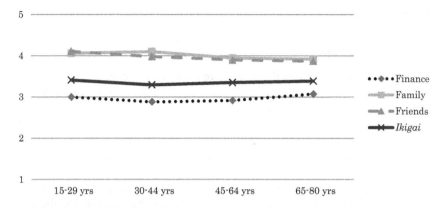

Figure 9.4 Mean levels of domain satisfaction by age group

Note: Mean levels of satisfaction on a 5-point Likert scale from 5 = "satisfied" to 1 = "dissatisfied". Only domains most relevant to the analysis are presented. Data on all domains is displayed in Table 9.2 in the Appendix.

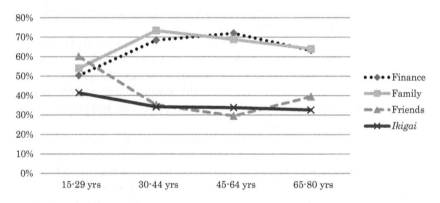

Figure 9.5 Subjective importance of domains for happiness evaluation by age group

Note: Percentage of respondents who selected the domain as important for their happiness evaluation. Only domains most relevant to the analysis are presented. Data on all domains is displayed in Table 9.3 in the Appendix.

increased over the life-course, while having a job and workplace relations were of lower importance for the oldest age group, where the majority has already exited the labor market. Interestingly, the share of the youngest age group who thought of having a job and job security as important for their happiness evaluation was lower than for the two middle-aged groups. This can possibly be explained by the fact that this group also comprises teenagers and respondents in their early 20s who are still in education and might not yet think about employment. Overall, the differences in importance placed on these eight life domains displayed here,

142 *Carola Hommerich and Tim Tiefenbach*

indicate that the young generation sets different priorities when evaluating their happiness.

Multivariate analysis

The impression we gain from the descriptive examination of the data is confirmed by the results of our multivariate analysis. The results are displayed in Table 9.1. Running separate OLS-regressions for the four age groups, we find differences in what significantly impacts the happiness levels of each respective group. In the following presentation of our findings, we focus on differences in the impact of domain satisfaction and importance, without explicitly discussing the control variables.

Comparing the impact of domain satisfaction across age groups, we find that the Heisei generation is the only group for which satisfaction with the financial situation has no significant relationship with happiness. For the other three age groups, the impact of financial satisfaction on overall happiness is positive and substantial. For the two middle-aged groups, it was also significant whether they thought of money as important when evaluating their happiness. This effect, however, was negative: They were less happy, if they thought of money as important. This means that a strong focus on material wellbeing reduces overall happiness, at least for respondents in the middle age bracket.

Being satisfied with whatever one feels to give life meaning (*ikigai*) impacts happiness positively for all but the oldest age group, with the effect being strongest for the youngest group. Whether a meaningful life was thought of as important, however, was unrelated to happiness. This means that being able to feel a purpose in life has a positive effect on happiness, even if the respondents did not think of it as important themselves.

Satisfaction with one's family has a significant positive impact across all age groups, while the size of the effect is somewhat smaller for the youngest group. For this domain, also thinking of family as important when evaluating happiness significantly correlates with higher happiness levels in all age groups.

Being satisfied with one's friends, however, shows to have no significant relationship with happiness across all age groups. This is contrary to Furuichi's hypothesis that friends are especially important for Japan's youth. Looking at the importance of friends for happiness evaluations, however, we find a different pattern. Young and middle-aged respondents who thought of friends as important when evaluating their happiness were significantly happier – independent from whether they were satisfied with their actual friends.

Discussion: satisfied now, but also happy tomorrow?

The results of our analysis support our hypothesis (H1) that different generational locations coincide with different structures of happiness. We find differences in which life domains impact happiness across age groups. This is true both for the satisfaction with as well as the importance placed on these domains.

Table 9.1 Results of OLS-regression on happiness

	15–29	30–44	45–64	65–80
	(1) Model 1	(2) Model 2	(3) Model 3	(4) Model 4
VARIABLES	*Happiness*	*Happiness*	*Happiness*	*Happiness*
Satisfaction finance	0.071	0.387***	0.418***	0.452***
Satisfaction job	0.151+	0.109	0.118+	−0.035
Satisfaction health	0.326***	0.160*	0.257***	0.219**
Satisfaction *ikigai*	0.497***	0.227**	0.322***	−0.125
Satisfaction family	0.374***	0.599***	0.602***	0.633***
Satisfaction friends	0.098	0.041	0.026	0.110
Satisfaction workplace	0.115	0.251***	−0.039	0.113
Satisfaction region	0.045	−0.059	−0.012	0.034
Importance finance	−0.179	−0.533***	−0.422***	−0.187
Importance job	−0.172	−0.127	0.071	−0.438*
Importance health	0.152	0.191	0.062	−0.198
Importance *ikigai*	0.163	−0.034	0.074	0.405*
Importance family	0.359*	0.438**	0.497***	0.811***
Importance friends	0.331+	0.138	0.297*	−0.008
Importance workplace	−0.079	−0.059	−0.195	−0.144
Importance region	−0.621+	0.078	0.228	0.199
Controls				
Household income	0.000	0.000	0.001**	0.001***
Married	1.081**	0.516**	0.045	−0.293
Women	0.290+	0.106	0.036	0.385*
Children under 6 yrs	−1.045+	0.051	0.478+	−0.052
Number of children	0.372	0.073	0.002	0.053
Regular employees		*Reference group*		
Kanrishoku	−1.695	0.193	0.001	0.495
Kaisha yakuin	1.783	−0.035	−0.070	0.157
Dantai yakuin	−0.486	−0.263	−0.232	1.227
Civil servant	0.746+	0.092	−0.026	1.484
Entrepreneur	−0.913*	−0.138	−0.124	0.280
Irregular employees	0.022	0.056	0.026	0.347
Homemaker	0.929*	0.481*	0.035	0.460
Student	0.405+	−0.258		
Unemployed (respondent)	−0.062	−0.278	−0.182	
Without work				0.399
Unemployed (in family)	−0.463	−0.206	0.263	−0.450
City very big (大都市)		*Reference group*		
City big (人口20万以上)	0.288	−0.368*	−0.047	0.272
City middle (人口10万以上)	0.238	−0.165	0.038	0.583*
City small (人口10万以下)	0.107	−0.195	0.093	0.258
City very small (町村)	−0.882**	0.042	0.156	0.235
Observations	404	684	876	455
Adj. R-squared	0.497	0.543	0.459	0.422
F test model	12.364	24.142	22.793	10.471

Note: *** $p<0.001$, ** $p<0.01$, * $p<0.05$, + $p<0.10$, unstandardized coefficients.

144　*Carola Hommerich and Tim Tiefenbach*

Our second hypothesis (H2), which we formulated to test Furuichi's claim that friends (*nakama*) are especially important for the happiness of the Heisei generation, was only partly supported. Our analysis showed that for all age groups satisfaction with friends had no significant impact on happiness. Thinking of friends as important for one's happiness, on the other hand, significantly enhanced the happiness levels of young and middle-aged respondents. This means that it is not the friendship as such but rather whether the respondent generally thinks of friends as important for an evaluation of wellbeing, that makes these two groups happier.

Our third hypothesis (H3) regarding differences in the existence of materialistic interests was fully supported by the data. In contrast to the three older age groups, it was only the Heisei generation for which satisfaction with their financial situation showed to have no significant relationship with happiness. Results of our descriptive analysis had already indicated that lower shares of the youngest age group think of money as important than of the three older age groups (see Figure 9.5). However, even though members of the youngest group state to place importance on their financial situation when evaluating their happiness, this did not significantly impact the outcome. Our data showed no significant relationship between financial importance and happiness for the youngest group, holding everything else equal. This distinguishes the Heisei generation from older generations and supports Furuichi's claim that the happiness of Japanese youth depends less on money than is the case for earlier generations. While this seems to point to an emancipation from a lifestyle circling around materialistic desires and – possibly – a return to more fundamental values like friendship, it might also simply be an indication of a generation that has adapted to a new economic reality. The non-materialistic attitude of the young is probably born of necessity, rather than an idealistic life choice of simplicity over abundance.

Nevertheless, the Heisei generation sets different priorities when evaluating their life. As a result, they might be more satisfied than can be expected by the standards older generations set for their own life evaluation. Their adaptation to a new reality can also be interpreted as a form of resilience that enables them to be happy with less – at least for now.

Whether their satisfaction today can translate into happiness tomorrow, however, is hard to tell. The longitudinal data quoted by Furuichi (and displayed in Figure 9.1) indicate a long-term change with the youngest age group being happier today than its peers some 20 or 30 years ago. While being less focused on material goods might make for a simpler and more content life for now, the question remains whether this is an actual value change that lasts over a life-time (cohort effect), or whether this attitude toward money and economic security might not change as this generation grows older and takes on more (financial) responsibilities (age effect). With the cross-sectional data used here, it is impossible to say whether we are looking at an actual effect of generational location. Future research that accompanies this generation as they grow older (in form of a panel survey) would be desirable in order to account for this.

While the results of the analysis presented here allow for the interpretation that material desires are not at the heart of young people's wellbeing, it remains

The structure of happiness 145

difficult to understand what actually makes them happy. While Furuichi suggests time spent with friends to be most decisive for the happiness of the young, it seems that the situation is more complex. Our results indicate that it is not the quality of actual friendships (here measured as satisfaction with friends) that contributes to happiness. Instead, it is only the question of whether friends are thought of as important that makes the young happier. This means that it is not actual time spent with friends that matters, but only the image of what friends should be that enhances wellbeing – something that is also possible to hold in the complete absence of friends. A more in-depth (qualitative) investigation into what expectations the young generation has towards friendship could help to further disentangle what seems like a riddle at this point.

Overall, what can be interpreted as resilience or a "realistic" approach to life can also be seen as a young generation who has "given up" and is in danger of arranging itself in a seemingly comfortable present, but is ill-equipped for coping with future risks. It seems necessary to return here to our own initial research premise according to which "happiness is not the same for everyone". Further research on this topic must differentiate between different subgroups, i.e. between young men and young women, between youths with different educational levels or from urban and rural contexts. Treating Japan's young generation as one group oversimplifies the different struggles to be found within.

Appendix

Table 9.2 Mean levels of domain satisfaction by age group

	15–29 years	*30–44 years*	*45–64 years*	*65–88 years*
Finance	3.0	2.9	2.9	3.1
Family	4.1	4.1	3.9	3.9
Friends	4.1	4.0	3.9	3.9
Ikigai	3.4	3.3	3.4	3.4
Job	3.0	3.3	3.3	3.1
Health	3.9	3.6	3.4	3.3
Workplace	3.5	3.5	3.5	3.3
Region	3.1	3.2	3.2	3.3

Note: Mean levels of satisfaction on a 5-point Likert scale from 5 = "satisfied" to 1 = "dissatisfied."

Table 9.3 Subjective importance of domains for happiness evaluation by age group

Domain	*15–29 years*	*30–44 years*	*45–64 years*	*65–88 years*
Finance	50.3%	68.4%	72.0%	63.2%
Family	54.0%	73.4%	68.8%	64.0%
Friends	60.2%	35.2%	29.5%	39.4%
Ikigai	41.4%	34.1%	33.8%	32.6%
Job	43.0%	52.9%	47.9%	17.9%
Health	54.2%	65.3%	75.5%	77.6%
Workplace	22.3%	23.2%	18.4%	5.9%
Region	4.9%	7.1%	11.3%	17.0%

Note: Percentage of respondents who selected the domain as important for their happiness evaluation.

Notes

1 Parasite singles = unmarried young people (mostly women) who live with their parents without paying expenses, despite having their own income. *Freeter* = originally a combination of "free" and "arbeiter" (worker), term to describe young non-regular employees. *NEET* = acronym to denote young people who are "not in employment, education or training". *Enjo kōsai* = compensated dating, especially of young (underage) girls. *Hikikomori* = social withdrawal of adolescents or young adults who do not leave the house or their room for weeks, months or even years.

2 The data stem from the *Kokumin seikatsu ni kan suru yoron chōsa* (Public Opinion Survey on the Life of the People) carried out annually by the Cabinet Office (2015), see also Figure 9.1.

3 Furuichi is not the first to point this out. He quotes Toyoizumi (2010) and Ōsawa (2011) who both discuss this seemingly puzzling data.

4 More information on the survey is available on the Cabinet Office's homepage: www5. cao.go.jp/seikatsu/senkoudo/senkoudo.html

5 As Figure 9.1 displays 5-year increments, it includes only one data point (2015) in addition to the data presented by Furuichi (2011). In the years in between, which are not displayed here, the share of satisfied 29-year-olds has steadily grown (2011 = 73.5%, 2012 = 75.4%, 2013 = 78.3%, 2014 = 79.1%), so this is a continuous upward trend.

6 The cabinet office labels the years in accordance with the Japanese fiscal year system, which runs from the beginning of April of one year to the end of March of the following year. Thus, the survey is from the fiscal year 2009. However, as the NSLP survey is always conducted at the end of the fiscal year, it was actually carried out in the calendar year 2010.

7 Note that questions on happiness and life satisfaction have already been included in questionnaires prior to 2009, but not necessarily as the main focus. For details, see Tiefenbach and Kohlbacher (2015b).

8 The exact scale reads: "satisfied" recoded as (5), "somewhat satisfied" recoded as (4), "neither satisfied nor dissatisfied" recoded as (3), "If anything, dissatisfied" recoded as (2) and "dissatisfied" recoded as (1).

9 Of course, also people who were born after 1981 still belong to this generation. The range we define here relates to our data set, which does not include respondents born later than 1981.

10 Ordinary least square regression (also called linear regression) is a technique to determine the statistical relationship between two or more variables. It calculates the extent to which the change in a dependent variable (in our case, overall happiness) is determined by a change in one or more independent variables. By controlling for the impact of the independent variables, the regression model tells us the single effect each independent variable has on the dependent variable. Please note, however, that the statistical technique alone does not allow for causal inference. Causal interpretations depend on the survey design, or might be derived from theory.

References

Asano, Tomohiko (2016) Seishōnen kenkyūkai no chōsa to wakamonoron no kyō no kadai [The Survey of the Youth Research Group and Current Topics of Discourses on Youth]. In: *Gendai wakamono no kōfuku – fuankan shakai o ikiru*. Masayuki Fujimura, Tomohiko Asano and Ichiyo Habuchi (eds.), 1–23. Tokyo: Kōseisha Kōseikaku.

148 Carola Hommerich and Tim Tiefenbach

Cabinet Office (2014) *Heisei 25-nendo wagakuni to shogaikoku no wakamono no ishiki ni kansuru chōsa* [International Survey of Youth Attitudes 2013]. Online available at: www8.cao.go.jp/youth/kenkyu/thinking/h25/pdf_index.html (accessed 19 May 2017).

——— (2015) *Heisei 27-nen kokumin seikatsu ni kansuru yoron chōsa* [Public Opinion Survey on the Life of Japanese Nationals 2015]. Online available at: http://survey.gov-online.go.jp/index-ko.html (accessed 19 May 2017).

Chōsa Jōhō (2012) Tokushū – ii janai no shiawase nara ba? Tōsei "wakamono" ron no kyojitsu [Special Issue: Why Not, It They Are Happy? Doubting the Controlled Youth Theory]. *Chōsa jōhō* 506: 2–39.

Diener, Ed, Robert A. Emmons, Randy J. Larsen and Sharon Griffin (1985) The Satisfaction with Life Scale. *Journal of Personality Assessment* 49(1): 71–75.

Easterlin, Richard A. (2006) Life Cycle Happiness and Its Sources. *Journal of Economic Psychology* 27(4): 463–482.

Frey, Bruno S. and Alois Stutzer (2002) *Happiness and Economics: How the Economy and Institutions Affect Well-Being*. Princeton: Princeton University Press.

Fujimura, Masayuki, Tomohiko Asano and Ichiyo Habuchi (2016) *Gendai wakamono no kōfuku – fuankan shakai o ikiru* [The Happiness of Today's Youth: Living in a Society of Uncertainty]. Tokyo: Kōseisha Kōseikaku.

Furuichi, Noritoshi (2011) *Zetsubō no kuni no kōfuku na wakamonotachi* [The Happy Youth of a Desperate Country]. Tokyo: Kōdansha.

——— (2013) Nihon no wakamono wa korekara mo shiawase ka [Will Japan's Youth Also Be Happy in the Future?]. *Asteion* 79: 88–102.

Goodman, Roger, Yuki Imoto and Tuukka Toivonen (eds.) (2012) *A Sociology of Japanese Youth: From Returnees to NEETs*. London: Routledge.

Hommerich, Carola (2009) *"Freeter" und "Generation Praktikum": Arbeitswerte im Wandel? Ein deutsch-japanischer Vergleich*. München: Iudicium.

——— (2017) Anxious, Stressed, and Yet Satisfied? The Puzzle of Subjective Well-Being Among Young Adults in Japan. In: *Life Course, Happiness and Well-Being in Japan*. Wolfram Manzenreiter and Barbara Holthus (eds.), 72–93. London: Routledge.

Kotani, Satoshi (ed.) (2017) *Nijūichi seiki no wakamono-ron – aimai na fuan o ikiru* [Youth Discourses of the Twenty-First Century: Living a Vague Uncertainty]. Tokyo: Sekai Shisōsha.

Linley, P. Alex, John Maltby, Alex M. Wood, Gabrielle Osborne and Robert Hurling (2009) Measuring Happiness: The Higher Order Factor Structure of Subjective and Psychological Well-Being Measures. *Personality and Individual Differences* 47(8): 878–884.

Loewe, N., M. Bagherzadeh, L. Araya-Castillo, C. Thieme and J. M. Batista-Foguet (2014) Life Domain Satisfactions as Predictors of Overall Life Satisfaction Among Workers. Evidence from Chile. *Social Indicators Research* 118(1): 71–86.

Mannheim, Karl (1998 [1923]) The Problem of Generations. In: *Essays on the Sociology of Knowledge*. Paul Kecskemeti (ed.), 276–320. London: Routledge & Kegan Paul.

MHLW (2014) *Heisei 26-nenban kōsei rōdo hakusho* [Heisei 26 White Paper on Labor Composition]. Tokyo: MHLW.

Murata, Hiroko and Miki Masaki (2013) Chūgakusei wa naze "kōfuku" nano ka – "chūgakusei, kōkōsei no seikatsu to ishiki chōsa 2012" kara [Why are Middle-school Students Happy? Insights from the 2012 "Survey on Life and Attitudes on Middle and High School Students]. *Hōsō kenkyū to chōsa* (3): 34–43.Nakanishi, Shintaro (2012) Itsu demo kōfuku de irareru fukō [Misery That Always Allows for Happiness to Enter]. *Kyōiku* 801: 49–58.

The structure of happiness 149

NHK Hōsō Bunka Kenkyūjo (2013) *NHK chūgakusei, kōkōsei no seikatsu to ishiki chōsa 2012: Ushinawareta 20-nen ga unda "shiawase" na jūdai* [NHK Survey of Middle School and High School Students 2012: The "Happy" Teens Who Were Born in Japan's Two Lost Decades]. Tokyo: NHK Shuppan.

Ōsawa, Masachi (2011) Kanō ni naru kakumei dai ikkai: "Kōfuku da" to kotaeru wakamonotachi no jidai [A Possible Revolution, Part 1: The Age of a Youth Who States "I am Happy"]". *At Plus*: 114–127.

Saito, Tamaki (2012) "Kawaranai" koto no "kōfuku" to "fukō" ni tsuite [On the Happiness of "Non-Change" and "Misery"]. *Chōsa jōhō* 506: 26–32.

Stewart, Marty E., Roger Watson, Andrea Clark, Klaus P. Ebmeier and Ian J. Deary (2010) A Hierarchy of Happiness? Mokken Scaling Analysis of the Oxford Happiness Inventory. *Personality and Individual Differences* 48(7): 845–848.

Tiefenbach, Tim and Florian Kohlbacher (2015a) Individual Differences in the Relationship Between Domain Satisfaction and Happiness: The Moderating Role of Domain Importance. *Personality and Individual Differences* 86: 82–87.

——— (2015b) Happiness in Japan in Times of Upheaval: Empirical Evidence from the National Survey on Lifestyle Preferences. *Journal of Happiness Studies* 16(2): 333–366.

Toivonen, Tuukka (2012) NEETs: The Strategy with the Category. In: *A Sociology of Japanese Youth: From Returnees to NEETs*. Roger Goodman, Yuki Imoto and Tuukka Toivonen (eds.), 139–158. London: Routledge.

Toyoizumi, Shūji (2010) *Wakamono no tame no shakaigaku: Kibō ni ashiba o kakeru.* [A Sociology for the Youth: Giving a Foothold to Hope]. Tokyo: Haruka Shobō.

van Praag, B., P. Frijters and A. Ferrer-i-Carbonell (2003) The Anatomy of Subjective Wellbeing. *Journal of Economic Behavior & Organization* 51(1): 29–49.

10 Life on the small screen

Japan's Digital Natives

Hidenori Masiko (translated by Yuka Ando)

There has been much talk on the so-called "Digital Natives" in Japan. Let us start by referring to some major categorizations stemming from these discussions. In Japan, generations are often named after decades in the Japanese calendar, resulting in terms like "Generation 76" (= born after Shōwa 50) and "Generation 86" (born after Shōwa 60). Some empirical studies have produced more detailed classifications, with more specific intervals for those who were born around the 80s.[1] The basis for the distinctions of these various age cohorts ("generations") are all rooted in the spreading use of the Internet. There exists a broad consensus that those born in the 90s are markedly different from those born before. Together with the prevalence of emails and messages, they left various constraints of time and place behind them. Postal mails became ridiculed as "snail mail". Note, however, that all of this was initially only true for middle-class kids in urban areas.

When those born in the 90s reached their teenage years, mobile devices became "part of their bodies", and they took new services such as social networking services (SNS) for granted. These young Japanese process information half-unconsciously with their thumb and through their voice. They think that keyboard input is awkward, if not primitive. For this new generation, script and sound are simply information, available when necessary and left when unnecessary. Information is fluent and weightless. Prompt-response communication dominates. They send and receive short sentences in short intervals via information and communication technology (ICT). Their physical location does not matter – it never has in their lives. Communication via ICT is forgotten immediately. There is a strong tendency for having everything "lighter and more compact", and this demand is thoroughly ensured in contemporary Japan.

Although those born in the 70s or the 80s are only one or two decades apart, they experience social relations and communication differently. Instead of filling in paper documents and transporting them physically from one place to another, the young generation uses digital documents that can immediately be transmitted. They use the mobile phone for exchanging brief and often fleeting information at short intervals. On the one hand, this situation is similar to places such as North America or South Korea where a digital space has been rapidly established, but on the other hand, the Japanese Archipelago has also its own unique developments. Both aspects will be discussed in this chapter.

Technical innovation and adaptation as a generation-making mechanism

In Japan, the idea of a so-called "Internet generation" has been proposed by Yoshiaki Hashimoto (Hashimoto 2010; Hashimoto 2011). There exists also a "four-generations model" that divides the so-called "Digital Natives" in more detail. It distinguishes between those who were born (1) from 1980 to 1982, (2) from 1983 to 1987, (3) from 1988 to 1990, and (4) after 1991 (Kimura 2012: 20, 83–141). This model regards these four types as forming a continuum rather than constituting clearly separate categories. In other words, the two decades in which the Digital Natives were born are seen to have involved a number of gradual changes. Those born before the so-called "Internet generation" are different, even though there are many early "PC maniacs" among them. They differ nonetheless, because the media they used at school (and at work) were basically analogous and only their private space was filled with information and communication technology. They acquired their ICT skills through conscious learning while living in a largely analogous world. ICT was for them, at least at the start, something extraordinary. For those who were born afterwards, ICT and the Internet are self-apparent. According to Hashimoto (2010: 53–59), the main difference between the Generation 76 and the Generation 86 is whether they are PC-based or cell-phone-based. For the Generation 76, PCs play the main role for collecting and processing information, while cell-phones are used only when leaving home. For the Generation 86, however, cell-phones are used not only for postings on the Internet, but also for writing reports such as university assignments. While they are able to use the numeric keypad on the phone at great speed, they have hardly any experience with PC keyboards, and they are often not very skilled in using it at university or at work.

Those who were born in the second half of the 70s and in the 80s had access to the Internet in their student days. Based on his face-to-face surveys, Kimura (2012: 110) concludes that they have an off-line life as a basis, and that online space constitutes an additional but subordinate layer. The majority of those born between 1983 and 1987 came to use cell-phones from the very beginning of their high school days. They mostly use emails and messages in order to contact their friends. They do so also as a means to reduce communication costs. This habit took shape when Internet costs at private households were still a matter of concern and flatrates did not yet exist. Unlike those born immediately after them, they encountered social network sites such as Mixi at the university, but their personal relationships were largely off-line-based. Online acquaintances were not yet widespread (Kimura 2012: 114).

Compared to the early members of the Internet generation, those born between 1988 and 1990 appear to be authentic Digital Natives. At the latest at the beginning of high school, they used emails and messages frequently, encouraged by the then-available flatrate system. Female junior and senior high school students created new information exchange spaces such as cellular blogs where they discussed fashion and other topics of shared interest. Access to the Internet and the

152 Hidenori Masiko

number of comments posted increased sharply (Kimura 2012: 115–116). At junior high school, PC learning was included in the school subject of home economy, and the Internet became an everyday affair. However, while PCs had now become standard in most households, they were either shared or used exclusively by the parents. It was rare for high school students to have their own PC. Mobile messages increased rapidly, and communication with friends now often included chatting (Kimura 2012: 117–118). The network of online connections expanded. The major distinction from those of the preceding age cohort is that those born between 1988 and 1990 came to use mobile devices also in order to access sites such as YouTube, Nico Nico, and so on. Male students accessed images of bikini-clad models not from co-shared PCs but from their own mobile device (Kimura 2012: 115–122).

This age cohort was followed by a new group who used the Internet again in different ways. They are in their mid-tweens today. Kimura (2012: 123–125) characterizes them as individuals who "could now use cell-phone blogs, mobile SNS and social games without having to worry about data restriction resulting from different provider contracts" and concludes that cell-phone-based social media now became more widely spread as an effect. A number of high school students (especially female students) created their own portal sites. This age cohort can also be considered to be Broadband Natives, so to say. From their elementary school days onwards, they devoted themselves to online games and chatting with those they met in the virtual space. Furthermore, their online network is to a large extent not related to their off-line network (Kimura 2012: 125–133).

Hashimoto Yoshiaki (2010: 96–105), who bases his analysis on the decennial divisions resulting in groups such as "Generation 76", "Generation 86", and "Generation 96", sums up the differences between these groups as follows:

> Generation 76: Flexible viewing of recorded TV programs. PCs have an output function and are used for writing, but provide also for relaxation and a device to connect to the world. Cell-phones screens are perceived as being small, and they are mainly used to exchange mails and to acquire information.
> Generation 86: Viewing TV programs in real-time, using them as a conversation topic with friends on the cell-phone. PCs are a device to check documents written by cell-phones. The PC is no longer an output device. Violation of privacy caused by having to share one PC with family members is avoided by using cell-phones. The phone becomes part of one's body and is used as a tool to access the Internet and to communicate with acquaintances.
> Generation 96: Enjoys video clips on the cell-phone and develops a lifestyle around this device. Both time and place are no longer relevant to them. They operate on various devices, using cell-phones, portable game consoles and music players such as the iPod.

Departing from the work by Hashimoto and Kimura, Takahashi, Honda and Terashima (2008), illustrate the different types of Internet users in Japan schematically. They distinguish between two factors: firstly, whether individuals were

Life on the small screen 153

Table 10.1 Classifications of digital habitus formation

	Born digital	Non-born digital
Digital life	Digital Natives	Digital Settlers
Non-digital life	Digital Immigrants	Digital Strangers

Source: Adapted from Takahashi, Honda and Terashima (2008: 72)

born or not born in the digital age and, secondly, whether or not they live a digital life. This results in a distinction between four groups (Table 10.1).

This classification is a criticism against the simple dichotomy of "Digital Natives" and "Digital Immigrants". Furthermore, it clarifies that not everybody "born digitally" also "lives digitally". Consider what characterizes these four types in more detail.

(1) Digital Natives: A group of young people that was socialized using information and communication devices such as computers and cell-phones every day and therefore acquired a high digital literacy. They actively collect information and communicate by using social media or shared video sites such as Nico Nico or YouTube.
(2) Digital Immigrants: For one reason or another, they did not have access to information and communication devices such as computers and cell-phones daily in their childhood even though they were born in an advanced information society.
(3) Digital Settlers: Those who were socialized with a limited exposure to the digital world. They acquired high digital literacy by using digital spaces only in more advanced periods of their lives. They were usually not brought up in environments where they had access to information and communication devices such as computers and cell-phones, neither at home nor at school.
(4) Digital Strangers: Those who have never experienced the digital world in their lives.

The generational transformations of senses and practices

In this section, I will explore how different exposure of the Internet and communication technology has affected body-senses and, as an effect thereof, various social practices.

Hashimoto's Generation 76 forms a continuum with the older generation since they both perceive PCs indispensable in order to be connected to the Internet, and in order to produce and transmit information. They also share the same bodily feeling that the screens of cell-phones are too small. Keyboards are taken for granted as an input device, and they feel comfortable and relaxed using PCs with their large displays. In contrast, the Generation 86 does not hesitate to input characters on cell-phones (as an everyday activity), and they are rather not so good

154 Hidenori Masiko

at keyboard input (which is to them a non-everyday activity). For the Generation 86, cell-phone screens are not small – PC screens are big. Large screens are used for activities such as proofreading (a non-everyday activity). Hashimoto (2010: 54–71) summarized these distinctions as follows: Generation 76: Write with PCs and read with cell-phones. A large screen is at least 40 Inches and above. Generation 86: Write with cell-phones and proofread with PCs. All PC screens are large.

According to Hashimoto the crucial point is what came first in an individual's life, a PC or a cell-phone? This has a range of effects such as using social media in solicitude and unconsciously also in the desire not to want to disturb others (Hashimoto 2010: 70–71). It might at first seem contradictory that the Generation 86 prefers direct telephone conversation more frequently than the Generation 76, but this is simply the result of different phone-charge systems across time (Hashimoto 2010: 66–69). While members of the Generation 76 spend their individual time on a PC at home, the Generation 86 enjoys individualism through cell-phones and uses emails and phone calls depending on their respective needs.

New sense of body and of time

Mobile devices have become part of the body of Digital Natives. They are carried around like wearable items and function as a kind of "extension" of their eyes, ears and brains. In other words, they are similar to glasses, or to wheelchairs for the physically disabled. The calculating and memorizing capability of computers has become a part of their body, and their body senses have been "enlarged" as an effect.

They have also physically adapted to their portable devices and are comfortable using only their thumbs and their voices for information input. Keyboard input is seen as primitive. Analogue writing with pencils is totally out of question. Thumb and voice (microphone/speaker/earphone) suffice for their subjective information activities (gathering/processing/sending), and for such activities, a PC is just a massive and clunky burden (that also overstrains all ten fingers and the eyes). Digital Natives use PCs only in their professional life.

Enjoying and sharing images (videos/pictures) freely in another time and space is also fluid and weightless, emerges only when necessary, becomes unnecessary immediately afterwards and quickly disappears. Enjoying and sharing images no longer require physical space like DVDs or art books to be stored at home. All of this is remindful of the "mass point" in physics.[2] Devices move in space automatically along with the movement of the users, and in this sense, they are "wearable" by definition. It is, therefore, not surprising that such mobile devices are nowadays also installed onto glasses and watches.

Data is just information that is fluid and weightless for Digital Natives. It emerges only when necessary, becomes unnecessary immediately afterwards, and then disappears. By exchanging (extremely) short messages and by shortening response time as much as possible (the "five-minute rule"), they send and receive short messages within short periods of time, wherever they happed to be physically (in bed, in the bathroom, while walking down the street, etc.).[3] Such

Life on the small screen   155

communication is usually immediately forgotten. The time used for these brief but endless acts sums up considerably during one day. Data shows that teens spend 39 minutes for emails and 78 minutes for messages per day during the weekend days, and that tweens use 36 minutes for emails and 52 minutes for messages (Sōmushō 2013). Consider also some more details about the so-called "five-minute rule". It represents a unique sense of time among Digital Natives and refers to a norm and a pressure within peer groups to respond to incoming information within five minutes. The "five-minute rule" is an unspoken convention that serves to not have friends worrying about either their acquaintances or their mutual relation. This makes this rule look like a considerate convention at first sight. In reality, how-ever, it ignores individual activities and lifestyles as it "enforces" an immediate response everywhere and anytime. Not responding "in time" can result in serious tensions. It is simply impolite not to answer right away. After all, one can engage in quick exchanges anytime, whether one is on the train or is eating with the family.

Some have observed that young people today use messages more frequently than they make phone calls. The reason therefore is that messages can control a sense of distance easier than calls. One has some leeway to respond (Ogiue-shiki BLOG 2009). The fact that two-thirds of young people answer messages immedi-ately cannot be ignored, though. As response to the question "Do you feel angry when you do not get a response right away?", 80 percent answered that "it doesn't bother me too much", but still 20 percent felt "very angry" or "a little angry", and the latter is an important fact. Interview surveys by Kimura (2012: 128–129) show several answers that confirm the application of the five-minute rule among the Digital Natives during their high school days.

These findings are confirmed by Matsushita, who writes:

> For those who send out mails, especially when they are high school students, it is hard to imagine that the receivers are not connected, or that they have their cell-phones off [. . .]. It is also difficult for them to think of a situation in which the receivers are too busy to answer the mails no matter where they are and what they are doing. [. . .] One of the merits about messages is that one does not have to respond immediately, but because of this, to respond quickly is valued, paradoxically. Furthermore, the senders feel worried whether a reply arrives or not, while the receivers feel pressured to communicate. It is not a rare case to send the same message to different people in order to receive one response.
>
> (Matsushita 2012: 48)

There are various ways to interpret such communicative behavior. Danah Boyd does not perceive young people's use of social media as an obsessive-compulsive disorder. Rather, she claims that "most of the teenagers are not addicted to social media [. . .] they are addicted to each other" (Boyd 2014: 130). Furthermore, Digital Natives are in a kind of "flow", in a happy immersion where the sense of time is lost and the power to concentrate increases. Matsushita (2012: 48), on the

156   Hidenori Masiko

other hand, points out that as a result of the prevalence of Mixi, the word "Mixi fatigue" (*mixitsukare*) has appeared. There are users who feel nervous when they do not receive any reactions from their diary. When they receive comments from others, their need for self-recognition is fulfilled. They are writing diaries in order to get comments – that is, the comments are more important than the diary itself. This shows traces of dependence, different from the "flow experiences" that Boyd describes. The sociologist Doi (2014: 2) states very clearly that mobile devices are indispensable for children nowadays in order to cultivate their friendships. Without them, it is difficult to maintain relations with others. As mentioned before, even though light, fleeting, and compact communication dominates, the total time spent on such communication is far from being short.

A generation that no longer knows analogous space

The Shōwa period (1926–1989) lasted for more than six decades and was divided by WW II. The latter 40 years consisted of the post-war reconstruction period, the high economic growth period, the oil shock, and the bubble economy. It is these 40 years that represent "Shōwa" for the average Japanese today. For those who were brought up in the subsequent Heisei period, the post-war reconstruction period and the high economic growth period are only imaginary events that can be "learned" from dramas and animations. They are called "retro" and are represented in places such as in the Shin-Yokohama Rāmen Museum.

Examples include "a rotary black phone", a fixed telephone in households that can be seen in anime such as *Sazae-san* and *Chibi Maruko-chan,* and an operator-assisted crank telephone that can be seen in Ghibli works such as *Tonari no Totoro*, creating an image of "the old days". In that sense, the transition from such a black phone, first placed and fixed at the entrance of the house, into the living room did not really change the acts of making phone calls. Only when cordless handsets became available, it was possible to make calls without worrying about the intrusion into one's privacy. This marks a huge turning point. The second turning point was the popularization of cell-phones in the 1990s. Subsequently, the costs to deliver voices, texts and images decreased dramatically. For the generation that knows only the present state of worldwide simultaneous information transmission through communication satellites and the Internet, it is literally impossible to understand the sense of frustration stemming from unsteady, short, expensive, or slow communication and information. To them, questions arise such as "How was information collected before there was the Internet?" or "How was information processed before there were PCs?" Only the generation that experienced the time when the Internet and PCs did not exist understands the various steps of innovation and the changes of practices it brought along. For those who grew up with digital technology, accounts of such development and diffusion are simply another tale from the past.

The verb *guguru*, i.e. searching information on your own by using Google, is used by a generation that is used to checking information on the Internet. It is impossible to understand for them how this could be done before there was

Life on the small screen 157

Google. In their adolescence, they learned how to ride a bicycle, drive a car and go to the distant places using public transportation. Along this process, they acquired the freedom given to adults. In a similar way, once they were allowed accesses to smartphones and PCs, their "analogous childhood" ended. They entered a new age, quickly forgetting the limitations that marked their lives before. Analogue devices disappear in early childhood. After this transition, they cannot experience exclusively analogous moments, unless they are far out in the mountains. They live in a space in which they are constantly connected, except for schools where cell-phones are not allowed (yet), and during some specific physical exercises.

Calculators installed on phones are used instead of the abacus and slide rules. Computation on paper is an archaic exercise, detached from everyday practices. The input is done through buttons and microphones without ever taking notes. Face-to-face communication and real voice communication is no longer really necessary. Records are not accumulated. Information flows through real time. If necessary, it can be accumulated as a lifelog on Facebook, which can be used for accumulation of data through time. Needless to say, books and magazines are not purchased. Looking for information in a bookstore or collecting it at a library is avoided as much as possible (but such information is appreciated on mobile devices no matter if it is purchased or not). In this way, the "minimalist lifestyle" becomes natural. One keeps only the necessary goods and information. Keeping or carrying around more than necessary is wasteful, and one can maintain a peaceful and quiet state of mind by ignoring (currently) unnecessary information. This is a life without waste. One can lead a consumer life based on home delivery (that makes excellent use of the Internet by the way), and get all the necessary information by adequate Internet searches. Data can be saved anywhere, without taking (too much) space, and there is no risk of the deterioration, destruction by fire, or theft. There seem to be only advantages of living such a life! It is hard to understand why pervious generations stick to things, and collect and store information. In the end, all of this is available everywhere, almost free of charge, if not outright gratis.

It is therefore only natural that the sense of embodiment has changed. Kawamoto Toshiro's (2005) book, titled *The Modern History of Easy and Convenient*, features the subtitle *The Future of Mass Consumption and Information Society*. In this book, he criticizes Japanese society in claiming that the mass production of goods has caused a mass consumer society that promotes mass consumption, and that, following this pattern, a mass information society has appeared that is eroding the mind and body, especially that of the younger generation. Kawamoto furthermore criticizes that the dramatic change of the information society represented by the quick popularization of i-mode cell-phones from 1999 onwards also led to changes in communication culture. One of the effects thereof is the emergence of what he portrays to be superficial if not outright destructive human relationships. At hindsight, however, the majority of his arguments turn out to be nothing more than some kind of crude youth discourse (*zokuryū wakamono-ron*), that is, statements filled with gender biases, discriminations against the younger generation

158   *Hidenori Masiko*

and glorifications of "mothers who are good at cooking" (Gotō 2008). However, it is true that the rapid and thorough spread of i-mode cell-phones within several years after their appearance did dramatically change the Japanese communication life and sense of embodiment. It crucially paved the way to the digital revolution. Even though most of Kawamoto's attention was directed at criticizing the young (and missing the "good old days"), his argument about the emergence of a mass-information society, the loss of relevance of distance and space, and the sense of 24-hour connection proved to be important predictions.

Research by Satō Kenji (2012: 218–221) reveals that messages are mainly used among close friends. They serve the function to maintain a balance between the appropriate intimacy and the necessary distance. His analysis is basically opposite to that of Kawamoto. Kawamoto (2005: 193) states, cynically, that the use of cell-phones "provides the illusion of being together with others and sharing life even when one is physically apart" and, furthermore, that such type of virtual relations requires "constant conformations of being connected with someone" since such relations "can be destructed like a house of cards at anytime". Friendships have become subjects of consumption. He continues in stating that "one is rather constrained by cell-phones, instead of making full use of them" and that "chatting is indispensable to maintain the belief that one is always connected with someone". However, what he calls the "sense of 24-hour pseudo-connection" is not to be treated cynically. Being virtually connected all the time is the reality or normality for the Digital Natives. It is wrong to interpret this as a loss of communal human relationships or as an attempt to gloss over feelings of loneliness and emptiness. This kind of interpretation is typical of the so-called "crude youth discourse". It sees technical innovation only negatively, and it fails to grasp new attitudes and behaviors adequately. For Kawamoto, all communication except for face-to-face communication is "pseudo-communication". This is evident in comments such as people "start feeling the reality in the virtual sense through the devices, not through the five physical senses". By writing this, he trivializes all communication using ICT as "deviant" or "incomplete" (Kawamoto 2005: 188–189), but he is oblivious of the fact that calligraphy-brush messages, too, are not face-to-face communication. Even if a message is handwritten, it is clearly no face-to-face communication. This also applies to radio broadcast (broadcast materials for the Open University of Japan, broadcast of the voice of Shōwa Emperor, etc.). This is just one example that shows that the criticism of the Digital Natives is often incoherent and contradictory.

It is also shortsighted to think that the Digital Natives are only interested in being virtually connected. Posting one's schedule on Twitter does not only constitute a case of simultaneous reporting in virtual space – it is also an invitation to join. A message such as "I'm going to eat at XX now" can also imply "why don't you come along and dine with me at XX" and not simply "I'm going to now give you a live coverage of the dishes I am going to eat at XX". Instead of inviting directly, Digital Natives speak to those who happen to be following these comments on Twitter. "I'm going to eat at XX now" works like a kind of advertising balloon. It may result in someone having a meal alone, or it may evolve into an unexpected huge party. In any case, nobody is hurt whatever way this event unfolds.

What deserves attention and what does stand out is the "embodiment" of cell-phones or smartphones. The neologism *sumaho rosu* ("smartphone loss") is probably more than a catchy buzz term. Losing one's phone is a grave loss. A smartphone is not simply a portable telephone. It is also an address book, one's schedule, transportation and location information, etc. It stores one's experiences such as communication with friends or memorable photos. In other words, a smartphone is a kind of doppelganger and an inseparable partner in one's life. One suffers tremendously if one looses it, or if it breaks down.

A glimpse at the practices of the Digital Natives

Although Japan is a leading electronic industrial country, it has fallen behind on the cell-phone/PC/home appliance market in the last decade. This development is now frequently explained by reference to the isolated and unique ecology of the Galapagos Islands. Hence, the term "Galapagosization" has come to be used when analyzing this situation. Just like the Shinkasen traffic control system, also Japanese phones and laptops have become extremely specified, resulting in high tech that is not required on foreign markets. Contrary to the case of industrial robots and automobiles, where Japanese industry continues to be internationally among the leaders, Japanese phones and laptops deviate extremely from the world standard on and expectations in such products. Due to the relatively large Japanese population and their considerable purchasing power, Japanese manufacturers have tended to specialize in domestic consumption. The Digital Natives are a crucial factor for understanding this Galapagosization phenomenon in Japan.

The Galapagosization of writing on the phone

The mixed orthography of kanji and kana had initially caused an enormous barrier to put written Japanese to practical use in information and communication technology. The Galapagosization of PCs was basically due to the unique orthography that is not based on the Latin alphabet and on Arabic numbers. In Japanese orthography, no empty space is left between words, and this facilitates the practice of the Digital Natives to express meaningful chunks of information in place of structured sentences. In line with such practice, a unique Japanese emoticon culture has developed. Consider some simple but widely known examples:

!(^^)!	= being overjoyed, /!/ on the left and right indicate raised arm while shouting *banzai* (~hurray)
(-_-;)	= cold sweat, /;/ represents sweat due to shock
(T_T)	= sad, crying face, /T/ represent tears running down the cheeks
m(_ _)m orz	= kneeling-down-on-the-floor kind of gratitude, the /m/ on the left and the right side represent hands placed next to the head, o is the head, r the upper body, and z the legs in kneeling position

160 *Hidenori Masiko*

These examples are clearly different from ASCII artwork or the western "smiley". In the Japanese computer culture, ideographic expressions with combined figurative structures are employed instead of using a phonetic alphabet. Hence, Internet slang cannot be described without referring to the unique Japanese kanji culture. The following examples require detailed knowledge about Japanese kanji. Not only foreigners but also elementary school pupils are at pains of grasping their meaning. For example, 氏ね *shine* (homophonous to 死ね, "die!") was created in order to avoid so-called "NG words" ("no good") as specified by netiquette in chats. There are also various plays on words and plays on the writing system. 厨房 *chūbō* (homophonous with 中坊) is an abbreviation of the derogatory term 中学生坊主 *chūgakusei bōzu* ("junior high school boy"); ネ申 is made up and the katagana *ne* and the kanji *saru* ("ape") to form the kanji 神 ("god"); 儲 (actually *mōke*, "profit") on the other hand is two kanjis 信者 (*shinsha*, "believer") merged into one. The complex system of kanji is used as grounds for language play, resulting in an even more complicated system. Digital Natives use emoticons, emoji and Unicode 6.0 emoji on cell-phones, mixing them with kanji kana mixed orthography and Arabic numbers in anarchic ways. The amount of different kinds of letters is beyond imagination for those who do not share this culture of communication. Messaging, too, shows traces of Galapagosization.

Literature on the phone – the case of the cell-phone novels

"Cell-phone novels" or "smartphone novels" are also worth mentioning as part of the Japanese cell-phone culture (see Calvetti 2015 for details). These novels are popular literature written, released and viewed via portable phones. They started appearing around 2000 and became popular especially among female high school students. Recently, a large number of these novels are no longer written exclusively by (often male) professional authors, but by young women. This is a typical feature of pop culture. The smartphone literature allows more artistic complexity, due to the larger screen and the higher resolution. This facilitated amateurs to join already established authors, and compose works without the support of professional editors. Compared to other types of literature, the cell-phone novels were considered to be somewhat "rough-around-the-edges", but Naito Mika (born 1971), known as "the queen of cell-phone novels", has enjoyed a professional career stretching over more than a decade by now. In this period of time, she has written more than 30 novels and novelized PC games. The cell-phone novels were once also published as books, and in 2007 they had more than ten million cumulative sales, including bestsellers that sold more than a million copies within a week after the release (Yoshida 2008: 49–55). Today, there is a pessimistic view claiming that the boom of cell-phone novels is over. Since 2008, none of them appeared in the bestseller rankings. However, the number of bestsellers decreased only because the profit-seeking big publishing companies started publishing many more titles, making it difficult for one particular title to become a hit. The boom is hardly over. Consider some numbers. In 2015, Noichigo (established on 30 May 2007), one of the cell-phone novels sites, reports to have sold 22 million

Life on the small screen 161

works, to have produced 218 professional authors, to have 600 million accesses to its promotion videos every month, 140,000 daily users of its platform, 720,000 members, and 490,000 submitted works that continue to increase by 5,000 new titles every month. Hence, the boom is only over for those who want to hit it big with one single work. Cell-phone novels are another unique product of the Japanese post-war pop culture. Needless to say, perhaps, this phenomenon is crucially driven by Digital Natives. Cell-phone novels are tools of self-expression. In contrast to manga, anime, and computer games, it is beyond the imagination that cell-phone novels will become popular outside of Japan. The cell-phone and smartphone novels, too, show signs of Galapagosization.

Digital job-hunting activities

One more phenomenon where practices have changed dramatically under the influence of the digital revolution is job-hunting. Traditionally, the simultaneous activities to find a full-time position at a private company for university graduates is called job-hunting (*shūshoku katsudō*, or simply *shūkatsu*). Huge companies receive ten thousands of applications. In order to deal with them, a number of companies now require an online application. As a consequence, *shūkatsu*, too, has moved into the virtual space and onto the smartphone. The number of job-seeking youth posting their student life on Facebook in order to appeal to human resource administrators has also increased dramatically. Matsushita Keita observes that:

Companies are now using computers and the Internet in various parts of the selection process in order to deal with the large amount of applications. The online systematization is progressing in various selecting processes such as information sessions, application submissions and employment examinations. Students are dealing with their *shūkatsu* 24 hours a day, using smartphones instead of just sitting and waiting in front of a PC in order to send an application or to make an appointment for an information session. They are also carefully checking the information about companies or job interviews appearing on social media such as Twitter and Mixi. Because the number of companies that use online submissions has increased [. . .], students have been freed from works that require an enormous amount of handwriting and repetition in order to avoid typographical errors. Besides, the number of the companies that distribute videos on the Internet for their seminars and information sessions is also increasing. [. . .] This allows students access to information sessions even without having made an appointment. Furthermore, questions can be directly asked during such sessions from those who have accounts for Ustream, Facebook or Mixi. These sessions are also archived and can therefore be watched repeatedly at any time. This kind of service is useful for those students who live far away from Tokyo or who could not make a reservation for an information session on a specific time. On the other hand, companies can also reduce their costs. For small and medium-sized enterprises,

162 *Hidenori Masiko*

it is impossible to offer a huge information session repeatedly, but this kind of service gives them a chance to appeal broadly to students. [. . .] Through the online systematization of the various screening processes, companies are freed from time and space. They can reduce the costs for personnel affairs and employment, and open their doors to more students to apply.

(Matsushita 2012: 152–153)

The long citation above shows not only that those who were born in the 1990s use the Internet via digital devices regularly, but also that recruitment practices have adapted to the Digital Natives. Matsushita (2012: 154–156) also points out that information was once acquired mainly through print and TV, then through homepages and information sessions, but that message-boards on social media such as Twitter have replaced both of these channels now. In the "old days" of *shūkatsu*, students used information passively. Information was one-sided, sent out from media, companies or university career centers. Today, the amount of information has sharply increased and is to be found everywhere on the Internet, where it needs to be accessed and analyzed by students. As an effect, those with a high digital literacy have an edge over those who are less savvy (Matsushita 2012: 156).

In a chapter on the "rising 'density' of job-hunting", Matsushita (2012: 157–190) examines the spread of smartphones and their impact. He reports that the pressure has grown to acquire smartphones that enable viewing PC sites for activities such as job-hunting. Since job-hunting includes collecting and sending out information, this can nowadays be done anytime during "spare time", while waiting, eating, or commuting. Those responsible for screening applicants are profiling their characteristics also by the actual state of social media use. Twitter and Facebook allow for the "self-branding" of candidates. This leads to a blurring of the border between job-hunting and private life. This results in new conflicts as an effect of the increasing "density" of job-hunting activities. Recruitment, too, is now freed from time and space.

Outlook

At the start of this chapter, it was stated that the Digital Natives initially originated in the urban middle-class and from there spread across all regions and social strata. Still today, not all young Japanese possess the same (high) digital literacy. In Japan, as in any other countries, too, one must therefore be careful to not universalize images and practices of the Digital Natives. A great number of such images have been propagated by marketing agencies seeking short-term profit by producing and circulating an optimistic perspective about the expanding market of the Digital Natives. This serves as a means to portray and to emphasize, in essentialist fashion, the uniqueness of the Digital Natives. Such practices serve the aim of promoting the idea of a vast and uncultivated market, creating as a side-effect an anxiety among the middle-aged generation for being left behind and being out of touch with technology and digital practices in contemporary Japan.

Life on the small screen   163

If the image of Digital Natives is considered to be an "ideal type" in the sense of Max Weber, then it helps to shed some light on broadly shared skills, practices and attitudes among the young generation. With regard to the use of information and communication technology, young Japanese are obviously different from the middle-aged generation, who were raised in a (predominantly) analogue world and later learned to adapt themselves, sometimes quite desperately, to the new technology in order to survive in a digitalizing world. The Digital Natives represent a new generation in the sense that they do not know the limitations of the analogue world, and in the sense that they experience the digital world as a basic or natural principle of everyday life.

Sooner or later, this generation will completely abandon writing on paper or whiteboards.[4] This is a generation for which handwritten letters are totally exotic – almost an art form. Those who were born and raised in the digital age come into contact with sounds, texts, and images often only after they have been converted into a digital form. Physical constraints such as location, availability of paper and pen, etc., are disappearing. Information is "free" in both senses of the word. The culture of vertical writing will disappear as an effect of the decline of paper publications. The current kanji-centered orthography practiced on the Japanese Archipelago will probably change as well. When the Japanese language can be processed as spoken information without written input composition, then not only existing language policies but also the discriminations resulting from unequal kanji proficiency will weaken or even totally disappear. Technological innovation will contribute to realize barrier-free communication. It is already being practiced and promoted by the Digital Natives.

It is irresponsible, however, to leave all the issues on the future of communication to the Digital Natives. The book *Did the Internet Make "Us" Happy?* (Mori 2005) underlines that there are also negative effects of the Internet and, what is more, that the Digital Natives cannot escape them. It would be ironic, if technologies innovated as products of good intentions and reform would bring about regretful effects. Everyone engaged in and using information and communication technology, not only the Digital Natives, must endeavor to stop vicious effects stemming from Internet-based communication and interaction.

Notes

1 Generation 76 is used often in the IT world since there are a lot of Internet-related entrepreneurs born around 1976. In advertising, terms such as Generation 86 and Generation 96 are used, following the model of Generation 76 (Hashimoto 2011: 146). Furthermore, members of the Generation 76 that are now entering their 40s at the time of writing are considered to be typical "Post-dankai Juniors", that is to say, are those people who experienced the glacial age of (non)-hiring (*shūshoku hyōgaki jidai*).
2 The reason why I mention the mass point in physics here is because the physicality of the phone is no longer relevant. The majority of mobile phones are today in the 100-gram range. Compared to the body weight of the users and in consideration to their physical strength and other items they carry along, phones are basically non-existent in a physical sense.
3 According to Takahashi (2014: 195–197), communication has been shortened with the introduction of LINE.

164   Hidenori Masiko

4 At the present time, handwritten memos are still prominent at the workplace. In school handwritten remains also dominant except for the mark-sheet-type examinations. However, even if plenty of handwriting remains today such as in writing down orders in the restaurant, etc., touch screen pads or ticket selling self-service machines are spreading rapidly. This trend will not retreat but continue to grow. School is therefore a noteworthy example of handwriting conservatism.

References

Boyd, Danah (2014) *Tsunagarippanashi no nichijō o ikiru – sōsharumedia ga wakamono ni motarashita mono* [It's Complicated: The Social Lives of Networked Teens] (translated by Momo Nonaka). Tokyo: Sōshiha.

Calvetti, Paolo (2015) Keitai shōsetsu: Mobile Phone Novels. Is It True That New Technologies Are Changing the Japanese Language? *Contemporary Japan* 1: 203–218.

Doi, Takayoshi (2014) *Tsunagari o aorareru kodomotachi – netto izon to iu mondai o kangaeru* [Children Engaged in Connection: Reflections on Net-Dependence and Bullying]. Tokyo: Iwanami.

Gotō, Kazutomo (2008) *Wakamono-ron o utagae!* [Doubting Discourse on Youth!]. Tokyo: Takarashimasha.

Hashimoto, Yoshiaki (2010) *Neo dijitaruneitibu no tanjō – nihon dokuji no shinka otogeru netto sedai* [The Emergence of the Neo-Digital Natives: A Net Generation as Japan's Unique Evolution]. Tokyo: Daiyamondosha.

——— (2011) *Media to nihonjin – kawariyuku nichijō* [Media and the Japanese: Changes in Everyday Life]. Tokyo: Iwanami.

Kawamoto, Toshirō (2005) *Kantan benri no gendai-shi – kōmitsudo shōhi, jōhō shakai no yukue* [The Modern History of Easy and Convenient: The Future of Mass Consumption and Information Society]. Tokyo: Gendai Shokan.

Kimura, Tadamasa (2012) *Dijitaruneitibu no jidai – naze mēru o sezu ni "tsubuyaku" no ka* [The Digital Native Era: Why Are People "Whispering" Without Mailing?] Tokyo: Heibonsha.

Matsushita, Keita (2012) *Dijitaruneitibu to sōsharu media – wakamono ga umidasu aratana komyunikēshon* [Digital Natives and Social Media: New Communication Produced by Youth]. Tokyo: Kyōiku Hyōronsha.

Mori, Ken (2005) *Intānetto to wa "bokura" o shiawase ni shitaka – jōhōka ga motarashita "risuku hejji shakai" no yukue* [Did the Internet Make "Us" Happy? The "Risk Hedge Society" Brought About by Information Technology]. Tokyo: Asupekuto.

Ogiue-shiki BLOG (2009) *"Gakkō-ura saito" to "netto ijime" no genjō – yori yutakana "kea" no tame ni* [The Current Status of "The Backside of School" and of "Internet Bullying". Towards a Richer "Care"]. Online available at: http://d.hatena.ne.jp/sei jotcp/20090919/p1 (accessed 5 January 2017).

Satō, Kenji (2012) *Keitai-ka suru nihongo – mobairu jidai no "kanjiru" "tsutaru" "kangaeru"* [The Cell-Phonization of Japanese: "Feeling", "Transmission" and "Thinking" in the Mobile Age]. Tokyo: Taishūkan.

Sōmushō (2013) *Jōhō tsūshin media no riyō jikan to jōhō kōdō ni kansuru chōsa* [Survey on the Time of Use of Information Transmission Media and on Information Behaviour]. Online available at: www.soumu.go.jp/iicp/chousakenkyu/data/research/survey/telecom/2014/h25mediariyou_1sokuhou.pdf (accessed 4 January 2017).

Takahashi, Akiko (2014) *Sōsharumedia chūdoku – tsunagari ni oboreru hitotachi* [Social Media Addiction: People Drowning in Their Connections]. Tokyo: Gentōsha.

Takahashi, Akiko, Kazuhisa Honda and Takuyuki Terashima (2008) Dejitaru neitibu to ōdiensu engējimento ni kansuru kōsatsu – dejitaru media ni kansuru gakusei chōsa yori [Discussion on Digital Natives and Audience Engagement: Based on a Student Survey on Digital Media]. *Rikkyō daigaku ōyō shakaigaku kenkyū* 50: 71–92.

Yoshida, Satobi (2008) *Kētai shōsetsu ga ukeru riyū* [Why Mobile Phone Novels Are Popular]. Tokyo: Mainichi Komyunikēshon Shuppan.

11 Dialect cosplay

Language use by the young generation

Patrick Heinrich

Introduction

At the end of the 1990s, Asahi Soft Drinks sought to rejuvenate its products, creating the new brand "Wonda" towards this end. They hired Tiger Woods for the first commercial in 1997, and afterwards cool anime producer Studio Ghibli. In 2014, it employed the Japanese girl group AKB48 for a new commercial of "Wonda Coffee Morning Shot". Its 48 members are from all across Japan. Asahi Soft Drinks placed them with a can of Wonda Coffee in their hand in front of famous local landmarks, and had them say in the respective regional dialects, "Hi everybody in Japan – we are totally supporting you".

On YouTube, a young viewer by the name of Chano Satō comments on one of these commercials, "although I am from Chiba, I have never heard the Chiba dialect before".[1] This is not surprising. The prevalent number of young Japanese no longer speaks dialect, and the Chiba dialect was actually one of the first targeted for extinction in the Meiji period (Hokama 1971: 75). Recent surveys reveal that a quarter of the Japanese population do not know whether a dialect was once spoken in the region where they grew up, and more than 70 percent report to use exclusively Standard Japanese in their lives (Tanaka et al. 2016). This number can be expected to be much higher among young Japanese. It is thus not far-fetched to assume that AKB48 members had to practice their lines for the commercial, and that they needed instruction in order to present themselves "locally" via dialect. We can also infer that speaking dialect is now somehow considered "cool".

The situation of AKB48 members purposefully learning to use dialect is noteworthy if we consider how dialects were viewed only half a century before. Consider an example. When the Heisei emperor and Shōda Michiko became engaged in 1958, this was big news. After all, she was the first commoner to ever marry into the imperial family. Empress Michiko had been born in Tokyo but fled to Gunma Prefecture as a 10-year-old in order to escape the Tokyo bombings of 1944. She returned to Tokyo in 1946, but the brief exposure to the Gunma dialect at young age had made her Japanese unacceptable to many. In particular, the fact that she did not use the nasalized variant of the velar plosive (*gagyō bidakuon*), pronouncing for example "east" as /higaʃi/ instead /hiŋaʃi/ made her the subject of criticism. Soon after she entered public life, newspapers disapproved of her pronunciation,

Dialect cosplay 167

writing "Cannot pronounce *gagyō bidakuon* – Princess Michiko's pronunciation of the Gunma Prefecture accent" (Tōkyō Shinbun, 27 December 1958, quoted from Shioda 2011: 135) until she purposefully corrected her (mis-)pronunciation. The media promptly approved of her newly acquired articulation.

The principle applied to everyone in Japan then. Speaking dialect was seen as a personal shortcoming, an embarrassment. The complete replacement of dialects in favor of Standard Japanese was propagated, a project that resulted for many in what became known as the dialect complex (*hōgen konpurekkusu*). According to Wikipedia (2016), this complex resulted "in neuroses and sometimes even in murder and suicide" but as the standard language skills "of the young improved, this dialect-based inferiority complex faded". Hence, not so long ago dialects were seen as awkward – the language used by the old folks, the ignorant, or the "countryside bumpkins". Now that the young no longer speak dialect, this image has changed. We have arrived at a situation where members of AKB48 pretend to speak regional dialect in a TV commercial.

In the following, I seek to explain how these changes have come about and what they imply for the young generation in present-day Japan. I do so by relating the effects of language standardization on dialect cosplay (*hōgen kosupure*). The first process is not directly related to the young generation, for they were born at a time when the standardization process was completed. However, the generations of their parents and grandparents have been crucially shaped by it, and their attitudes and behaviors towards language contrast with that of the young generation. The second part of this chapter depicts a novel way of speaking Japanese among the young generation, i.e., dialect cosplay.

Language standardization and its social effects

Every language has the double tendency of diversifying and unifying at the same time (Bakhtin 1987). A living language breathes, so to speak. In the course of modernization, the centripetal forces become prevalent and language becomes less diversified or, in the terminology of Bakhtin, it becomes more "monoglossic". In modern societies, language has to be adapted to an industrial and literate society. It has to ensure access to a nationally unified labor market and enable social mobility for everyone. This, together with the novel idea of the nation, results in language standardization. In Japan, like in most other modern societies, a vernacular language variety was chosen, codified, functionally developed and then spread as "standard language" through the modern education system (Heinrich 2012). Quasi as a side effect, the establishment of Standard Japanese resulted in the creation of "dialects", which were seen to be "wrong", "backward", or "uncultivated" (Masiko 2003: 68–70). Dialects came to be perceived as the exact opposite of standard language.[2]

Along these lines of thought, Standard Japanese was not spread as "an additional variety", but dialect was "corrected" into Standard Japanese through language education. This left everybody not (fully) proficient in Standard Japanese suddenly speaking "incorrectly". This had consequences for such speakers,

168   Patrick Heinrich

because we ultimately speak in order "to do things" and "to be someone". Speaking dialect dramatically restricted the possibilities of "what could be done" and "who you could be". In a large number of contexts, use of dialect indexed speakers negatively. This logic affected all dialect speakers, including speakers of the Tokyo dialect, because Standard Japanese was an artificially created variety that had been nobody's native language (Heinrich and Yamashita 2017; Nomura 2013).[3]

Consider the sociolinguistic situation at the time. A good source for the use of Japanese before standardization is the *Linguistic Atlas of Japan* (Kokuritsu Kokugo Kenkyūjo 1966–1974). Informants surveyed for the atlas were born between 1879 and 1903. Their language revealed much variation. "Good morning", for example, was *ohayō gozaimasu* in Standard Japanese, but from north to south researchers found *ohayō gozansu* in Iwate, *ohayō gozarisu* in Miyagi, *hayainee* in Chiba, *ohayō gansu* in Kanagawa, *ohayōsan* across Kansai, *oyaō gowasu* in Tokushima, *okinasattaka* in Shimane, *ohayō arimasu* in Yamaguchi and *ohin narimashitaka* in Kagoshima (Sanada 2001: 135). (By the way, these are the very expressions that are used by members of AKB48 in the commercial). Language standardization before 1945 meant to replace such language by Standard Japanese. Placing stigma on dialects and on dialect speakers was a key mechanism towards this end.

Standard Japanese spread from Tokyo across Japan. However, Tōhoku in the north, Shikoku in the west and Kyūshū in the south initially lagged behind. The standard was subsequently spread with yet more fervor there. As an effect, it was already noted in the mid-1970s that Tōhoku dialect speakers spoke dialect in their hometown but had shifted to Standard Japanese in the neighboring municipality (Jugaku 1978). In Ōsaka, Kyōto and the surrounding Kansai plain, the local dialects were maintained relatively well even when Standard Japanese was spread there (Kumagai 2016).[4] Put simply, Kansai speakers did not buy into the language ideology, claiming that their way of speaking was "wrong" while speaking a language associated with the archrival Tokyo was "correct". We will return to this issue further below.

Standard language spread changed its rational after 1945. It now became seen as an important means for democratizing Japanese society. The idea of "Standard Japanese" was relaxed, shifting from a strict 100 percent adherence to the norm (*hyōjungo*) towards the recognition of efforts to follow the norm in the best way possible (*kyōtsūgo*).[5] Towards the end of "language democratization" the Japanese National Language Institute was established, and the numerous surveys on standard language spread it subsequently conducted give us insights into how different generations in Japan speak.

Let us quickly consider two studies to illustrate the language standardization process, firstly an analysis of attitudes towards dialects and standard (Tanaka and Maeda 2012), and then a longitudinal survey of standard language and dialect proficiency (Kokuritsu Kokugo Kenkyūjo 2013). In a study clustering types of speakers on the basis of attitudes towards dialect and standard language, Tanaka and Maeda (2012) show three important findings. In order to capture the dynamism

Dialect cosplay 169

of change, I contrasted their findings with a similar survey carried out in the mid-1970s (Jugaku 1978).

- Individuals using exclusively (or almost exclusively) standard language have been centered in Greater Tokyo for many decades, but we can witness more recently a spread of such types of speakers into the regions surrounding it (Northern Kantō, Koshinetsu, Hokuriku, and Tōkai). Many individuals in Greater Tokyo and its surrounding regions have difficulties identifying the dialect once spoken in their home region.
- Speakers of dialects have predominantly been centered in the Kinki region (Ōsaka, Kyōto, and its surrounding), and recently the use of dialect has been spreading from there into the neighboring regions of Chūgoku and Shikoku.
- In Tōhoku and Kyūshū, informants report to be differentiating between dialect and standard language according to the sociolinguistic situation in which they speak, thus coming closest to the post-war policy ideal of *tsukaiwake*, i.e., a differentiated use of standard and dialect according to context (formal/informal).

We need to be careful when drawing conclusions from these results as they simply reflect what people *state* about their language use. Let us therefore consider how standard language and dialect proficiency has changed after 1945.

Tsuruoka in Yamagata Prefecture was chosen as a case by the Japanese National Language Institute because the linguistic distance between the local dialect and Standard Japanese was large there, and because the city was also geographically isolated. The first survey of 1950 showed that Standard Japanese had not widely spread. The survey was repeated in 1971, 1991, and in 2011 (see Kokuritsu Kokugo Kenkyūjo 2013). Consider the results for *karasu* (crow). Whereas 40 percent of the oldest informants of the first survey (born in 1896) came up with the Standard Japanese expression, the youngest informants (born in 1916) averaged already 60 percent. Slightly less than 60 percent of the oldest informants (born in 1901) produced the standard variety term in 1971 versus 97 percent of the youngest informants (born in 1961). In the third survey, 84 percent of the oldest persons surveyed (born in 1934) answered with the standard variety term while the youngest (born in 1994) accounted for 99 percent. Finally, in the last survey 99 percent of the oldest locals consulted (born in 1934) answered with the standard term, while everybody born afterwards used without fail the standard term. In other words, the standardization process was completed, as everybody could produce the standard language form then.

In preparing the 2011 survey, the National Institute of Japanese Language suspected that most informants were by now speaking Standard Japanese, and it therefore added a new question. Participants were now also asked whether they could imitate (*mane dekiru*) the local dialect. The result showed that informants had retained only partial knowledge (Kokuritsu Kokugo Kenkyūjo 2013: 7). It disclosed that there was basically no knowledge that *iki* ("breath") had been *eki* in the local dialect, that *eki* ("train station") had been *iki*, and that *hebi* ("snake")

170   Patrick Heinrich

had been *febi*. Less that 10 percent remembered that *karasu* ("crow") had been *karashi* and that *uchiwa* ("fan") had been *utsuwa*. Almost 90 percent remembered that *neko* ("cat") had been *nego*, though. In the short time span of 60 years, Japan had thus transformed from a dialect-speaking society, where the standard language was learned at school and where speakers were linguistically insecure, into a standard language speaking society where only isolated dialect token were remembered (e.g., *nego*).

While language use between all age cohorts was very similar in the 2011 survey, the linguistic experiences between the generations differ. An analysis of all four surveys shows that the greatest advances in language standardization were made between 1950 and 1970. The remaining gap to full standardization was closed between 1970 and 1990. Everybody born afterwards, that is, everybody born in the Heisei period, has been linguistically socialized in a standard language speaking society. We can therefore infer that those born in the Heisei period have not experienced linguistic insecurity due to speaking dialect, and that they have not made efforts to rid themselves from speaking dialect in order to pass as a speaker of "correct language".

Being born in the Heisei period means growing up in a society where standard language is commonplace (*kyōtsūgo wa atarimae*). This is a fundamental difference from the experiences of the older generations, who had to learn to adapt and change their speech, or suffer the consequences for not speaking adequately. Growing up after 1990 has crucially shaped language attitudes and language uses. As a matter of fact, Japanese sociolinguists are in agreement that the start of the Heisei period coincides with the start of a language de-standardization process (see e.g., Inoue 2011; Sanada 2000). While de-standardization (*datsu-hyōjungoka*) in itself is not a generation-making mechanism, the differing attitudes and uses of language nevertheless set Heisei period-born Japanese linguistically apart from older generations.

From trying to pass as a standard speaker to dialect cosplay

Nobody has better summarized what it means not to speak according to language norms than Pierre Bourdieu. In his seminal essays on language, Bourdieu (1991) showed how speakers of regional and social dialects were undermining their own standing in society by recognizing a form of language as "legitimate" that they were not able to produce. That is to say, he showed how ideas about what constitutes "correct" or "good speech" were more widely spread than such speech was actually possessed. Bourdieu (1991: 45) called such speakers "dominated speakers". According to Bourdieu (1991: 52), dominated speakers "strive desperately for correctness" and, being conscious of the fact that they do not speak according to the standard norms, are left at times " 'speechless', 'tongue-tied', 'at a loss for words', as if they were suddenly dispossessed of their own language." While a great number of Japanese have at one point or another found themselves being "tongue-tied" or linguistically uncomfortable, this is not an experience that the

Dialect cosplay 171

young generation has had. It is true that Kansai retained the local dialect, but it retained it because they take pride in it. Speaking Kansai dialect does not result in being tongue-tied. (Quite the contrary is often true).

Those born in the Heisei period differ linguistically. Most have never faced difficulties due to dialects. In the rare case that they experienced language problems, these were quickly settled. Consider some excerpts taken from language biographies I collected from university students in the Tokyo Metropolitan area in 2012.

(1) I am of course totally fluent in Japanese, but sometimes I feel that I cannot express myself very well. I mean, I can say what I think and feel, but I do not always find the exact expression. Recently, for example, I wanted to tell my friend "you need a rest", but I did not really know how to say that. All I could think of was *"karada o yashinau ga hitsuyō"* (literally, "it's necessary to cultivate your body"), but you can't really say that to a friend. It's exaggerated.

(Female graduate student)

(2) My family is Japanese, and I was born in Tochigi. Like other prefectures, too, Tochigi has a dialect. But there is not such a strong accent in my hometown of Utsunomiya, and I find it quite easy to speak standard language. I do not speak dialect with my parents and neither with my friends.

(Female graduate student)

(3) I was born in San Francisco, because my father worked there at the time. My parents are Japanese. Both of my father's parents are from Kagoshima and both parents of my mother are from Fukushima. But my parents were born in Tokyo and grew up there. They therefore speak almost no dialect. Only my mother occasionally uses dialect when she speaks with her parents, that is, with my grandparents, because both speak Fukushima dialect. When I was two, we returned to Japan, and we first lived in Chiba. When I was four, we moved to Ibaraki, where we have been living ever since. When I was in elementary school, some people told me that I pronounced some words differently, and that I have an accent. I guess this was part of the Fukushima dialect. I then tried to speak as "normally" as possible, and so I lost this accent.

(Male undergraduate student)

(4) I was born in Tokyo and grew up in Chiba. My father is from Kyōto and my mother is from Tokyo. Since the city where we live is a sleeping town near Tokyo, there is no Chiba dialect there. My father sometimes speaks dialect, but my mother says that I speak without dialect and that my father did not take any influence on my language. I went to kindergarten and elementary school in Chiba, but went to Tokyo for middle school and high school. My classmates in middle and high school all came from Tokyo, Saitama, Kanagawa, Chiba and Ibaraki, but I think we always spoke without dialect.

(Female undergraduate student)

We find little exposure to or influences of dialects in the language lives of these students. If they have a language problem, it's more likely that it stems from

172   Patrick Heinrich

speaking too formally (1), or if dialect is involved, it is quickly settled for good (3). There may be a local dialect where one lives and grew up, but this dialect is spoken by others (2). It does not affect one's own life. Among peers, dialect has never been an option (1–4). If relatives occasionally speak dialect, it remains a rather detached and weak experience (4). The young generation is quite unique in these experiences, and as a matter of fact, all biographies I collected were quite similar in this respect. There was no "linguistic drama" in their lives.

In general, the young generation speaks Standard Japanese. In case they grew up in a more marginal geographical area such as Tōhoku or Kyūshū, they may remember some tokens of dialect (e.g., *nego*). For young Japanese, the standard language no longer indexes learnedness, erudition or modernity. Standard Japanese literally stands for nothing. All of their peers speak it. This constitutes a new problem because Standard Japanese is somewhat "dull" as the seminal Japanese sociolinguist Takesi Sibata (1999[1965]: 206)[6] already noted more than 50 years ago, describing it as "a coarse framework; its flavor is bland. If this is not so, it would be difficult for speakers of various languages and dialects to master [it]" which is why standard language "slims itself down to the bare minimum". It is the experience of speaking only a "coarse" and "slim" language and of never having experienced the anxiety of potential embarrassment that paves the way for the partial return of dialects in the form of dialect cosplay.

Dialect cosplay

Three things are required for dialect cosplay to emerge. Firstly, it necessitates a newfound appreciation of dialects. Speakers have to be free from the fear that using dialect is a potential cause of embarrassment. Secondly, dialect cosplay requires bits and pieces of knowledge about dialects (token knowledge). Thirdly, dialect cosplay requires knowledge about local stereotypes. Let us consider these three points in this order.

Appreciation of dialects

In a nation-wide survey conducted in 2010, informants were asked about their attitudes towards Standard Japanese and their local dialect (the place where they had live longest until the age of 15). They were asked to what extent they appreciated these two varieties. The survey yielded the following results.

The results displayed in Figure 11.1 have a number of important implications. To start, Tokyo aside, local dialects are more popular than Standard Japanese across Japan today. Secondly, the further the local dialect is linguistically distant from Standard Japanese, the more popular is it. Tōhoku, Shikoku and Kyūshū were regions where standardization efforts were particularly fervent, and standardization took longer to realize (see above). There is a simple pattern here. The more a dialect once had been stigmatized, the more popularity it enjoys today. Elements of dialects are thus used for pepping up standard language speech, but knowledge of dialect is scarce among the young.

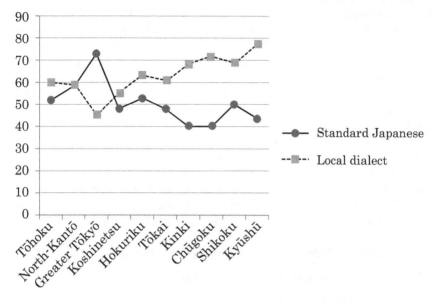

Figure 11.1 How much do you appreciate your dialect and the standard language?
Source: Adapted from Aizawa (2012: 30)

Remaining knowledge of dialects

Dialect proficiency has dropped considerably. As a rule, the younger the speaker, the lower their knowledge of dialects is, and the more pronounced they perceive the differences between standard and dialect (Sanada 1996). There is one exception to this pattern, namely Kansai. Japanese has two prestigious spoken varieties, namely that of Tokyo and that of Ōsaka/Kyōto. While Standard Japanese has been based on the Tokyo language, a standardization process also involves the *acceptance* of the codified standard (Haugen 1966). This acceptance and the subsequent linguistic behavior are not uniform in Japan. In Kansai, speakers never bought into the ideological claim that Standard Japanese was "correct" while the Kansai dialect was supposed to be "wrong". As a result, Kansai dialects were maintained in all informal domains and to some extent also in formal domains (Kumagai 2016). The Ōsaka dialect is more popular than the Tokyo dialect across Japan but for the Metropolitan region, and it is in particular popular with younger people (Sanada et al. 2007: 33–35). All of this implies that the processes of standardization and de-standardization evolve(d) differently in Kansai. To start, young speakers in Kansai have remained active speakers of the local dialect, and they also innovate their spoken language largely independently from Tokyo. Young people's language use in Kansai is then spreading into the neighboring prefectures. In other words, de-standardization in western parts of Japan draws to a considerable extent

174 Patrick Heinrich

on the Kansai dialect. Yasumizu (2014) shows how present-day youth language is diffusing more or less in concentric circles both from Tokyo and from Kansai. In Kansai, the city of Ōsaka serves as the center of diffusion, and older elements of youth language such as *makudo* (MacDonald's) have been spreading from there throughout the greater Kansai area (Ōsaka, Fukui, Nara, Wakayama, Kyōto, Hyōgo) and it is currently also replacing the Tokyo based *makku* also in Shiga, Mie and in all four prefectures of Shikoku Island. At the time of writing this chapter in summer 2017, MacDonald's Japan was actually showing this distribution on the paper mats that are placed on its plastic trays. The more recent Ōsaka youth language term *sebuire* (Seven Eleven), too, is also spreading throughout Kansai, but it has yet not reached Shikoku (Yasumizu 2014: 134).

Let us consider next an example of how dialect is used when dialect proficiency among the young is low, that is, everywhere outside Kansai. Sanada (2000: 127–128), for example, explains the return of the interjectory particle *-bē* in Tōhoku dialects among young speakers. Originally, this particle has three functions.

(1a) The particle indexes that the speaker is making a guess:

- *aitsu wa iku-bē* (I guess that guy went)

(2a) It is used to make a solicitation:

- *issho ni iku-bē* (will you go with me [please]?)

(3a) It is used to express an intention:

- *ashita koso iku-bē* (I will go tomorrow, too!)

While it has been noted that the particle *-bē* is seeing a comeback among younger speakers in the Tōhoku region, it has also become clear that the particle is used only in order to make a guess, as in (1a). This new use pattern of the dialect particle *-bē* can easily be explained when taking into consideration that the expression of guessing, on the one hand, and those of solicitations and intentions, on the other hand, have different inflections in Standard Japanese.

(1b) In order to make a guess, the volitional form of the copula is used:

- *aitsu wa iku darō* (I guess that guy went)

(2b) Solicitations are expressed by the volitional from of the verb:

- *issho ni ikō* (Will you go with me [please]?)

(3b) Intentions are also expressed by the volitional form of the verb:

- *ashita koso ikō* (I will go tomorrow, too!)

Young speakers' use of *-bē* corresponds to expression for (1a) only, because (2b) and (3b) use a different grammatical construction in Standard Japanese. In other words, young speakers insert the dialect feature *-bē* into their otherwise Standard

Dialect cosplay 175

Japanese repertoire. The dialect particle is not part of their mental language system (matrix language). It is simply an element inserted into an otherwise Standard Japanese utterance. Kinsui (2003), therefore, calls dialect particles used in this way *kyara gobi* ("character suffixes"), i.e., suffixes attached to standard language utterances in order to invoke or play a particular social role. Such use requires stereotypical knowledge about the speakers of various dialects.

Dialect and social stereotype

The use of character-invoking particles and inflections is not based on anybody's actual use of dialect. It is mimicking the language of dialect speakers. Such use of dialect implies crossing a line between one's bare self (*su no jibun*) in order to assume the role of somebody else. Due to the specific sociolinguistic profile of young Japanese speakers, nobody doubts their Standard Japanese proficiency when they engage in dialect cosplay. Hence, it involves no risk of embarrassment and no social stigma. Not much knowledge about local identities is required either, in order to leave one's bare standard language speaking self behind. Consider an inventory of dialect elements and the corresponding social stereotype among young speakers of Japanese.[7]

Table 11.1 illustrates (albeit in a simplified manner) how local stereotypes and some partial knowledge of dialects can be applied to stylize one's utterance. That is to say, any given utterance can be rendered "simple-minded", "naïve", "funny", "frightening" or extremely "manly" by just adding the respective *kyara gobi* at the end.

It is also a noteworthy fact that individuals engaging in dialect cosplay do not simply play with the regional dialect where they grew up, but that they may choose to use any Japanese dialect in order to assume a role. That is to say, dialect cosplay

Table 11.1 *Kayra gobi* and associated stereotypes

Region / Stereotype	Simple-minded (*suboku*)	Funny (*omoshiroi*)	Frightening (*kowai*)	Manly (*otokorashii*)
Tōhoku	-dabe, -dabesa, -ppeka, ndadomo			
Kansai		-yan, -yaro, -ja, -nandeyanen		
Chūgoku			-yake, -kee, -jaken	
Kyūshū				-ken, -tai, -desutai, -degowasu

Source: Adapted from Tanaka (2011: 17–18, 28)

176 *Patrick Heinrich*

is no longer simply a new way of indexing one's regional background. Dialect use has become layered, involving *nise hōgen* ("fake dialect") and what is called *jimo hōgen* ("homesick dialect").[8] "Fake dialect" refers to using a regional dialect with which one is not regionally associated, e.g., using elements of the Kansai dialect when you are actually from Kyūshū. The "homesick dialect", on the other hand, is engaging in dialect cosplay with one's home dialect. (This is what the AKB48 members did in the commercial). In particular, fake dialect strongly plays with regional stereotypes in order to stylistically pep up utterances (Tanaka 2011: 21–23). What is missing in the linguistic practices of the young generation is the "conventional" use of dialects – Kansai being the usual exception.

It has now become clear how much things have changed for the young generation. The difference between its employment of dialect and the conventional use of dialect is considerable. Recall that conventional dialect is "a form of a language spoken in a particular geographical area or by members of a particular social class or occupational group, distinguished by its vocabulary, grammar, and pronunciation", constituting thereby "a form of a language that is considered inferior" (Collins 2017). This definition only holds true for older generations in Japan. Young Japanese apply their fractured knowledge of dialects in order to stylize their utterances. This constitutes a new form of diversity that is the direct result of their language repertoire formation. While most Japanese from the older and middle generation acquired and use(d) dialect in private domains such as the family, among peers or in the neighborhood, the young generation has always used the standard language in these domains (Kansai aside). In a way, Standard Japanese is the "vernacular" of the young generation, the language they speak with the least effort. The older generation, and partly also the middle generation, added the standard language later in life, usually at school and at work. As a consequence, they are sometimes insecure about what is dialect and what is standard – or in their minds what is "wrong" and what is "correct" language use.

The young generation, on the other hand, picks up scattered elements of dialects through its rare and fleeting contacts with local speech. Young people's dialect cosplay is a manifestation of (1) using language in novel ways, but, what is more, it is also (2) exploring a novel way "of being someone through language". Language no longer gives the speaker away as it did in the past ("you speak dialect and are therefore not cultivated", or "you speak dialect X so you must be from the X region"). Young people in Japan have turned this principle on its head. They apply language in a way that allows them to take on specific roles and identities ("imagine me being from X and having the stereotypical characteristics of this place"). Playing a stereotypical role presupposes (fractured) knowledge of a regional code, but yet more crucially, it requires knowledge of how language is in the service of characterizing individuals. The young generation is savvy about how identities are constructed and what socially constructed identities do to individuals. They are reflexive.

New linguistic self-representations by the young generation

Dialect cosplay "crosses" into other people's language repertoires in order to evoke stereotypical images. The evocation of stereotypes is the reason why such

Dialect cosplay 177

kind of language use is never practiced in interactions with the "real speakers" of these varieties (Heinrich 2017). Dialect cosplay cannot be used in such situations, because it would be offensive to use a mock-version of *their language* in order to evoke social stereotypes. This principle ties dialect cosplay firmly to its users, i.e., to the young generation that grew up in the post-standardization society of the Heisei period. It makes dialect cosplay their "we-code", functioning as a linguistic demarcation line between the young generation and the older generations.

Dialect cosplay is the young generation's strategy for being "linguistically diverse" despite having grown up "linguistically uniform". They could have been diverse in many other ways, though. The young generation could have relied simply on its very own linguistic innovations (youth language) or on the incorporation of non-Japanese elements (e.g., English, Korean, Chinese). It is a noteworthy fact that young Japanese chose to draw so heavily on Japanese dialects, i.e., on varieties that were once heavily stigmatized and carried with them the danger of social marginalization and exclusion. As a matter of fact, research on attitudes towards dialects by Tanaka and Maeda (2012), and others, always point to a high popularity of dialects that have once been severely suppressed (e.g. Tōhoku and Kyūshū). It is, therefore, only logical that the least popular dialect for the young generation is that of Tokyo (see Figure 11.1). The language of powerful social actors is out, because power is uncool, and young speakers seek to speak in cool ways (Maher 2005). The practioners of dialect cosplay do not simply use language in novel ways – they purposefully "break the code". They feel empowered by doing so. Dialect cosplay is not simply about fun (*goraku*). Dialect is not merely becoming a toy (*omocha-ka*) or an accessory (*akusesorī-ka*), as Tanaka (2007) believes. Dialect cosplay is also a rejection of the values and attitudes that accompanied language standardization – attitudes, to recall, that discredited the varied ways of speaking Japanese and placed a stigma on non-standard speakers.

We have seen above that those engaging in dialect cosplay have mastered the art of linguistically doing things the "legitimate way", i.e., of using Japanese according to standardized norms. Young speakers' deviance from these norms through acts of transgression makes these norms visible. It reveals their metapragmatic knowledge about the way "things are getting done with language" in Japan, that is, it reveals an awareness that the legitimate language is in the service of power. This metapragmatic knowledge sets the young apart from older speakers of Japanese. The latter, to recall, have been and often remain insecure about "speaking correctly", and they are firm in the belief that some ways of speaking are "correct" while others are "wrong". Their linguistic behavior testifies to such beliefs day in and day out. It is this attitude and the countless code-choices that resulted from such attitudes that resulted in the language standardization process in the first place. The young generation, on the other hand, is critical of how language is employed in order to exercise authority. They break the code – and enjoy doing so – because it is a symbol of power and a tool of dominance of the strong over the weak. Born on the shorter end of the power divide, in a society where the older generations are privileged over the young generation, the young have grown sensitive to such inequalities.

178   *Patrick Heinrich*

The "feel for the game" of talking and texting Japanese has changed. The old relation is contested, not explicitly ("I do not approve"), but implicitly through linguistic deviances and transgressions. The exercise of hiding one's regional and social background through the use of standard language has been replaced by a practice where the ability to be quirky, fast and innovative is supreme. In a word, it has been replaced by an ability to be cool and to speak in cool ways (Maher 2005). For young speakers, plurality, variety, contingency and ambivalence have taken the place once occupied by universality, homogeneity, monotony, and clarity in language.

The relation between language, identity, and authority is no longer fixed and solid. Terms like "new dialect" (Inoue 2008) and "neo-dialect" (Sanada 1997) do not capture what is at stake in the use of dialect elements by young speakers. The young generation has moved beyond the stage of new dialects and neo-dialects. The everyday common language of young Japanese today is a "relaxed" use of (Standard) Japanese that is stylistically "pepped up" with dialect elements. Such use is not a new linguistic system – as terms like "new dialect" and "neo-dialect" suggest – it is a new linguistic practice stemming from new and critical attitudes towards language and identity. Dialect cosplay is not a fixed speech repertoire shared in a given community. It is a verbal style that is based on language attitudes that are widely shared among young Japanese due to their unique position in Japan's sociolinguistic history.

What has really changed for the young generation is the presentation of self through language. Consider what Erving Goffman had to say about self-representation:

> When an individual enters the presence of others, they will commonly seek to acquire information about him or to bring into play information about him already possessed. They will be interested in his general socio-economic status, his conception of self, his attitudes towards them, his competence, his trustworthiness, etc. [. . .] Information about the individual helps to define the situation, enabling others to know in advance what he will expect of them and what they may expect of him.
>
> (Goffman 1959: 13)

Young Japanese enjoy flouting this mechanism of social coexistence outlined by Goffman. They do so for two reasons. Firstly, the language in which they were socialized no longer indexes anything (except for Kansai). Standard Japanese says nothing about social background or trustworthiness in an informal setting, but is socially empty. Secondly, young Japanese are critical of power and symbolic violence, as is obvious from their use of once heavily stigmatized dialect elements. They reject the mechanism through which some were silenced, made uncomfortable or insecure on the basis of their divergence from language norms. According to Goffman's theory of individuals as social actors, people seek to be coherent by playing the appropriate role for specific contexts and tasks. By employing dialect cosplay, however, young Japanese purposefully act "incoherently" in linguistic

Dialect cosplay 179

interaction (Heinrich 2017). What is more, they are conscious thereof. They embrace "anti-roles" and "anti-language" as a means to distance themselves from the dominant norms and expectations. This is a clear break with the practices of those born before the Heisei period.

Young Japanese speakers in super-aging Japan

This book seeks to explore whether those born in the Heisei period have made unique experiences, and whether they have come up with distinctive cultural and emotional responses. Language undoubtedly constitutes such a unique and generation-specific experience. Language reinforces the boundary between the young generation and those born before them. Practices such as dialect cosplay and the language attitudes that undergird them are distinctive. The young generation is engaged, active, and creative, and it is so in new and unconventional ways. They are re-working and re-using existing materials, images, attitudes, stereotypes and varieties – they are *bricoleurs* of language, and they are so whole-heartedly. Linguistically, they are not driven by ambition ("Speak well!" or "Be someone!"), but by a desire to be quirky and cool. They embrace and rework dialects once regarded as odd and embarrassing. They are not embracing English in order to inform the world about Japan, as official language policy encourages them to do (Liddicoat 2013: 49–59). The young are not consumed by ambition. They have little choice, though. The modernist dream of ever more progress is largely absent in their lives. Japan has been stagnating for as long as they have lived.

For young Japanese, getting along in post-growth and super-aging Japan means having smaller dreams and making the best from what is available to them (Furichi 2011). Being young in a super-aging society makes them feel distant from the modernist dreams of their parents and grandparents. At the same time, this super-aging, former Number One society leaves them abundant material to engage with in their very own ways and with their very own set of attitudes. Metaphorically speaking, Japan is like an abandoned wardrobe and young Japanese enjoy exploring its content with an aloofness and coolness that is new. We can see this in the way they recycle language in order to put it into new uses, citing and quoting from a world they know quite well from school, TV, or accounts of older family members. But this is also a world to which they have never belonged. Young Japanese know this very well. They are conscious about this generational divide. This becomes most evident by the fact that they are "playing" to be part of it.

Notes

1 Online at: www.youtube.com/channel/UCwmCgpZW-hEiMkBZWud1k7A (accessed 24 February 2017).
2 Before language modernization, spoken language was inevitably "dialect". It is therefore of little surprise to find that the concept of *hyōjungo* (standard language) predates that of *hōgen* (dialect) in Japan.
3 An analysis of the *Linguistic Atlas of Japan* (Kokuritsu Kokugo Kenkyūjo 1966–1974) reveals that only 62% of the Tokyo dialect vocabulary surveyed corresponded exactly to

180   *Patrick Heinrich*

that of Standard Japanese. This number stood at 41% for Osaka and 16% for Kagoshima at the start of the language standardization process.

4 Hokkaidō as a settlement colony and the Ryūkyū Islands where the Ryukyuan languages were displaced differ in various ways from this situation and will not be discussed further here (see Hirayama and Ono 1997 on Hokkaidō, and Anderson 2015 on the Ryūkyūs).

5 Sibata Takesi, who had been pushing for the relaxation of standard language norms, (1999[1965]: 201) made clear that this was an important issue if democracy was to take root, writing that "[t]he basis of democracy is discussion. Discussion means using words. It was impossible to have a fair discussion with one person being quite because of his dialect, and another spouting off just because he can speak Standard Language."

6 Some Japanese scholars prefer the *kunrei*-style transcription of their names. Their choices are respected in the text and the list of references.

7 Playing roles through language includes also playing the role of foreign speakers of Japanese by, e.g., adding *aruyo* and the end of an utterance in order to invoke the image of a Chinese speaker of Japanese. Note that such use is often outright racist and is for instance used by extreme right wing groups who add *-nida* (from Korean verb inflection *-mnida*) to statements in order to ridicule or degrade ethnic Koreans in Japan or those sympathetic to them.

8 *Jimo* is a clipped form of *jimoto de asobu*, i.e., "having a good time in your hometown". It is used as a fixed expression when students studying in big cities go back home in order to have a good time there, enjoying food, nature, or hot springs. The advantage of going back home usually also implies that all of this is free of cost. When out of money but in need of spending a good time, *jimoto asobi* is a popular strategy among young Japanese.

References

Aizawa, Masao (2012) Hōgen ishiki no ima o toraeru: 2010-nen zenkoku hōgen ishiki chōsa to tōkei bunseki [Research on Present-Day Dialect Consciousness. Nationwide Survey in 2010 and its Statistical Analyses] *Kokugoken purojekuto rebyū* 3(1): 26–37.

Anderson, Mark (2015) Substrate-Influenced Japanese and Code-Switching. In: *Handbook of the Ryukyuan Languages*. Patrick Heinrich, Shinsho Miyara and Michinori Shimoji (eds.), 481–509. Boston: Mouton de Gruyter.

Bakhtin, Mikhail (1987) *The Dialogic Imagination* (edited and translated by Michael Holquist and Caryl Emerson). Austin: University of Texas Press.

Bourdieu, Pierre (1991) *Language and Symbolic Power*. Cambridge: Polity Press.

Collins (2017) *Free Online Dictionary*. Online available at: www.collinsdictionary.com (accessed 21 April 2017).

Furuichi, Noritoshi (2011) *Zetsubō no kuni no kōfuku na wakamono-tachi* [The Happy Youth of a Desperate Country]. Tokyo: Kōdansha.

Goffman, Erving (1959) *The Presentation of Self in Everyday Life*. London: Penguin Books.

Haugen, Einar (1966) Dialect, Language, Nation. *American Anthropologist* 68: 922–935.

Heinrich, Patrick (2012) *The Making of Monolingual Japan: Language Ideology and Japanese Modernity*. Bristol: Multilingual Matters.

——— (2017) New Presentations of Self in Everyday Life: Linguistic Transgressions in England, Germany and Japan. In: *Identity and Dialect Performance: A Study of Communities and Dialects*. Reem Bassiouney (ed.), 381–407. London: Routledge.

Heinrich, Patrick and Rika Yamashita (2017) Tokyo: Standardization, Ludic Language Use and Nascent Superdiversity. In: *Urban Sociolinguistics*. Dick Smakman and Patrick Heinrich (eds.), 130–147. London: Routledge.

Dialect cosplay 181

Hirayama, Teruo and Yone'ichi Ono (1997) *Hokkaidō no kotoba* [Language of Hokkaidō]. Tokyo: Meiji Shoin.

Hokama, Shuzen (1971) *Okinawa no gengoshi* [Okinawa's Language History]. Tokyo: Hōsei Daigaku Shuppan.Inoue, Fumio (2008) *Shakai hōgengaku ronkō: Shin-hōgen no kiban* [Studies in Social Dialectology: Foundations of New Dialects]. Tokyo: Meiji Shoin.

—— (2011) Standardization and De-Standardization in Spoken Japanese. In: *Language Life in Japan*. Patrick Heinrich and Christian Galan (eds.), 109–123. London: Routledge.

Jugaku, Akiko (1978) Hyōjungo no mondai [Standard Language Problem]. In: *Iwanami kōza nihongo* (volume 3). Ei'ichi Chino (ed.), 52–55. Tokyo: Iwanami.

Kinsui, Satoshi (2003) *Vācharu nihongo – yakuwarigo no nazo* [Virtual Japanese: The Mysteries of Role Language]. Tokyo: Iwanami.

Kokuritsu Kokugo Kenkyūjo (1966–1974) *Nihon gengo chizu* [Linguistic Atlas of Japan]. Tokyo: Ōkurashō Insatsukyoku.

—— (2013) *Dai-4-kai Tsuruoka-shi ni okeru gengo chōsa kekka to gaiyō* [Results and Overview of the 4th Language Survey in Tsuruoka City]. Tokyo: Kokuritsu Kokugo Kenkyūjo.

Kumagai, Yasuo (2016) Developing the Linguistic Atlas of Japan Database and Advancing Analysis of Geographical Distributions of Dialects. In: *The Future of Dialects*. Marie-Hélène Côté, Remco Knooihuizen and John Nerbonne (eds.), 333–362. Berlin: Language Science Press.

Liddicoat, Anthony J. (2013) *Language-in-Education Policies: The Discursive Construction of Intercultural Relations*. Bristol: Multilingual Matters.

Maher, John (2005) Metroethnicty, Language, and the Principle of Cool. *International Journal of the Sociology of Language* 175/176: 83–102.

Masiko, Hidenori (2003) *Ideorogī to shite no "nihon"* ["Japan" as Ideology]. Tokyo: Sangensha.

Nomura, Takashi (2013) *Nihongo sutandādo no rekishi* [History of Standard Japanese]. Tokyo: Iwanami.

Sanada, Shinji (1996) Shiga-ken Imazu-machi, Fukui-ken Kaminaka-machi gengo chōsa hōkoku [Shiga Prefecture, Imazu-Town and Fukui Prefecture, Kamakura-City Language Survey Report]. *Ōsaka daigaku bungakubu kiyō* 36: 31–64.

—— (1997) *Nishi-nihon ni okeru neo-hōgen no jittai ni kansuru chōsa kenkyū* [Empirical Research on the State of Neo-Dialects in Western Japan]. Ōsaka: Ōsaka University.

—— (2000) *Datsu-hyōjungo no jidai* [The Age of De-Standardization]. Tokyo: Shōgakukan Bunko.

—— (2001) *Hyōjungo no seiritsu jijō* [Circumstances How Standard Japanese Was Formed]. Tokyo: PHP Bunko.

Sanada, Shinji et al. (2007) *Hōgen no kinō* [The Functions of Dialects]. Tokyo: Iwanami.

Shioda, Takehiro (2011) Constraints in Language Use in Public Broadcast. In: *Language Life in Japan*. Patrick Heinrich and Christian Galan (eds.), 124–139. London: Routledge.Sibata, Takesi (1999 [1965]) The Advent of the Age of Common Language and the Fate of Dialects. In: *Takesi Sibata: Sociolinguistics in Japanese Contexts*. Tetsuya Kunihiro, Fumio Inoue and Daniel Long (eds.), 196–206. Berlin: Mouton de Gruyter.

Tanaka, Yukari (2007) *Chakudatsu sareru "zokusei" – hōgen "omocha-ka" genshō* [Distinctive Features Put On and Off. Dialect Decoming a Toy Phenomenon]. Online available at: http://skinsui.cocolog-nifty.com/sklab/files/JASS19tanaka.pdf (accessed 12 April 2017).

—— (2011) *Hōgen kosupure no jidai* [The Age of Dialect Cosplay]. Tokyo: Iwanami.

182 Patrick Heinrich

Tanaka, Yukari, Naoki Hayashi, Tadahiko Maeda and Masao Aizawa (2016) *Ichiman-nin kara mita saishin no hōgen, kyōtsūgo ishiki* [Latest Trends in Nationwide Language Consciousness and Standard Language of 10,000 People]. Tokyo: NINJAL.

Tanaka, Yukari and Tadahiko Maeda (2012) Washa bunrui ni motozuku chi'iki ruikei no kokoromi [Regional Typology Based on Individual-level Clustering of Dialect Usage]. *Kokuritsu kokugo kenkyūjo ronshū* 3: 117–142.

Wikipedia (2016) *Hōgen konpurekkusu* [Dialect Complex]. Online available at: https://ja.wikipedia.org/wiki/方言コンプレックス (accessed 5 April 2017).

Yasumizu, Kanetaka (2014) "Zenkoku wakamonogo chōsa" ni okeru gengo denpa moderu [Language Diffusion Model in the "Nationwide Youth Language Survey"]. In: *Shutoken gengo no kenkyū shiya*. Harumi Mitsui (ed.), 129–151. Tokyo: NINJAL.

12 No family, no school

Young people in literature by young Japanese writers

Dan Fujiwara

Introduction

Some 20 novels, all written by young authors who were under the age of 20 at the time, have won literary awards such as the Bungei, Bungakukai, Gunzō Shinjin Bungaku or the well-known Akutagawa Prize since the late 1970s in Japan. The primary aim of these awards, whose jury is composed of highly influential writers and critics, is, as we know, to reward new talents in order to prepare them for a successful career.[1] Many writers who are today well-established and highly active on the Japanese literary scene are former recipients of these awards. Examples include Murakami Haruki (the Gunzō Shinjin Bungaku Prize for *Kaze no uta o kike, Hear the Wind Sing*, 1979), Murakami Ryū (the Akutagawa Prize for *Kagirinaku tōmei no chikai buru, Almost Transparent Blue*, 1976), or Ogawa Yōko (the Akutagawa Prize for *Ninshin karendā, Pregnancy Calendar*, 1990).

Nevertheless, it was not until the late 1970s that an author under the age of 20 received any of these awards. In 1978, the jury of the 21st Gunzō Shinjin Bungaku Prize rewarded Nakazawa Kei (born 1959), then an 18-year-old high school student, for a novel entitled *Umi o kanjiru toki* (*When I Sense the Sea*, 1978).[2] The awarding of such an important literary prize to a teenage girl was a major literary event, and it caused the novel to become a great commercial success.[3] Published as a book by Kōdansha immediately after it had appeared in the June 1978 issue of the literary magazine *Gunzō, Umi o kanjiru toki* sold in a single year more than 600,000 copies. In 2014, the novel was adapted for the screen by Japanese director Andō Hiroshi.

Nakazawa Kei's novel is not an isolated case. In that same year, Matsuura Rieko (born 1958) was awarded the 47th Bungakukai Shinjin Prize. In the 1980s, three teenagers received awards, with three more being crowned in the following decade. The period from 2000 to 2009 was exceptional because altogether 13 prizes, including the Akutagawa Prize, went to 12 novels whose authors were under 20 at the time.[4] Note also in this context, that no teenage author has been awarded any of these literary prizes since 2009 at the time of writing this chapter.

In the following, I examine the practice of awarding prizes to such young authors, focusing in particular on the extraordinary events between 2000 and 2009. The aim is thereby not to comment on the link between literary maturity

184   *Dan Fujiwara*

and the age of a given author. The primary reason for addressing this subject is to simply examine these novels from a narrative perspective, since the central characters in most of these works are teenagers.[5] Of course, the theme of adolescence has always attracted Japanese novelists, but it should be noted that these authors were *already adults* and often well established when they published works on this topic. In short, their approach to teenagers was clearly nostalgic. Today, probably for the first time in the history of contemporary Japanese literature, there is a relatively large number of works featuring literary self-portraits of adolescence, where teenagers portray themselves, using their own words. What then are the features that these young authors put to the fore when they talk about people of their own age? What are the words they use to depict themselves? What kind of discourses can we read in these words? What differences exist between the representation of teenagers by these young authors, who were children and teenagers in the late 1980s, and that of the works by authors from previous generations? This chapter seeks to clarify these issues by studying a corpus of literature written by young authors (see Appendix).[6]

Given the age of the characters depicted in the novels examined here, attention needs to be placed on the importance of the family and of school. Family and school are generally managed by parents and teachers, in short by adults, but they also exist *for* children and might be the principal structure of their everyday life – at least until they become morally and financially autonomous. Given the generational differences that characterize family and school, these are places of transmission where conflicts between generations are often inevitable.

It may appear appropriate to analyze the fundamentally antagonistic relationship between young people and adults in the family and the school. However, while examining the corpus, it soon became clear that such an approach would not be fruitful. Family and school appear to not matter. Consider an example. Emiko, the main character of Nakazawa Kei's *Umi o kanjiru toki* (*When I Sense the Sea*), says in 1978:

> My mother was intelligent; too intelligent even. I trusted her and hated her at the same time. I was hungry for a bestial affection, the kind of physical warmth that animals produce by rubbing each other. Even high school did not fill this feeling of emptiness. This group life in which young people gathered together and expended their energy on, was merely a picture of the youth of ten years ago.
>
> (Nakazawa 1978: 17, translation mine)

As I will illustrate in the following, the novels written by the youngest authors examined in this chapter (who are part of the generation that has been educated by the generation to which Nakazawa Kei belongs) acknowledge the feelings of emptiness and frustration expressed by Emiko. They even assign such feelings to the past. They reveal, however, that a feeling of antipathy today no longer shapes the relationship developed by the adolescent characters with adults, but that these relationships are characterized by a general indifference, difficulty, or even impossibility of having confrontations with adults. The question with which we are faced when studying our corpus is not "how do adolescents face the adult world", but rather "how do adolescents exist and act in a society where inter-generational conflicts no longer exist".

Family breakdown: the failure of parents as married couples

Although teenagers are quite autonomous in various aspects, they nevertheless depend on their parents, in particular financially. Even in the realm of fiction, it is impossible to analyze representations of adolescence without taking into account the ambiguous relationship that teenagers have with their parents. This relationship is characterized by limited autonomy and partial dependence, with one of these aspects being the consequence of the other.

First of all, it should be noted that, perhaps surprisingly, most of the adolescent characters featured in the corpus of young literature appears to be largely uncon-cerned with parents. In fact, in about ten works (that is, exactly half of the corpus), parents do not appear as characters in the narrative at all. They live separately from their children and are merely mentioned in passing by the narrator or the fictional adolescent characters. For example, the main character, who is also the first-person narrator of *Sōgi no hi* (*Funeral Day*, 1978) by Matsuura Rieko (born 1958), states:

> By the way, we don't know much about the privacy of people who work as "weepers or laughers of funerals". Is it a hereditary profession?
> I said to myself: "I have already told you! I chose this job myself! No one imposed it on me. I don't know much about my parents. I believe they did the same job, but it's none of my business".
> (Matsuura 1993: 27, translation mine)

In a similar vein, Lui, the main character and first-person narrator of *Hebi ni piasu* (*Snakes and Earrings*, 2003) by Kanehara Hitomi (born 1983), says the following in reply to a question by her boyfriend:

> "So Lui *is* your real name. How about family? Do you have any parents?"
> "People always assume I'm an orphan, but yes, I do have parents. They live in Saitama."
> (Kanehara 2006: 109–110, translated by Karashima)

It is important to stress that the lack of interest that is so obvious in these utterances does not stem from negative feelings toward the parents. In these particular examples, the two female characters, despite being teenagers, are already earning a living and enjoy material autonomy, and this may justify such a vague account of their rela-tionship with their parents. It is equally true that other characters in the corpus, who show little interest in their parents even when living with them, express no antipathy towards them, neither explicitly nor implicitly. Parents simply do not matter.

186 Dan Fujiwara

In the other half of the corpus, where parents appear as characters and influence the narrative development, they no longer function as a married couple due to separation, divorce, or other problems that divide them. And this is precisely what constitutes the general background of all these works, especially those published between 2000 and 2009. At this point, it is necessary to take a closer look at the social consequences of these circumstances. That is to say, we need to examine the life of the adolescent characters as being systematically contextualized by a single-parent family model in which the figure of the mother is prominent.

The first such exemplifying this trend is *Shiruetto* (*Silhouette*, 2001) by Shimamoto Rio (born 1983). The novel tells the story of an impossible love between two teenagers, in which the heroine, whose father "completely disappeared when she reached the age of reason" (Shimamoto 2004: 28), lives with her mother. Although the family, in its conventional meaning, has broken down, the heroine has no particular conflict with her mother. Rather, the mother is simply "occupied with her work" and "lets her daughter do what she wants" (Shimamoto 2004: 28). The family drama, if it exists, can be seen in the life of a classmate with whom the heroine falls in love. This notwithstanding, even the classmate's family drama is depicted through anecdotes, without affecting the development of the main narrative. Shimamoto's novel is an instructive example of the essential nature of the relationship that the generally female, adolescent character develops with her mother – the bond between the two female characters definitively remains, for better or worse, indissoluble.

This strong bond between two females varies from one novel to the other. However, when we read the corpus from a chronological point of view, there is a clear evolution in the nature of this bond. In her 1978 novel, *When I Sense the Sea*, Nakazawa Kei described the relationship between the heroine and her mother in the following terms:

> My mother can only cling to me as I do to her. She thinks that such a situation occurred because of me, and I expect her to have a more human affection. But we must remain dependent on one another. My mother finds her own daughter both precious and vulgar without being able to manage these contradictory feelings. I see in her both a woman who humiliates me, and a mother who persists in protecting me.
>
> (Nakazawa 1978: 127–128, translation mine)

This conflictual relationship between mother and daughter – presented here as inescapable – can also be seen in *Mizericōdo* (*Mercy*, 2000) by Īzuka Asami (born 1983). In Īzuka's novel, the heroine and first-person narrator depicts her life as entirely devoted to the prayers she recites with her mother in a chapel that she (and her mother) inherited from the mother's parents. The narrative evokes an unfortunate family past. The heroine's aunt, that is, the older sister of the mother, gave birth to a mentally handicapped girl. She then left the family, abandoning her baby to the heroine's mother, and this caused the mother to adopt a much more religious life, something that the father was unable to bear. It caused the end of

No family, no school 187

the parental relationship. Recalling the period when her father left the family, the heroine says:

> I had to make a decision. Should I follow my father or my mother? Of course, I would have liked to live with my father rather than with this fanatical woman who spoke to her own daughter using polite forms of speech. However, I dared to stay with this woman. I had already been baptized. Even if it was carried out without my will, I vaguely resigned myself to the idea that this sacrament compelled me to live my life as a servant of God. That is why I had to choose an existence that consisted in living and dying while devoting myself to prayer like my mother. Having heard my decision, my father nodded and left the house the next day.
>
> (Īzuka 2000: 61–62, translation mine)

Why did the heroine make such a contradictory choice, even when it conflicted with her true feelings? Is it, as the novel's name suggests, in order to obtain "mercy", because she hoped to save her mentally handicapped cousin? Whatever the case may be, this novel illustrates through its extreme characters the two main interrelated features that characterize all works in the corpus – the disappearance of the father and the indissolubility of the mother-daughter bond. What appears to be new in comparison to Nakazawa's novel, however, is the fact that the heroine establishes a significant distance from her mother by referring to her using an honorific suffix -*san*, which in Standard Japanese is used to refer to people outside the family or outside intimate relationships. Thus, the mothers who appear in the novels published between 2000 and 2009 are discreet and observant figures, but do not take part in the main narrative. As a matter of fact, they are often not aware what their daughters are doing. This is also the case in another novel by Shimamoto, *Ritoru bai ritoru* (*Little by Little*, 2006) and in *Insutōru* (*Install*, 2001) by Wataya Risa.

Despite this markedly feminine dimension of the parent-child relationship seen in the corpus examined here, the father is not totally absent. However, when he emerges in the narrative, he does so as a disappearing figure. In the late 1980s, *Kawaberi no michi* (*The Road along the River*, 1987) by Sagisawa Megumu (1968–2004) already demonstrated this paradoxical presence of the father. Gorō, a 15-year-old schoolboy, lives with Tokiko, his 23-year-old stepsister by a different mother. Although they have already lost their respective mothers, their father barely bonds the two young people together. He no longer lives with them either, having settled elsewhere with his mistress. Thus, the father-child relationship is reduced to a financial one. Gorō visits his father every month to receive money.

Here, it should be noted that although the relationships between parents and children might become conflicting, it is as if the adolescent characters wanted to avoid or ignore any risk or potential confrontation with their parents. What is the consequence of this kind of pseudo conflict? One answer to this question can be found in Minami Natsu's (born 1990) novel *Heisei mashinganzu* (*Heisei Machine Guns*, 2005). At the beginning of the narrative, tension develops between Tomomi,

188   *Dan Fujiwara*

a 15-year-old schoolgirl who is the first-person narrator, and her father, who has little interest in his daughter's life and who gradually introduces his mistress into the house following the departure of his wife (from whom he is separated but not yet divorced). The heroine has complex feelings towards her father. They are mingled with disappointment and frustration. To add, she is haunted by the figure of the Demon (*shinigami*) that appears in her dreams. Having become the target of "bullying" at school due to her family situation, the heroine no longer visits school and seeks to convince her mother to return home. However, the mother accepts neither this idea of her daughter's nor that of a divorce. She remains determined to live alone. Thus, the heroine changes school and learns to accept her father's double life. Everything happens as if each of them – the father, the mother, and the daughter – continued along their own path without trying to face each other.

In his 1994 book, Kawamura Minato (born 1951), one of Japan's most influential literary critics, formulated the subsequent hypothesis on the trend of broken families in contemporary works of literature:

> Japanese literature between the 1980s and the 1990s shifts the center of gravity of its main features from family breakdown to the feelings of orphans. Family disintegration and the isolation of the individual must not merely be the themes of future literary works but rather the premises.
>
> (Kawamura 1994: 223, translation mine)

More than 20 years have passed since the publication of these lines, which commented on works of Yoshimoto Banana (born 1964) and Shimada Masahiko (born 1961), among others. Indeed, "family breakdown" and "orphan feelings" have become a standard topic of Japanese literature today. The novels of the corpus examined here are no exception to this trend. However, what is different, and new, in the case of our corpus is that the young fictional characters are not simply talking about family breakdown, but more particularly about their parents' failures as married couples. What is most evident in the works published from 2000 to 2009 is the fact that the parents are not portrayed as a unitary generation, i.e., as parents. The parents are more individualized, encouraging the adolescents, due to the complicated circumstances, to find other solutions than the conventional confrontation with their parents. In this prototypical sense, parents no longer exist.

Friends first?

Like family, school is a place whose main function is barely described in the works of literature in our corpus. In half of them, school is never mentioned, and when it is, it is simply evoked to characterize the social status of adolescent characters as high school students. School rarely functions as a place where the narrative's main events take place. Given such a context, it is no surprise to find that teachers do not appear as elaborated, fully described characters either. Their narrative function is secondary at best, if they are not entirely absent. Just like the

No family, no school 189

parents, the teachers act as mirrors to the indifference felt by adolescents to issues of generational difference and to questions of authority. The absence of teachers as characters in the narrative, or their purely functional presence as symbols of indifference, is counterbalanced by the importance of the relationships established by the adolescent characters with their peers in school or outside school. Actually, the majority of narratives center on friendly, affective or antagonistic relations between classmates.

From this point of view, *Kirishima bukatsu yamerutte yo* (*Kirishima Is Quitting the Club*, 2009) by Asai Ryō (born 1989)[7] is a key example for this trend.[8] In reading this novel, it becomes apparent that peer relationships at school are not merely the narrative subject, but that this relationship influences the very organization of the narrative itself. This novel is composed of six chapters, and each of the chapters is named after one of the characters and narrated from their point of view.[9] In so doing, the novel provides for six different perceptions of one and the same event, namely the fact that their classmate Kirishima is quitting the volleyball club. Each chapter deals with one episode that often has no direct link to the main event. The main event, announced solely in the title of the novel, is not dealt with in any chapter. The narrative is structured in such a way as to lead the reader to gradually imagine the peers' relationships. These take on a variety of different forms, ranging from sympathy, rivalry, love, and friendship to indifference. The primary interest of this narrative structure is not necessarily to describe the event (the departure of the captain of the volleyball team), but to reveal the network of classmates.

Let us next consider the gender of the five narrators of this novel. While three of the narrators are boys, who describe episodes focused on peer relationships, the other two are girls, who deal with entirely unrelated subjects. One relates her failure in love, and the other one to the depression of her stepmother, who lost her husband and daughter in a car accident. This difference between male and female narrators, while seemingly stereotyped, is a core theme shaping all novels of the young authors examined here. In reading the novels, we find that the male narrators are generally interested in peer relations, whereas female narrators tend to distance themselves from classmates and explore themes of love or family problems (such as the father-mother relationship discussed above). Thus, the heroines of the novels by Wataya Risa (born 1984) and Minami Natsu (born 1990) are lonely and refuse to go to school in order to avoid frequenting their peers – in other words, in order to avoid other girls. Hatsumi, the heroine of *Keritai senaka* (*I Want to Kick You in the Back*, 2003) by Wataya Risa, says:

> I hate being a leftover, but I hate being part of a group even more. Once you're caught up in one you have no choice but to patch yourself into it, and that's a sorry thing to have to do. I was in a group in middle school, and it was suffocating. Having to gossip incessantly, forces yourself to get excited over things you couldn't care less about, and cling to boring subjects just to keep the chatter going . . . just ten minutes of that felt like an eternity.
>
> (Wataya 2015: 25, translated by Karashima)

190   Dan Fujiwara

Hatsumi does not fit in at school, and she struggles to find her place through her studies or through her relationships with classmates. She is more interested in her classmate Ninagawa, not because he is a passionate *otaku* of a very popular female singer, Ori-chan, but because he can accept his loneliness by reading women's magazines during class. Intimate relationships, when they are tackled in the narrative, in particular by female characters, tend to remain alone just like Hatsumi being fascinated by Ninagawa's perfect loneliness or to revolve around relationships with young adults rather than peers. This is also very clearly the case in the novels of Shimamoto Rio discussed above.

There is a very clear difference between the relationships that are created by boys, and those created by girls. Boys remain inside the school system, whereas girls remain outside, lock themselves up at home – or, although rarely, explore the outside and adult world. It needs to be emphasized here that the peer relations developed by young male characters are established almost exclusively between boys.[10] Ultimately, school hardly constitutes a shared space for boys and girls. Encounters between the two sexes do not occur there.

Failed escapes, or another strategy for becoming a teenager?

Addressing the Japanese youth of his day, Terayama Shūji (1935–1983) repeated his *iede no susume* ("encouragement to run away from home") from the 1960s to the 1970s. From 1963 onwards, the charismatic artist began to launch this provocative appeal, and he varied it in different forms such as essays, poems, plays or films.[11] His famous theatrical company *Tenjō sajiki* (Ceiling Gallery), which was created with young people having fled from their family and school, is one of the outcomes of this avant-garde artistic movement. Terayama's work combined youth, artistic imagination and the act of running away from home. For adolescents in present-day Japan, at least those described in the novels of our young authors, this slogan no longer makes much sense. Note in passing that *iede no susume* is also an excellent caricature of Fukuzawa Yukichi's (1835–1901) *Gakumon no susume* (*An Encouragement of Learning*, 1872–1876).

Despite not being part of Terayama's generation, we find in our corpus a number of adolescents, who either run away from home or who stop going to school. *Sakana no yō ni* (*Like a Fish*, 1991) by Nakawaki Hatsue (born 1974) is an example thereof. The novel depicts the feelings of a young male narrator who leaves his house, going up a river to find out why his older sister left home. However, in most cases the adolescent characters run away for such a brief period of time that their absence at home hardly matters. Even though it is clear that our adolescent characters do not want to stay at home nor at school, they have other ways to deal with this unwillingness. They hang around, finding places to stay for a more or less short period of time, rather than breaking up with their family or abandoning school completely.

We can see in the works published before 2000 that some characters go to quite distant places. However, these journeys almost systematically lead to a dead end.

No family, no school   191

For example, Nakazawa's heroine follows her boyfriend to Tokyo in the hopes of having a child with him. However, she returns to her mother already after a few weeks. Yūichi, the main character-narrator of *She's Rain* (1984)[12] by Hiranaka Yūichi (born 1965), travels to Kōbe for a romantic date with one of his classmates, but he ultimately decides to not pursue a relationship with her on the pretext that he does not want to force her to commit to him.

In the works published from 2000 to 2009, it is clear that attempts of running away are shorter and less ambitious from the outset. In Wataya's *I Want to Kick You in the Back*, the main character Hatsumi only goes to the house of a classmate whose parents are absent. Asako, the heroine of *Install* (2001), another work by the same author, decides not to go to school and spends her days in a large fitted-wardrobe of a neighbor's apartment to manage, along with a 12-year-old boy, a pornographic conversation website. The heroine of Shimamoto's *Silhouette* visits her boyfriend's apartment every week, whereas the main character-narrator of Kanehara's *Snakes and Earrings* moves in with her boyfriend Ama, after being seduced by the tip of his tongue which "was clearly split in two like that of a snake" (Kanehara 2006 1). Our teenage characters also explore other places, including tearooms, fast-food restaurants, recording studios, beaches, and bookstores. It is important to note that these young people are seemingly not interested in escaping or wandering around for a long time. They never really quit. Unlike running away and breaking away from one's family, the aim of these escapades is not to leave the family or school, but to find a space where young people can create an everyday life other than that of the family and of school.

In comparing two field surveys on Japanese youth in 1980 and 2004, sociologist Watabe Makoto (born 1952) notes that in the 25 years between the two surveys, Japanese teenagers have significantly lost interest in acts that aim to divert the norms imposed by family and society (traveling alone, for example) (Watabe 2006). Watabe concludes that effective and reinforced control by adult people works so well that young people have become wise and irreproachable. They no longer dare to cross any boundaries. This conclusion is undoubtedly true, and it also seems to be valid for the observations I made in the corpus. At the same time, we must also take the appearance of a new paradoxical social and family context into account, a context in which the adolescent characters happen to find themselves. Their desire to leave the family and school is less strong than that of their parents. It is the fathers (and sometimes mothers as well) who leave their family, before the children do. For young people, neither family nor school is worth leaving. More than running away, the issue here is the impossibility of running away. Adult control no longer works. Therefore, teenagers can simply stay at home or stay among themselves.

This is why our young characters, during their wanderings or detours, describe their age as a period of emptiness and immobility. Nothing happens. In a similar way as the heroine of Nakazawa's novel, that of Matsuura Rieko's novel also said in 1978, in a skeptical tone (Matsuura 1993: 66): "It seems to me that nothing has changed since I was 15 years old. Will something change once I'm 20?" In a similar vein, we can also read the following bitter inner monologue of the main

192   *Dan Fujiwara*

character at the end of Sagisawa's (1992: 38) novel: "I don't want to become anything". *Kaion* (*Noise of Destruction* 1995) by Shinohara Hajime (born 1976) depicts the dream of Taki – a cocaine-loving teenager – through the image of a deserted city with constantly resonating destruction noises. And we can also quote the ironic final words of Minami Natsu's *Heisei Machine Guns*:

> I wanted to know who should be the target, the real face of my opponent to fight.
> In my dream, the Demon loads the machine guns while holding a big knife in his hand. I rained bullets on everyone. The Demon, when I looked at him closely, had very black decayed teeth.
>
> (Minami 2005: 110, translation mine)

Reception

In contemporary Japanese society, the age of 20 is significant – not only because it is at this age that one legally becomes an adult in Japan – but also due to the term *jūdai* in Japanese.[13] *Jūdai* refers to persons from 10 to 19 years of age, and it shows that Japanese society tends to regard this age as a full social category in the same way as other age groups (*nijūdai* for tweens, etc.). This categorization is artificial, of course. We also know that any attempt to describe its characteristics or to come up with a general, acceptable definition is difficult. However, when a person is regarded as a "young talent" in the field of art, sport or other specific practices or performances in Japan, a notion of immaturity or, on the contrary, of prodigy and therefore eccentricity, also accompanies the selection process. Concretely speaking, whenever authors under 20 are awarded, the issue of their age is inevitably discussed. We can read this, explicitly or implicitly, between the lines of comments by jury members, or in various texts written by journalists and literary critics about them.[14]

The perception of winners under the age of 20 varies from one jury to another and ranges from suspicion and astonishment to hesitation and indulgence. Etō Jun (1932–1999), undoubtedly one of the most influential literary critics of the conservative current in contemporary Japan, commented on Hotta Akemi (born 1964), who received the 18th Bungei Prize at the age of 17, with the following words: "I could not help but change my unfavorable opinion on rewarding a 17-year-old girl who has no responsibility in society" (Etō 1981: 295). We can also witness a general feeling of embarrassment among the jury members of the 21st Gunzō Shinjin Bungaku Prize, who wondered whether they sympathized too much with the fact that the laureate, Nakazawa, was just 18 years old.[15] Some jury members of the 64th Bungakukai Shinjin Prize (1987)[16] expressed their surprise by observing the writing style used in the awarded novel, *The Road along the River*. The work showed great maturity considering the age of its author. Sagisawa was 19 years old at the time.

From the 1990s onwards, however, we find more frequently comments that positively emphasize the fact that the work by the young laureates describes the way of life of youth today. Consequently, also their style of writing is praised. In 1993, Hatakeyama Hiroshi, commenting on *Noise of Destruction* by Shinohara Hajime, wrote: "In *Kaion*, it is clear that the abstract notions of 'protestor' or 'fear' are used without being well defined. The description of the opacity of our contemporary society are superficial. However, I also perceive living expressions that exceed these defects" (Hatakeyama 1993: 20). Shōno Yoriko also relativizes these apparent "defects" in Shimamoto's *Silhouette*: "This innocent youth, despite the defects that the author reveals through the use of stereotyped and worn-out expressions, is undoubtedly the driving force behind this work". (Shōno 2001: 164).

Much can be learned about the reception of these works if we compare comments by jury members with comments written by readers on various Internet sites. In spite of their anonymous or pseudonymous character, the latter comments can justify, in one way or another, the evolution of the jury members' perception of the works of our corpus. Of course, the opinions of the readers are often divided, but it is, nevertheless, possible to trace these conflicting opinions to the same basis. While there are some readers who regard the works in the corpus as "banal" and as a well-known expressions of Japanese youth today, others appreciate the same works for this very reason, feeling assured of being able to find an accurate expression of their own identity and universe. The comments on Wataya's *Install*, for example, are quite symptomatic. Many readers seem not to be surprised by the story that describes a high school student who escapes the reality of exam studies and prefers to enter a virtual world of managing a chat-room on the Internet. This allows some to argue their indifference, while others express their sympathy, especially in relation to the fact that the novel deals neither with love nor with family – although it deals with youth.

Outlook

Today, leaving family and school, being in conflict with parents and with teachers does not constitute an issue of Japanese adolescents (as presented in the works of literature discussed here). The years of adolescence (extending from the late 1970s to 2009 in our corpus) do not necessarily involve a break with the family and the school as a ritual and formative passage that allows adolescents to become adults and enter society. The texts we discussed here suggest a completely different representation of adolescence, one that is not characterized by inter-generational conflict. In contemporary Japan, adolescence has no end (Galan 2014) and even no beginning, *because* family and school do not function. In other words, they invite us to consider not only how to live through adolescence, and how to leave it behind, but also how to access adolescence. The apparent failure of running away, as we saw above, demonstrates, to some extent, that young people are looking for other ways of becoming adolescents. Feminine and perceived from the inside, this Japanese literary adolescence takes us away from those well-known pictures with which Japanese youth has often been identified. In this regard, it is important to emphasize, from a sociological point of view, that most of the narratives of

194   Dan Fujiwara

our corpus are set in provincial towns from which also the great majority of our young authors hail. Far from the highly urbanized culture of the megalopolis, the universe described in the works by Japanese adolescent authors may provide us, through its eccentric character, with another model to reflect on Japanese youth today – a youth that does not need to rebel against social mores because the society they find themselves is in disarray, and because contemporary Japanese society might anyhow be unable to provide any model of life for this youth.

Appendix

Corpus of young literature (ordered by date of publication)

Year	Author	Novel	Award
1978	Nakazawa Kei (born 1959)	*Umi o kanjiru toki* [*When I Sense the Sea*]	21st Gunzō Shinjin Bungaku
	Matsuura Rieko (born 1958)	*Sōgi no hi* [*The Day of the Funeral*]	47th Bungakukai Shinjin
1981	Hotta Akemi (born 1964)	*1980 Aiko jūrokusai* [*1980, Aiko 16-year-old*]	18th Bungei
1984	Hiranaka Yūichi (born 1965)	*Shīzu rein* [*She's Rain*]	21st Bungei
1987	Sagisawa Megumu (1968–2004)	*Kawaberi no michi* [*The Road along the River*]	64th Bungakukai Shinjin
1991	Nakawaki Hatsue (born 1974)	*Sakana no yōni* [*Like a Fish*]	2nd Botchan Bungaku
1993	Shinohara Hajime (born 1976)	*Kai-on* [*Noise of Destruction*]	77th Bungakukai Shinjin
2000	Satō Tomoka (born 1983)	*Nikushoku* [*Carnivore*]	37th Bungei
	Īzuka Asami (born 1983)	*Mizerikōdo* [*Mercy*]	91st Bungakukai Shinjin[17]
2001	Shimamoto Rio (born 1983)	*Shiruetto* [*Silhouette*]	44th Gunzō Shinjin Bungaku[18]
	Wataya Risa (born 1984)	*Insutōru* [*Install*]	38th Bungei
2002	Shimamoto Rio (born 1983)	*Ritoru bai ritoru* [*Little by Little*]	25th Noma Bungei Shinjin
2003	Hada Keisuke (born 1985)	*Kokureisui* [*Black Cold Water*]	40th Bungei
	Kanehara Hitomi (born 1983)	*Hebi ni piasu* [*Snakes and Earrings*]	27th Subaru Bungaku[19]
2004	Kanehara Hitomi (born 1983)	*Hebi ni piasu* [*Snakes and Earrings*]	130th Akutagawa
	Wataya Risa (born 1984)	*Keritai senaka* [*I Want to Kick You in the Back*]	130th Akutagawa
2005	Minami Natsu (born 1990)	*Heisei mashinganzu* [*Heisei Machine Guns*]	42nd Bungei
2006	Nakayama Saki (born 1989)	*Henrietta* [*Henrietta*]	43rd Bungei
2009	Asai Ryō (born 1989)	*Kirishima, bukatsu yamerutte yo* [*Kirishima Is Quitting the Club*]	22nd Shōsetsu Subaru Shinjin
	Gōbaru Sōichirō (born 1992)	*Semai niwa* [*Small Garden*]	109th Bungakukai Shinjin[20]

196 *Dan Fujiwara*

Notes

1 Only unpublished texts sent in as a response to a call for manuscripts are the subjects of the examination of these literary awards for new talents. The Akutagawa Prize differs in this respect and rewards only works that have already been published. Generally, major publishing houses such as Bungei Shunjū are organizers or partners of these prizes. They offer cash prizes (500,000 yen in the case of the Bungei Prize) to the winner and publish not only the awarded works but also the first works after the award.
2 The jury members were Sasaki Ki'ichi (critic, 1914–1993), Sata Ineko (novelist, 1904–1998), Shimao Toshio (novelist, 1917–1986), Maruya Sai'ichi (novelist and critic, 1925–2012), and Yoshiyuki Junnosuke (novelist, 1924–1994).
3 The Gunzō Shinjin Bungaku Prize is one of the most esteemed literary prizes for new writers in Japan. Many novelists who are famous today, including Haruki Murakami (born 1949), started their career with this award.
4 Kanehara Hitomi won the Subaru Prize and the Akutagawa Prize for her *Snakes and Earrings*.
5 That is why I call these literary works "teenager in his/her own words" (*adolescent par lui-même*) (see Fujiwara 2013: 9).
6 With a few exceptions, like that of the Akutagawa Prize, this corpus has been made up from the works that won literary prizes organized by so-called "five major literary magazines" (*junbungaku godai bungeishi*), all well-known literary magazines in Japan today.
7 Asai Ryō won the Naoki Prize in 2012. He is the youngest winner of this literary prize that was created in 1935 by Kikuchi Kan, known also as the creator of the Akutagawa Prize.
8 The novel was adapted for screen by Yoshida Daihachi (born 1963) in 2012. The film, entitled "The Kirishima Things", won the 36th Japan Academy Prize for Picture of the Year (*Nippon akademī-shō*) in 2013.
9 The six chapters of *Kirishima bukatsu yamerutte yo* are entitled: "Kikuchi Hiroki", "Koizumi Fūsuke", "Sawashima Aya", "Maeda Ryōya", "Miyabe Mika", and again "Kikuchi Hiroki".
10 This brings to mind the notion of "male homosocial desire", as developed by Eve Kosofsky Sedgwick (1950–2009).
11 In 1963, Terayama gave a number of lectures literally entitled *iede no susume* ("call for fugue") at Japanese universities, which then resulted in him publishing a book on this activity. The author proposed to entitle it *Call for fugue*, but his editor declined because they thought it to be too provocative in tone.
12 The novel *She's Rain* has been adapted for screen by Shiraha Mitsuhito in 1993.
13 However, a new law on the right to vote, which lowers the minimum age to 18, was adopted in June 2015 and came into effect in summer 2016.
14 Usually, the jury's comments are published together with the rewarded works in the magazine that organizes the prize.
15 See endnote 3 for the names of the jury's members.
16 The jury members were: Kuroi Senji (novelist, born 1932), Hino Keizō (novelist, 1929–2002), Miyamoto Teru (novelist, born 1947), Hatakeyama Hiroshi (novelist, 1935–2001), and Nakagami Kenji (novelist, 1946–1992).
17 Izuka Asami received a special prize and was not the laureate.
18 Shimamoto Rio received a special prize and was not the laureate.
19 Kanehara Hitomi might be a border case. She was 20 years old when her *Snakes and Earrings* won the Subaru Bungaku Prize in November 2003. However, it is sure that the text had been finished before, as her birthday is in August and the deadline for the Subaru Bungaku Prize is in March.
20 Gōbaru Sōichirō received a special prize and was not the laureate.

References

Etō, Jun (1981) Dai-ichigi no zaihi [The Question of Existence of the Essence]. *Bungei* 20: 294–295.

Fujiwara, Dan (2013) "L'adolescent par lui-même": Une nouvelle figure de la littérature japonaise contemporaine? ["Teenagers by Themselves". A New Figure in Contemporary Japanese Literature?] *Japon pluriel* 9: 449–456.

Galan, Christian (2014) Sortir ou rester, et comment? Quatre pistes possibles pour l'étude des hikikomori [Staying in or Going Out, and How? Four Possible Keys to Understanding hikikomori]. In: *Hikikomori, ces adolescents en retrait*. Maïa Fansten, Cristina Figueiredo, Nancy Pionnié-Dax and Natacha Vellut (eds.), 94–111. Paris: Armand Colin.

Hatakeyama, Hiroshi (1993) Karoyakana Funade [Smooth Sailing]. *Bungakukai* 47: 20.

Īzuka, Asami (2000) Mizerikōdo [Mercy]. *Bungakukai* 54: 50–88.

Kanehara, Hitomi (2006) *Hebi ni piasu* [Snakes and Earrings]. Tokyo: Shūeisha Bunko (translated by David James Karashima, 2005). London: Vintage.

Kawamura, Minato (1994) *Sengo bungaku o tou* [Rethinking Post-War Literature]. Tokyo: Iwanami Shinsho.

Matsuura, Rieko (1993) *Sōgi no hi* [Funeral Day]. Tokyo: Kawade Shobō Shinsha.

Minami, Natsu (2005) *Heisei mashinganzu* [Heisei Machine Guns]. Tokyo: Kawade Shobō Shinsha.

Nakazawa, Kei (1978) *Umi o kanjiru toki* [When I Sense the Sea]. Tokyo: Kōdansha.

Sagisawa, Megumu (1992) *Kaerenu hitobito*. Tokyo: Bunshun Bunkō.

Shimamoto, Rio (2006) *Ritoru bai ritoru* [Little by Little]. Tokyo: Kōdansha.

Shimamoto, Rio (2004) *Shiruetto* [Silhouette]. Tokyo: Kōdansha.

Shinohara, Hajime (1995) *Kaion* [Noise of Destruction]. Tokyo: Bungei Shunjū.

Shōno, Yoriko (2001) Hontōni kore de yokatta no ka [Doubtful Results]. *Gunzō* 56: 164.

Watabe, Makoto (2006) *Gendai seishōnen no shakaigaku* [Sociology of Contemporary Japanese Adolescence]. Kyoto: Sekai Shisōsha.

Wataya, Risa (2003) *Keritai senaka* [I Want to Kick You in the Back]. Tokyo: Kawade Shobō Shinsha (translated by Julianne Neville, 2015). New York: One Peace Books.

13 Visualizing elders by young artists

Age and generational differences

Gunhild Borggreen

The anthropological turn in art

It has become increasingly difficult to pursue an individual career as an artist in Japan after the economic bubble burst in the early 1990s. While some dream of becoming a new star of the Neo Pop art scene, many artists of the young generation today focus on aspects other than becoming rich and famous. They begin to explore other formats where art can be utilized as a means to participate in various societal practices. Methodologically, this interest of young artists in Japan to engage in social practices may be seen as a part of the so-called "anthropological turn" in contemporary art, a development that began in the late 1990s. Art critics such as Hal Foster (1996) and Miwon Kwon (2000) began to theorize how parts of contemporary art could be seen as an "ethnographic practice", in which artists combined their aesthetic ideas with a concern for everyday life of their surrounding society. The anthropological longing for reading "culture as text" was combined with reflexivity in critical art projects (Kwon 2000: 75). Artists were inspired by ethnographic fieldwork methods, and dismissed the conventional modernist mode of "pure art", a conception of art as autonomous and secluded from the surrounding society with the sole purpose of providing visual and aesthetic pleasure. Instead, the "artists as ethnographers" may engage in fieldwork methods such as participatory observation, interviews with local informants, and recording field notes on issues related to everyday life. Such art practices do not necessarily aim for specific political outcomes, and they often focus on engaging local communities and on non-artist participation (Hjorth and Sharp 2014). The processes and results of such fieldwork endeavors are designed and interpreted through the artist's aesthetic strategies and modes of presentation.

I will adopt this "artist as an ethnographer" approach in the following analyses of Japanese artworks that deal with generational issues. There are numerous societal challenges related to being young in Japan today, and some of the issues are addressed in artworks by Japanese artists as a means of examining everyday life conditions and of providing new modes of reflection. In my analyses, I present two such art projects that are conceived and produced as ethnographic encounters – one art project entitled *My Grandmothers* (2000–2004) was created by the artist Yanagi Miwa (born in 1967) in collaboration with young female informants.

Visualizing elders by young artists   199

The second art project is entitled *Ojisan no kao ga sora ni ukabu hi* ("The day a middle-aged man's face floats in the sky", 2013–2014). It was produced by the artist action team Me (members are born between 1979 and 1983) in collaboration with citizens of Utsunomiya City in Tochigi Prefecture. These two art projects relate to issues concerning demographic changes and generational differences in various ways, either as a way to account for young peoples' imaginations of old age, or as a means to engage in inter-generational activities. These two art projects have been chosen here to exemplify two different artistic strategies – Yanagi Miwa, taking an ethnographic approach, uses the information from her conversations with young informants to visualize issues of generational conflict, while the art action team Me involves local citizens of all ages in practical activities with the purpose of making them perceive their everyday environments in a new perspective. Yanagi Miwa's work can be seen as an instance of reflection on social aging as a problem or as an opportunity for the future of young generations, while the work by the artist unit Me is an example of how young artists are involved in creating new values in the art system, and subsequently also in society at large. The latter approach resonates with theories of sociologist Miura Atsushi (2014), who identifies a movement towards a society-oriented behavior and altruistic interaction in contemporary Japanese society. This shift can be found in many art projects from the 1990s onwards. It is, therefore, possible to argue for the emergence of a new movement or genre of contemporary art that reflects the situation of the young generation in Japan today.

State of the art: generations in art history research

Before venturing into analyses of specific artworks, let us quickly consider some historical and critical discussions that relate to generational differences in contemporary Japanese art. In the era of the student protest and political activism in the 1960s, the young generation came to symbolize new modes of lifestyle and political organization, which influenced the art world, too. While neither KuroDalaiJee (2010) nor other studies on the 1960s art scene in Japan, such as Chiba Shigeru (1986) and William Marotti (2013), explore generational gaps as a motivation behind concrete artworks, they include age-related terminology in their analyses. They frequently use expressions such as "young people", "young artists", or "a new generation of artists", which indicate the notion that new art forms emerged from young artists in the 1960s.

More explicit attention to generational differences within the Japanese art scene can be seen in the early 1990s, where the sociological concept of *shinjinrui* ("the new human type" or "new breed") is activated within contemporary art as a means of identifying new trends. The *shinjinrui* generation within contemporary art was made up of artists who were born in the 1960s and grew up during the era of economic growth of the 1970s and 1980s. They included young male artists such as Tarō Chiezō (born in 1962), Itō Gabin (born in 1963), Nakahara Kōdai (born in 1961), Yanobe Kenji (born in 1965), and Murakami Takashi (born in 1962) (Nakahara, Murakami and Yanobe 1992). Identified as part of a Neo Pop Art movement,

200 *Gunhild Borggreen*

the *shinjinrui* generation of artists represented the growing affluence of a new consumer society. They were seen as maintaining a youthful lifestyle by indulging in mass consumption, popular culture and in entertainment formats such as manga and anime. This may be said to be particularly true for Murakami Takashi, who chose the blurring of boundaries between "pure art" and commercial pop culture products as an artistic strategy. This can be seen in Murakami's (2006) own business model, or in that of the commercial art gallery owner Koyama Tomio (2008). Due to the large commercial success of the Neo Pop artists from the *shinjinrui* generation, many young artists from the following generation attempted to follow their style, hoping to repeat their economic success and recognition. These younger artists are usually identified as the 00 generation (*zero zero jenerēshon*), because they emerged on the art scene around the turn of the new millennium. In 2006, *Bijutsu techō*, one of the leading Japanese art magazines, launched a special issue on the zero zero generation as a means to update the notion of what the editors refer to as *mienai jidai* ("the invisible era") of the first decade of the 2000s. More than half of the 108 artists mentioned in the special issue are born in the second half of the 1970s or in the early 1980s. According to art critic Sawaragi Noi (2006), the zero zero generation has been informed and restrained by a number of domestic and international events across the world since 1989, which has resulted in a certain kind of introversion among this generation of artists. In addition to the attention from *shinjinrui* generation art critics such as Sawaragi Noi (born in 1962), the *dansō junior* generations of artists were also supported by a curatorial and promotional support from *shinjinrui*-generation artists such as Murakami Takashi, who encouraged younger artists to develop their own Neo Pop style (Rothkopf 2007: 152).

The artists who were supported by Murakami included female artists such as Takano Aya (born in 1976), Ban Chinatsu (born in 1973), and Aoshima Chiho (born in 1974). These artists are identified with a certain kind of *kawaii* ("cute") aesthetics or modes of expression that were closely associated with popular culture, especially *shōjo bunka*, girl culture (Sawaragi 1992: 98). The notion of girl culture highlights *shōjo* ("girls") as a segment of society that denotes a transitional phase from childhood to adulthood. Anthropologist Sharon Kinsella concludes from a survey conducted in 1992 that most young people conceive adulthood as involving responsibility (*sekinin*) and a lack of free time. Kinsella notes that there is no ideal in Japan that links maturity to individual emancipation, and that a cute lifestyle is seen as a way of acting vulnerable and immature and thus unable to carry out social responsibilities for family or for the workplace. Many of the girls indulging in *kawaii* are deliberately extending the period of *shōjo* in order *not* to grow up and become a *shakaijin*, "member of the society" (Kinsella 1995: 242–243).

In a later study, Kinsella (2007) argues how young females, who appeared to be engaged in "derivative" *kawaii* culture such as *enjo kōsai* ("compensated dating") or *terekura* ("telephone chat lines"), were blamed in the media for the economic crisis and general misfortunes that Japan suffered in the so-called "lost decade" of the 1990s. As Kinsella points out, such views by the media gave rise to

Visualizing elders by young artists 201

the impression of a dangerous female conspiracy against the patriarchal society, carried out through (alleged) acts of sexual deviance, violence, and sub-cultural non-conformity. Such discourses may have been the reason why the *kawaii* style became prominent in art criticism during the 1990s. Art critics and museum curators identified cute aesthetics as part of an ironic, subversive and even feminist element in contemporary art by female artists of different generations, such as Nishiyama Minako (born in 1965) (Nakai 1997; Hasegawa 2002), or Sawada Tomoko (born in 1977) (Borggreen 2015). Sharon Kinsella also notes that the status of "bad" schoolgirl attitudes was not established through empirical evidence of such behavior, and she suggests that much of the *kawaii* revolt may have been taking place only on the front pages of popular reviews and newspapers and not as actual acts of cultural resistance (Kinsella 2012).

From "lost decades" to the age of sharing

Amidst the "lost" and "invisible" decades of 90s and 00s, things did happen in the contemporary art scene. Consider an example that caught attention beyond the world of art. Sociologist Mōri Yoshitaka (2005) refers to one of the first artist-driven social actions, the Shinjuku Cardboard House Art Movement, where the artist Take Jun'ichirō (born in 1968) in 1995 began to paint the cardboard boxes that homeless people in Shinjuku used for shelter in an underground passage near Shinjuku station. Due to the economic crisis and the rising unemployment or under-employment then, a new cohort of young people appeared on the streets with no place to stay (Yoshida 2015). The project expanded and came to include other artists, students, and *freeter*, who also painted the cardboard houses of homeless people over a course of several years, drawing attention to the increasing numbers of homeless people in Japan. As Mōri (2005: 25) notes, the west Shinjuku underground area became a space for expression as well as an alternative public sphere, and "a project of visualization of those who were forced to be invisible in urban space".

Carl Cassegård (2013) in his examination of youth movements and trauma also analyzes the Shinjuku Cardboard House project. For Cassegård, the term *freeter* is used to refer to young people who live in a "precarious existence". He defines *freeter* as those who

> belong to a stratum of people who may drift in and out of studies, unemployment, dispatch work or other forms of irregular work or states of withdrawal. Students, young academics, artists, and young homeless people can all be part of this stratum, as well as dispatch workers, part-time working housewives and social withdrawers.
>
> (Cassegård 2013: 4)

He mentions the Shinjuku Cardboard House project as an example of artists and *freeter* collaborating with other activist movements, in this case NPO groups supporting homeless people. While the political activists saw the Shinjuku cardboard

202 Gunhild Borggreen

village as a space for promoting political participation in a public sphere, the artists were less directly politically motivated. They appreciated the space as a "no-man's land" that existed apart from mainstream society. The Shinjuku Cardboard House struggle ended tragically in 1998, when an attempt from the authorities to evict the space resulted in a fire that killed five homeless people. All cardboard houses were destroyed either by the fire or by water during this incident. While Cassegård (2013: 138–139) notes that the artists themselves explicitly deny any political commitment, he also argues that "art can be political even where it fails to conform to the models of instrumental or prefigurative politics".

In the wake of such cultural activism, many critics maintain that despite the increasing number of art projects with an explicit social or political agenda, it remains difficult to see these projects as having any real effect on the political landscape, and no societal changes are registered as a result of artistic interventions. In his recent book, John Clammer (2014) devotes a chapter to the sociology of art in contemporary Japan, and he includes many references to the Neo Pop artists of the 1990s. Clammer (2014: 187) also mentions the Shinjuku Cardboard House art project and other socially motivated art projects, but concludes that these activities had "very little impact on the injustices of Japanese society, its corporate structures or ineffective government". Mōri (2005) and Cassegård (2013) argue that incidents such as the Shinjuku Cardboard House project and other *freeter*-based activities during the 1990s paved the way for the present-day social activism in Japan. Note also in this context that the "introversion" identified by Sawaragi Noi (2006) among some young artists in the early 2000s was challenged when young people in Japan began to display political and social resistance in the streets in the form of global anti-war movements from 2003 onwards. Mōri maintains that these anti-war protests in public space were more like street parties with techno music and dancing, and he identifies the cultural practice as one of the main differences from the political activism and demonstrations carried out by the youth of the 1960s. Mōri (2005: 22) also argues that these new cultural practices were initiated and organized by *freeter*, many of whom were artists, musicians, and DJs who aspired to work in the creative industry, but who would seldom manage to secure a permanent employment in the declining labor market.

The social contributions of *freeter* and young artists in general fit the tendency towards altruism and sharing that sociologist Miura Atsushi (2014) identifies in his overview of consumption patterns in Japanese society. Miura presents a number of significant changes in Japanese society in the early 2000s as parts of the consumer society's transformation from a third to a fourth stage. According to such a shift, luxury brand names are exchanged with simple and casual products, and the craze towards western, urban, and individualistic lifestyle is now turned more towards local, regional, and decentralized organization of everyday life. There is less emphasis on goods and more focus on services, and a general move from self-oriented and egoistic behavior towards society-oriented and altruistic interaction. According to Miura, the Japanese society in the 2000s started to exhibit a general tendency away from possessiveness towards a culture of sharing.

Visualizing elders by young artists   203

He identifies this as a new model of consumerism, which reverses the individualistic tendencies of the past and which rebuilds connections between people.

Miura defines his generational categories slightly differently than the editors of this book, as Miura names all people born in the 1970s *dankai junior* (Miura 2014: 192). He notes that *dankai junior* were the generations most supportive of the second-stage consumption patterns. Miura uses the term "New People" for the *shinjinrui* concept that emerged in the late 1980s, and he regards them as the main force behind the third-stage consumerism. Miura argues that the emergence of a fourth stage of consumerism is due to the emergence of the *dankai junior* generation, who grew up with affluence but began to value quality over quantity when they were in their 30s, that is, from the 2000s onwards. Miura does not mention the youngest generations (those born in the 1980s), even though he speculates on what a future "fifth stage" of consumerism would look like. Based on the prediction that there will be three seniors for every one young person in Japan in 2035, he projects a type of sharing, where three elders (who in many cases might be living alone) could support one young person with housing, food and connections to the job marked in return for favors such as shopping, Internet support, or helping out around the house. These notions of sharing are based on the experience of the fourth stage of consumer society that is already underway. The fourth stage is seen to involve four basic principles: (1) a conversion towards sharing across different fields of the society, such as lifestyle, business, and community building; (2) the creation of a new public sphere by having people open their private spheres little by little; (3) a revival of Japanese rural regions to attract young people from the urban areas; and (4) the encouragement to shift from an economic preoccupation towards a lifestyle where attention to money is replaced by attention to relations with other people (Miura 2014: 198).

Similar tendencies of society-oriented behavior within the art world is documented in a five-year research project conducted by the Tokyo Art Research Lab under the directorship of Kumakura Sumiko at Tokyo University of the Arts. Published in the report *Nihongata āto purojekuto no rekishi to genzai 1990–2012* (*Japan's Art Projects, Its History and Present State, 1990–2012*), the collaborative research team outlines a number of community-based and socially engaged art projects across Japan (Kamakura 2013). The term *āto purojekuto* ("art project") is applied as an overall concept for different types of activities. These are in general described as being co-creative and concerned with social conditions of a particular time and place. Five defining characteristics for the concept of "art projects" are identified: (1) art-making as a process is highlighted and actively disclosed; (2) art projects seek to be site-specific within the social context of the site; (3) art projects are developed as long-term engagements with spreading effects; (4) they focus on a collaboration of people of various backgrounds while inducing such collaboration through communication; and finally, (5) art projects show interest in and engage with social fields outside the world of art.

The research report includes a number of contexts in which socially engaged art projects can be found, including art museums and universities, but also alternative spaces, social institutions, companies and business communities, as well

204 *Gunhild Borggreen*

as in *machizukuri* ("town-community making") activities and processes. More importantly, perhaps, the report lists a number of art-project activities in which young people are involved, including the volunteer organizations of large-scale art festivals such as the Echigo-Tsumari Art Triennale in Niigata Prefecture or the Setouchi Art Triennale in the Inland Sea, where young volunteers interact with local inhabitants. Young artists who move to regions outside the urban centers become "go-betweens" in the existing communities and contribute to the establishment of new cultural activities. In some places, art projects become part of *machizukuri* processes, attracting also tourists and increasing a sense of "civic pride" among local citizens. Such effects are important. If local inhabitants find their own community appealing, it will not only attract young people from the outside, but also make individuals who have moved away want to return. Art museums such as Mito Art Museum engage in new art projects by inviting young artists to collaborate with curators, and they have established many art project activities for school children in the area. A young generation of artists as well as local school children engage in various ways in community-based or socially concerned art projects that emphasize collaborative, site-specific, and communicative activities.

When young artists and members of volunteer organizations in connection with art festivals move from the urban centers to regional and rural areas, some conflicts are bound to emerge. The director for the Echigo-Tsumari Art Triennale, Kitagawa Fram, summarizes his experience from the first installment of the art festival in 2000. He reports how conservative and elderly rural farmers in the Echigo-Tsumari area were skeptical about the art projects in their region. They initially dismissed the young artists and volunteers as "strange" people who belonged to urban centers. As a reaction to such skepticism, the young people then developed a new strategy in order to establish and maintain personal relationships across generations. They applied a new sense of self-awareness of their own position in order to create mutual empathy. As Kitagawa (2014: 20) concludes, "this cross-pollination of individuals of differing generations, background, and contexts is now a strong foundation of the Echigo-Tsumari Art Triennale."

After the triple disaster of earthquake, tsunami, and nuclear meltdown in 2011, the socio-aesthetic trajectories of the contemporary art scene are again shifting towards new types of relational aesthetics. While the government promoted discourses of national unity in the months after the disasters, contemporary artists explored the potential for disclosing social issues through the performative and participatory aspects inherent in relationships and networks, regardless of whether these were virtual on social media or community-based in the Tōhoku region. Artists would contribute by donating profits from their art productions to relief work, or they would offer their knowledge of creative practices to form artist-run activities for specific communities or groups, i.e., organizing art workshops for children or establishing and maintaining art cafes. In areas where the disaster had destroyed conventional infrastructures and institutions, art was seen as a means of unifying people under new formats, or to serve as an outlet for memories or

Visualizing elders by young artists 205

experiences of loss. An example of such a kind of project is the artist Nishiko (date of birth unknown) and her *Repairing Earthquake Project*, for which Nishiko traveled to areas in the Tōhoku region that had been affected by the tsunami. Talking to local inhabitants, Nishiko listened to their experiences during the tsunami, and initiated other activities that established personal relationships between the artist and people from the local community (Nishiko 2012). During this phase of creating relationships, Nishiko also began collecting items in the debris that were broken in order to repair them and to mend objects that were not claimed by others. Several art institutions such as the Yokohama Triennale and the Art Tower Mito hosted workshops in which Nishiko performed actual repair works on these objects, and exhibited the artifacts she had mended (Takehisa 2012). Other examples of artists who engage with local communities in the aftermath of the 2011 disasters include Katō Tsubasa (born in 1984), who reconstructed the local lighthouse in the town of Iwaki by using waste material from tsunami debris and asked local inhabitants to help raise the structure by pulling ropes (*hiki-okosu*). The artist group Nadegata Instant Party (Nakazaki Tōru, born in 1976; Yamashiro Daisuke, born in 1983; and Noda Tomoko, born in 1983) organized local festivals for volunteer supporters, and other collective art groups worked in similar manners (Hattori 2015). As a reaction to the disaster, young artists felt empathy and established new ways to contribute to the recovery of everyday life of the people in the affected areas.

Grandmothers in performance and photography

In this section, I would like to present two different art projects that deal with issues of age and generational gap. The case studies show how artists employ an ethnographic approach to registering and transmitting the results of fieldwork observations and interviews, combined with artistic practice. Both projects include a significant element of collaboration. The first example is a series of artworks by Yanagi Miwa entitled *My Grandmothers*, created between 2000 and 2004. Yanagi Miwa's works are hybrid digital photographic images that display computer generated manipulation of urban or rural landscapes that are inhabited by various female figures. The series *My Grandmothers* consists of 19 photographic works, all of which feature a portrait of an elderly woman (in a few cases two or more). The project is conceived in close collaboration with young women in their 20s, who had been working as models in Yanagi's previous projects, or who had responded to an add on her Internet site. The participants were asked to imagine themselves in a specific situation 50 years into the future when they would have become "grandmothers" and to formulate their vision in a short text. It is the participant or informant herself who enacts her own future vision in the image with the help of heavy make-up in order to make her look aged. The participant in the picture is also the author of the accompanying text, which functions as an anchorage to fix the meaning of the image to the specific context. The texts are written in a first-person-singular monologue voiced from the fictitious figure in the image.

206 Gunhild Borggreen

The artist herself presents the series on her website by stating that,

> the *My Grandmothers* series is a project which visualizes the self-perceived notions of several young women when asked to imagine what type of woman they themselves might become 50 years later. Borrowing from these models' ideas, these works are not only images of my own fictitious grandmothers, for they also stand as collaborative portraits of the ideal elderly woman. I bless all the grandmothers of the future.

(Yanagi 2000)

Yanagi herself is born in 1967, and thus represents the *shinjinrui* generation, who grew up during the age of economic affluence. The younger models she collaborates with in this series were in their 20s at the time of the creation, which means they are born in the late 70s or early 80s, the "Post-Bubbles" of the *dansō junior* generation described in the first chapter of this book.

All the portraits are fictitious but based on an ethnographic method, in which a young Japanese woman conveys to the artist her thoughts about her own future. These images cannot be understood as straightforward empirical data from ethnographic interviews because they are saturated by the aesthetic choices of the artist. The text, too, is often poetic and allusive. The quality of the series lies in its strong visual manifestation of a specific imagination of a concrete future situation – not just airy dreams or vague aspirations. The concept relies on the young informant to share her visions for the future, and to visualize, formulate, and collaborate with Yanagi in order for these visions to materialize on photo.

Some of the works in the *My Grandmother* series relate specifically to generational issues. The work entitled *Hiroko* from 2002, for example, deals with the way in which professions or trades are handed down from one generation to the next, a topic which may contain issues of conflict because the young generations do not always appreciate the way in which their parents or grandparents run the business, or they might oppose the limitations in their own choice of career paths by being obliged to take over the family business. In the work *Hiroko*, the profession in question is related to escort services and prostitution. The image features a slim, elderly woman in front of a large window in what appears to be a hotel room. There are open suitcases and take-away food containers on the table, and there is a view of an airport on an artificial island in the background outside the window. Holding a teacup in her hand, the elderly woman appears to be facing and perhaps talking to a younger woman seated with her back to the viewer on the hotel bed. The younger woman is wearing a towel around her body and has her hair bleached, and parts of it rolled in curlers. In the background, a television set is displaying scenes from a pornographic video, and the accompanying text suggests that both women are employed in the sex industry. The text implies that the younger woman on the bed is the "granddaughter of the last Dominatrix of Legends" and that this trip is not a vacation, even though the granddaughter does get pampered. The elderly woman teaches her grandchild on the development of the trade (Yanagi 2004: 73): "When I was about your age, private sexual

Visualizing elders by young artists 207

services were still illegal. [. . .] I had to fight against all forms of discrimination and unfair laws for an incredibly long time." In writing the text and imagining the monologue of herself 50 years ahead in time, the young informant in *Hiroko* expresses an awareness of the family-based transmission model in which knowledge of various skills is handed down through generations. It also highlights the possible social and cultural tensions in this tradition. In the text, the figure of the elderly prostitute says (Yanagi 2004: 73): "And now, when I see the blindness of today's youth who lay down on the foundation that I built so long ago, I know that I will never be able to retire."

Another example from the *My Grandmothers* series is *Minami* (Yanagi 2000). It reveals how a young informant imagines the *kawaii* features associated with present-day popular *shōjo* culture will continue to be pertinent for her also 50 years into the future. In this imaginary setting, the figure of *Minami* has attained the powerful position as the CEO of an entertainment park called Minami Island. She is an elderly woman with her hair dyed pink and dressed in what looks like a cosplay costume of a pink toy animal. The mask of the costume is placed on the table next to her, and it resembles a rabbit or cat adorned with all the signifiers of *kawaii* aesthetics. The elderly woman is reclining in an armchair with her feet (in plushy pink animal paws) on the table, indicating that she is not observing the good manners of keeping her feet on the ground. On the contrary, she seems to state that she does whatever she wants. Two younger women flank the older woman – both are dressed in elegant business suits and wear discreet jewelry. They try to hand a notebook and several telephones to the older woman in the chair. The background offers a view through a large window, through which an amusement park is visible, and on a dresser in the left-hand side of the image a large amount of soft toy characters in the same appearance as the costume can be seen. The accompanying text identifies the elderly woman as the president of the Minami Island Company, which is a global enterprise with a new branch coming up in Hawai'i and is planning to expand business also to Los Angeles and Paris.

Despite her apparent financial success and independency, the elderly woman finds herself restricted in her freedom in other ways. She states:

> My secretaries are certainly efficient, but they can really be a pain in the neck. No matter where I go, they always track me down and bring me back to this room. What's wrong with the president of the company to go out dressed up in this costume, anyway? Wearing these things isn't just a hobby – it's a way for me to stay fit.
>
> (Yanagi 2004: 70)

This seems to suggest a stubborn elderly woman, who is used to getting her will and doing as she pleases. This statement may be seen as an ironic paraphrase of the self-indulgence attributed to the *shinjinrui* generation. At the same time, the viewer may also imagine that the elderly woman has been outside, straying around dressed in her pink costume, perhaps due to dementia and age-related memory failure. In any case, she was brought back to the office by the two younger

208 *Gunhild Borggreen*

women. While the face of the elderly woman is bathed by the sunlight from outside the window, the two younger women are cast in shadow, indicating their discreet function as attendants or wardens. The text and narrative of the image of the young collaborator associates old age with being bossed around.

Another aspect of the generational element in Yanagi's series is that of reproduction. In these imaginary future scenarios, the elderly woman is never part of a conventional family. She has no husband or family around her. The grandmother figure in the work *Yuka*, for example, has a laughing face, a cigarette in her hand, and brilliantly red hair as she sits in the sidecar of a motorcycle in full speed across the Golden Gate Bridge in San Francisco. The character states in the accompanying text (Yanagi 2000): "As for the kids and grandkids back in Japan, well, I just don't see them anymore. I bet my own grandchildren wouldn't even recognize me – or me not them, for that matter." Instead, Yuka has a young boyfriend, who wants to marry her (which she declines). Another figure, *Mika*, has lived isolated on an island for ten years with a group of her young female students, not knowing if they are the last people on earth. Mika has only one wish (Yanagi 2000), "that somehow all the life forms that live on this island give birth to the next generation". Since there are no men around, this wish seems to imply different means of procreation than conventional heterosexual reproduction. In other words, many of the informants who participate in this artistic project do not see themselves as a conventional grandmother in the future, but as independent women who make decisions for themselves and who create alternative relationships outside conventional family structures. This is a deliberate selection made by Yanagi, as she claims she did not want to include participants in the project if their vision of themselves as grandmother was too conventional. Nevertheless, the independent and single lifestyle of the imaginary grandmothers seem to echo the trends already registered in current Japanese society, where a decline in the fertility rate is part of the conditions for what is known as a hyper-aged society (Goodman 2010: 210). In this way, Yanagi Miwa's collaboration with young women reflects issues of social and political importance that concern young women today in their imagination of the future.

A middle-aged man's face in the sky

While Yanagi Miwa ventured into collaboration with a number of participants or informants in order to co-produce the imaginary visualization of future grandmother generations, other young artists appropriate different collaborative strategies. Artist collectives as a social and aesthetic construction is not a new phenomenon in Japan. They have been around since the early modernist period. Examples include the avant-garde group MAVO, active in the 1920s, as well as artist groups such as Gutai, Neo-Dada Organizers, Hi-Red Center, and many others from the 50s and 60s. Recent groups such as the Tokyo-based Chim↑Pom, formed in 2005, take up many of the aesthetic strategies of the avant-garde by organizing happenings in public spaces. As mentioned above, collaborative art projects with a social activist inclination by young *freeter* emerged already 20 years ago.

Visualizing elders by young artists 209

The contemporary art action team Me (which means "eye" in Japanese) engages in other types of collaboration and sharing. It belongs to the kind of art projects that Cassegård identifies as more concerned with new forms of exchange and experience of everyday life forms rather than having an explicit social agenda. The group was formed in 2012 and has three core members: Kōjin Haruka (born 1983), Minamigawa Kenji (born 1979), and Masui Hirofumi (born 1980). They engage a number of technicians and other people with practical skills for the execution of their projects. The group is active in creating site-specific installations of great complexity at art festivals in Japan such as the Setouchi Art Triennale in 2013 and 2016, and the Echigo-Tsumari Art Triennale in 2015. These young artists challenge the ego-centered art production of the post-bubble era by working as collective groups rather than as individual artists. They defy the notion of art as consumption products and brand names as did artists associated with the Neo Pop movement. Young artist groups and collectives share authorship for the artworks and thereby transform the systems of consumption from an individualized lifestyle of the *shinjinrui* generations towards a community-oriented, altruistic and shared engagement with art.

Over almost two years in 2013–2014, the art action team Me realized the art project *Ojisan no kao ga sora ni ukabu hi* ("The day a middle-aged man's face floats in the sky"), which was commissioned by the Utsunomiya Art Museum but took place outside the museum, in the streets and the public space of Utsunomiya city. The project was realized throughout a series of workshops and production phases that included groups of local citizens. Kōjin Haruka, one of the members of Me, had a dream when she was a junior high school student in which a giant head or face of a middle-aged man, an *ojisan*, was floating in the sky and changed peoples' perception of their surroundings (Kōjin 2015: 51). The art project was an attempt to realize this dream, and it signifies also a general reflection on the potentials of providing new visions to the familiar surroundings of everyday life.

In his account in the accompanying exhibition catalogue, Me's art director Minamigawa Kenji refers to the first meeting that was set up between the artists and about 20 people from the town who had responded to flyers on the art project and attended the meeting. A local shop owner commented that they already knew about various types of art designed towards citizens' participation, but he did not want to repeat such a kind of project. He would much more prefer to engage in serious art (*honki no geijutsu*) (Minamigawa 2015: 53). The process of creating a large face of an *ojisan* that could float in the air was elaborate and carefully carried out by the artists in close collaboration with different groups of inhabitants of Utsunomiya. The group opened a headquarters called *Kao shūshū sentā* ("Face collection center") in a redesigned shop on Yuniondōri (street), in which various meetings, workshops and documentation exhibitions were held. The next step was a series of face collection workshops that took place over seven days between October and November 2013. In this phase, the artists went around the town with a mobile photo booth made of an old set of cart wheels mounted with wooden boxes, a white screen, and a red and white canopy, and asked middle-aged male citizens for a photo of their face to serve as a model for the large-scale balloon.

210   *Gunhild Borggreen*

In total, ten workshops were held. They covered various activities, spanning from testing possible locations for the balloon launch, a children's festival, live music concerts, producing badges, and painting faces on small lamps. Local people were included in different groups such as the face-collection group or the launch group.

On two different days in December 2014, a huge three-dimensional balloon-like object illuminated from the inside painted with the face of a middle-aged man was launched over the town of Utsunomiya and floated in the air until 9 o-clock in the evening. Except for the people who had been involved in the process, inhabitants of Utsunomiya did not know about this event in advance, and so they would stop and look at this unusual and surprising sight. According to the artists, who observed and collected reactions from Utsunomiya inhabitants, many people were surprised, some people laughed, others started crying, and it was possible to sympathize with all these feelings. One person could recognize the face of his old friend in the sky and called him on the phone after not having been in touch with him for many years. The face floating in the sky was an extraordinary intervention in the routine everyday life, a vision of something that *could* happen, and actually *did* happen. According to the artists in Me, this is an example of a personal element (a dream of a junior high school student, an individual person's face) appearing in the public sphere – a public sphere that is not only the sky over Utsunomiya, but the entire earth and universe. They state that this is one of the functions of art in society. Whereas science needs to prove the existence of things in a scientific manner, art can just show it (Kōjin and Minamigawa 2016).

Let's return once more to the preparatory workshops. One of the workshops was dedicated to the important aspect of choosing only one face from a total collection of more than 200 different *ojisan* models. At this meeting about ten people spanning the age groups from 20 to 70, who did not know each other in advance, had to agree on selecting one face as the one being best suited for the project. The meeting lasted for five hours, and included exchanges on how to understand the concept behind the project, as well as discussions on how they should carry out the decision process (Minamigawa 2015: 52). In other words, the collaborative aspects of decision-making and conceptualization were highlighted as equally important as the actual artifacts of lamps, badges, and balloons. Documentation of the many workshops and other activities in the form of photographs and field notes created by the participants was a central part of the project, and they are featured in the catalogue. This is an example of a co-creative form of artistic activity, which is not limited to the exhibition of artworks, but engages non-artist members of a community to conceive and execute the art project together as a means to engage with contemporary society. The *Ojisan no kao ga sora ni ukabu hi* project did not aim at producing a physical and permanent monument that could account for the joint efforts of the citizens' creative forces. Rather, the outcome of a long and complex preparation process was a brief and ephemeral aesthetic experience where a giant three-dimensional representation of a familiar face of one local citizen hovered in the sky above the city for a short time. For the young artists in the art action team Me, the project was a conceptual and philosophical project. They sought to create interventions into everyday life in order to make people aware of their familiar surroundings, albeit from a new perspective. They wanted to make them appreciate and value the place they live, and to consciously share these values with others.

Outlook

By looking at the different generations of artists in contemporary art, it is possible to detect a transformation in the artistic strategies and aesthetics that follows some of the overall trends in Japanese post-bubble consumer society. Although not all artists fit easily into a rigid definition of generational categorizations, in general terms, the *shinjinrui* generation resonates to what Miura identifies as the third stage consumer society, in which individualized consumption was promoted as personalized, creative consumption of specific brands and luxury goods. The drawback of this was an increase in the number of people who felt isolated and alone, and this was then further amplified when many people lost their jobs or failed to get a (decent) job in the post-bubble economy. This sentiment can also be seen in the "introvert" reactions of the "zero zero generation" of artists that followed the *shinjinrui* group. The precarious conditions of the late 1990s paved the way for *freeter* and young artists uniting with political activists in order to improve conditions for and make visible some of the victims of a hyper-aged late capitalist society. Miura identifies a new model as a fourth stage of consumer society, which focuses on reversing the individualistic tendencies of the *shinjinrui*-informed third-stage consumerism and instead rebuilds connections between people. The "lost decade" as well as the earthquake, the tsunami, and the nuclear disaster of 2011 have spurred a wave of volunteers and NPO engagement in rebuilding local communities. There is less emphasis on goods and more focus on services, and a general move from self-oriented and egoistic behavior towards society-oriented and altruistic interaction.

Miura recognizes that the four stages of consumer behavior do not replace each other, but rather make up additional layers to already existing patterns. For the same reason, it may be doubtful how widespread Miura's rather optimistic perception of a new model of consumerism in Japanese society is. Many styles and concepts of art exist at the same time and add new layers on existing patterns, which makes it possible for consumption-based Neo Pop art to exist in parallel with the emergence of socially concerned projects founded within *freeter* communities or with community-based art projects conducted by collective art groups. Those who call for an immediate impact of socially engaged art projects on the political and legislative institutions in Japan are perhaps asking the wrong questions. Art rarely produces concrete results that can be instrumentalized and measured in terms of their political or social effect. On the other hand, art is necessary for creating new perceptions and visions among people in their everyday life, and therein rests art's potential for social change.

212 Gunhild Borggreen

Acknowledgments

I would like to thank Kōjin Haruka and Minamigawa Kenji from the contemporary art action team Me for insights into their artistic practice during a personal interview in Kitamoto, 27 June 2016. I want to thank the Novo Nordisk Foundation for supporting the research trip that made the interview with the group possible.

References

Borggreen, Gunhild (2015) Cute and Cool in Contemporary Japanese Visual Arts. In: *Socioaesthetics: Ambience – Imaginary*. Anders Michelsen and Frederik Tygstrup (eds.), 129–151. Leiden: Brill.

Cassegård, Carl (2013) *Youth Movements, Trauma and Alternative Space in Contemporary Japan*. Leiden: Brill.

Chiba, Shigeru (1986 [1997]) *Gendai bijutsu itsudatsu-shi 1945–1985* [A History of Deviations in Contemporary Art, 1945–1985]. Tokyo: Shōbunsha.

Clammer, John (2014) *Vision and Society: Towards a Sociology and Anthropology from Art*. London: Routledge.

Foster, Hal (1996) *The Return of the Real: The Avant-Garde at the End of the Century*. Cambridge: MIT Press.

Goodman, Roger (2010) Silver-haired Society: What Are the Implications? *Social Anthropology* 18: 210–219.

Hasegawa, Yuko (2002) Post-Identity Kawaii: Commerce, Gender and Contemporary Japanese Art. In: *Consuming Bodies: Sex and Contemporary Japanese Art*. Fran Lloyd (ed.), 127–141. London: Reaktion Books.

Hattori, Hiroyuki (2015) Chi'iki shakai to āto no kōryū kara umareru sōzōsei [Creative Forms Born from the Interchange Between Local Communities and Art]. *Bijutsu techō* 67: 102–103.

Hjorth, Larissa and Kristen Sharp (2014) The Art of Ethnography: The Aesthetics or Ethics of Participation? *Visual Studies* 29(2): 128–135.

Kamakura, Sumiko (2013) *Nihongata āto purojekuto no rekishi to genzai 1990–2012* [Japan's Art Projects: Its History and Present State, 1990–2012]. Tokyo: Arts Council Tokyo.

Kinsella, Sharon (1995) Cuties in Japan. In: *Women, Media, and Consumption in Japan*. Lise Skov and Biran Moeran (eds.), 220–254. Honolulu: University of Hawai'i Press.

——— (2007) Female Revolt in Male Cultural Imagination in Contemporary Japan. In: *Female Revolt on Male Cultural Imagination in Contemporary Japan*. Barbara Ruch (ed.), Kyōto: Medieval Japanese Studies Institute.

——— (2012) Narratives and Statistics: How Compensated Dating (*enjo kōsai*) was Sold. In: *A Sociology of Youth: From Returnees to NEETs*. Roger Goodman, Yuki Imoto and Tuukka Toivonen (eds.), 54–80. London: Routledge.

Kitagawa, Fram (2014) *Art Place Japan: The Echigo-Tsumari Art Triennale and the Vision to Reconnect Art and Nature* (translated by Amiko Matsuo and Brad Monsma). New York: Princeton Architectural Press.

Kōjin Haruka (2015) Atarimae no yō ni soko ni aru [It Is Like Naturally There]. In: *Utsunomiya Bijutsukan kangai purojekuto 2013–2014 – "Ojisan no kao ga sora ni ukabu hi" kirokushū*. Utsunomiya Bijutsukan (ed.), 51. Utsunomiya: Utsunomiya Bijutsukan.

Kōjin, Haruka and Minamigawa Kenji (2016) Personal interview. Kitamoto (Japan) (27 June).

Visualizing elders by young artists 213

Koyama, Tomio (2008) *Gendai āto bijinesu* [Contemporary Art Business]. Tokyo: ASCII Media Works.

KuroDalaiJee (Kuroda Raiji) (2010) *Nikutai no anākizumu – 1960 nendai nihon bijutsu ni okeru pafōmansu no chika suimyaku* [Anarchy of the Body: Undercurrents of Performance Art in 1960s Japan]. Tokyo: Guramu Bukkusu.

Kwon, Miwon (2000) Experience vs. Interpretation: Traces of Ethnography in the Works of Lan Tuazon and Nikki S. Lee. In: *Site-Specificity: The Ethnographic Turn*. Alex Coles (ed.), 75–83. London: Black Dog.

Marotti, William (2013) *Money, Trains, and Guillotines: Art and Revolution in 1960s Japan*. Durham: Duke University Press.

Minamigawa, Kenji (2015) Ojisan no kao ga sora ni ukabu hi made [Until the Day When a Middle-Aged Man's Face Floats in the Sky]. In: *Utsunomiya Bijutsukan kangai purojekuto 2013–2014 – "Ojisan no kao ga sora ni ukabu hi" kirokushū*. Utsunomiya Bijutsukan (ed.), 52–54. Utsunomiya: Utsunomiya Bijutsukan.

Miura, Atsushi (2014) *The Rise of Sharing: Fourth-Stage Consumer Society in Japan* (translated by Dana Lewis). Tokyo: International House of Japan.

Mōri, Yoshitaka (2005) Culture = Politics: The Emergence of New Cultural Forms of Protest in the Age of freeter. *Inter-Asia Cultural Studies* 6(1): 17–29.

Murakami,Takashi (2006) *Geijutsu kigyōron* [How to Start an Art Business]. Tokyo: Gentōsha.

Nakahara Kōdai, Murakami Takashi and Yanobe Kenji (1992) Posuto hobī āto Japan [Post Hobby Art Japan]. *Bijutsu techō* [Art Notebook] 44: 68–81.

Nakai, Yasuyuki (1997) Pinku no mukōgawa – Nishiyama Minako-ron" [On the Other Side of Pink: On Nishiyama Minako]. In: *Nishiyama Minako-ten – pinku, pinku, pinku*. Nishinomiya-shi Ōtani Kinen Bijutsukan (ed.), 5–10. Nishinomiya: Nishinomiya-shi Ōtani Kinen Bijutsukan.

Nishiko (2012) *Repairing Earthquake Project. First Phase/Jishin o naosu purojekuto. Daiichi dankai*. Online available at: http://nishiko55.com/eq/ (accessed 6 March 2018).

Rothkopf, Scott (2007) Takashi Murakami: Company Man. In: ©*Murakami*. Elizabeth Hamilton (ed.), 128–159. Los Angeles: Museum of Contemporary Art.

Sawaragi, Noi (1992) Rori poppu – sono saishōgen no seimei [Lollipop. A Minimum of Life]. *Bijutsu techō* 44: 86–98.

——— (2006) "Naikō" no gihō, kizoku naki "hyōshō" [The Technique of "Introversion", the "Symbol" of no Return]. *Bijutsu techō* 7: 101–107.

Takehisa, Yū (2012) Artists' Interview: Nishikō. In: *3.11 to ātisuto – shinkōkei no kiroku/ Artists and the Disaster: Documentation in Progress*. Justin Jesty (ed.), 127–128. Mito: Art Tower Mito.

Yanagi, Miwa (2000) *My Grandmothers*. Online available at: www.yanagimiwa.net/My/e/ (accessed 28 September 2016).

——— (2004) *Miwa Yanagi*. Frankfurt am Main: Deutsche Bank Art.

Yoshida, Miya (2015) The Hidden Homeless: From Bio-Politics to Popular Culture in Contemporary Japanese Society. In: *Socioaesthetics: Ambience – Imaginary*. Anders Michelsen and Frederik Tygstrup (eds.), 86–97. Leiden: Brill.

Conclusions

14 Social rejuvenation and change

The resilient generation of the Heisei period

Christian Galan and Patrick Heinrich

Many things have happened in the past 30 years in Japan. These events have destabilized and transformed society. We wrote in our introduction to this book that "something happened in the Heisei period", and we have now clarified the scope of what has happened in the first part and the cultural and emotional reactions of Japanese youth to these changes in the second part. The chapters of this book support the hypothesis laid out in our introduction. The generating-making mechanism that is at work since the beginning of the 1990s is different from the mechanisms that produced the older generations in post-war Japan (the parents and the grandparents).

It is noteworthy to recall in this context that there have been few major historical watershed events between the 1950s and the 1980s. There were of course the student movement of the 1960s and the oil crisis of the 1970s, but none of this resulted in any fundamental social change (Oguma 2009; Tsutsui and Mazzotta 2014). Rather, after some time of doubts and questioning, post-war Japanese society was reinforced after these events. In contrast, two major historical events took place in the Heisei period – the bursting of the bubble in the early 1990s, the consequences of which were only really felt from the second half of the 1990s, and the triple catastrophe of Fukushima in 2011. The effect of the bubble burst had a profound impact "on Japanese politics, society, and culture" and was altogether "little short of devastating" (Tsutsui and Mazzotta 2014: 66). The shocking and frightening character of Fukushima, and the reactions it has provoked in the population, resulted in Fukushima being regarded as a landmark event or a historical turning point (see e.g., Karel, Paravel and Castaing-Taylor 2015; Cadicott 2014). However, at least for our discussion at hand, Fukushima may be less important. As can be seen across all chapters of our book, the defining event – the one that affected the daily life and the future of all young people and that profoundly changed Japanese society – is the prolonged economic crisis. The bust bubble caused a *dénouement* (an untying) of the contradictions between nation-imagining ideology and the actual social life.

Some chapters in this book show that, far from being broken, the intergenerational bond has probably never been so strong in Japan. This is the result of the fact that the inter-generational bond can no longer be seen as a given. It is no longer experienced as a non-negotiable obligation (filial piety, Confucius, etc.).

218 *Christian Galan and Patrick Heinrich*

The relations between generations may now become internalized and desired. Inter-generational continuity emerges today in unexpected places – for example, in the fact that 90 percent of grandfathers report to enjoy spending time with their grandchildren or with Japanese fathers enjoying taking a bath with their little children (Ishii-Kuntz, this volume). Inter-generational relations have also changed because parents and grandparents are older today than they were a few decades ago (Coulmas, this volume). The triple catastrophe of Fukushima in 2011 may have played an important role in the fact that relations between generations are operating in both directions, from young to old and vice versa. The younger generation and the old generation have been united as a "community of destiny", that is, by material living conditions often marked by precariousness and uncertainty (see Gonon, this volume). If Fukushima has had an impact on generations, it is more as an event promoting inter-generational rapprochement and strengthening inter-generational solidarity. Also in this sense, it is more accurate to portray young Japanese as a "generation of the economic crisis" rather than as a "Fukushima generation".

Absence of a generation conflict

Behind the talk of defining "generations" inevitably lurks the issue of "generation conflict". In contemporary Japan, inequality between generations cannot be denied, although it is rarely addressed (see Imamura, this volume). This may be seen as surprising, because one cannot help but notice that the older generations have mortgaged the future of young people. Japanese society is sacrificing its young generation (Mizushima 2007). The young are obliged to pay the pensions of the old and to take care of them, but young Japanese will have to carry the burden of their own wellbeing alone, without being given the same conditions that older generations found when they were young, i.e., without the security and the wealth of the post-war Shōwa years. Social aging is amplifying this trend as it naturally functions to disempower young people, most obviously in elections. This notwithstanding, young Japanese are accused of refusing to play their part, i.e., they are accused of refusing to work, refusing to participate in politics and elections, of choosing individualistic lifestyles, of refusing to pay the debt, of no longer wanting to have children, of no longer being solidary. In short, they are accused of no longer "being Japanese". From the point of view of the older generations, the young generation lacks "responsibility"; from the point of view of the young, the older generations lack "foresight". Yet, in the case of a "real" generation conflict there would be antagonism – present or in the making – between young and old. There would be a struggle between the (old) majority of the electorate who, by their sheer majority in number ensure the rule by the LDP, and, in doing so, vote against any deep-rooted and transformative change. The young would form, organize, and demand their interests to be reflected in Japanese policies but this is not the case (Imamura, this volume). They seem to have cut ties with the rest of society.

The way in which the young generation "makes sense" of contemporary Japan does present a break with previous generations, but this "break" does not mean "conflict" or "opposition". Rather than having a conflict at hand, we are witnessing

Social rejuvenation and change 219

a redefinition of the concepts of "generation", "adulthood", "age", or the binary "active/inactive". The current "sense of crisis" concerning youth and inactiveness is due to the fact that this redefinition is currently underway. As an effect, life benchmarks are uncertain, unstable, and at times also troubling. The chapters in this book show something more complex, deeper, and more epoch-making than a generation conflict. We are not dealing with a confrontation of young and old that is naturally resolved when the young grow older. Change is more fundamental and more substantial, too. There will be no calming down, no getting back, no adjustment to the older generations by the young. It seems that the young have crossed a line of no return.

The fact that phenomena such as economic crisis and demographic decline characterize age cohorts of different ages at a shared point of time does not necessarily mean that there is conflict or solidarity between all individuals of an age cohort. With regard to work, for example, Imai (this volume) shows that solidarity has collapsed within companies between those employed regularly and those employed irregularly. Such a collapse of solidarity, and not a potential conflict between generations, is the result of Japan's crisis. Contemporary Japanese society has become indifferent and relationless (*muen*), not antagonistic. At the turn of the present century, post-war Japanese society as we knew it imploded. Some of its components have yet to realize this (parts of the urban middle-class, parts of the political class, parts of the mainstream media), while others are living this new reality on a daily basis and know nothing else (most young and poor, many women, parts of the working class, inhabitants of declining rural communities). Japanese society is divided, as Imamura (this volume) shows for the case of Japanese women. For some – the poorest, the most isolated, the oldest, and the most precarious – hope about relief in the future has vanished (Murakami 2002). The result is not a conflict between "have and have-not", or between young and middle-aged and old, but a rise of uncertainty, a lack of confidence, and resulting thereof an attempt to somehow stick to past models, benchmarks, and norms (see Coulmas; Imai; Gonon, this volume). A pervasive and "nagging sense of insecurity" characterizes large parts of Japanese society, in particular, the young (Genda 2006).

The humiliation bestowed upon young people by not being able to access adulthood (according to the old criteria) is somewhat similar to the humiliating circumstances in which many old people find themselves, namely being forced to live in precarious conditions. Solidarity is vanishing everywhere. Japanese society is sacrificing their old generation, too (Allison 2013: 143–153). Being young in an economically stagnating and demographically declining society involves being concerned about old age already in young years, and this may very well work against a potential generation conflict. If there is a conflict, it is most likely a direct conflict between parents and children, not incidentally the most prominent topic of Heisei period literature by young authors (see Fujiwara, this volume). This is no insignificant finding. Grandparents and grandchildren share a certain individual and mutual sympathy between them (see also Borggreen, this volume). This sentiment is undoubtedly reinforced by communal experiences such as shared economic difficulties and social indifference, but also by Fukushima.

220 *Christian Galan and Patrick Heinrich*

Relationless society (*muen shakai*) also results in strengthening bonds within one's social network. Masiko (this volume) reports that young people may actually not be hooked on their cell-phones as such – they rather seem to be hooked on one another. Indeed, never has there been so much (phatic) communication as we find today between members of the young generation in virtual space. This virtual space allows them to escape the analogous society and to engage with a large number of like-minded (young) individuals. This has resulted in a very distinct and novel way of communicating on all levels of interaction, and such communicative habits in themselves already set the young generation apart.

Born this way

Japanese society is changing in many ways. An important aspect of the transformation of Japanese society is the rather dramatic break in the modality of how adulthood is accessed today. As a result of this break, those who have become "adults" in the Heisei period are different from "past adults". The "classical" transition to adulthood was connected to gaining independence and assuming responsibility (Coulmas, this volume). Existing categories and terminology for this transition (*shakaijin*, lifestyle, consumption, partnership and family, responsibility, financial independence, etc.) no longer match the social realities of those who grew up in the Heisei period, though. There is no longer a simple and straightforward match between biological age and the social age – at least not in the terms that this relation was seen in post-war society. As an effect, the "Heisei generation" is no longer characterized by what has characterized generations before. This, in turn, is exactly what is held against the young by the media and other popular methods of criticism against them. This book has shown that this criticism is not valid, because it applies patterns of transition, models, or expectations on the young that have lost their significance or are no longer valid. Hommerich and Tiefenbach's account (this volume), for example, shows that "happiness" means something quite different to the young generation. Possessions are deemed to be less important towards this end – a trend that is both strengthened as well as reproduced by the "lightweight" digital lifestyle of "access" versus the outmoded lifestyles centered on "possession" (Masiko, this volume).

Something happened indeed. The rules of the game have changed, and the young generation must be seen and studied along this new set of rules. Doing so, as we attempted to do in this volume, shows that the young are "a generation" in every sense of the word, from the most banal to the most intellectual, and from the most common to the most radical. They constitute "a generation", firstly, because they are the children of their parents (they are family members "born after" their parents). Secondly, they are a generation in the sense of a sociological cohort that gathers all young people living at the same time. They share traits that concern aspects of identity and attitude. Thirdly, they constitute a "social generation" in the sense of Mannheim, that is to say, they form a "community of experience" and a "cultural community" (as explored in Part I and Part II of this book, respectively). In a word, those born in the Heisei period constitute a generation due to a rupture between them and the older generations. The break between them is very

Social rejuvenation and change 221

much like the break created by a "new generation" of computers or cell-phones. In these cases, the novelty does not rest in a new sense of quality. They only constitute a "new generation" if the new model is fundamentally different from the old one in terms of its makeup, its functions, the ways it is used, its materials, or its mode of construction. You clearly have "something else", and everybody knows it. This is also what we have in the case of the Heisei generation. They are a "new generation" of Japanese in this very iconoclastic sense.

Young Japanese of the Heisei period, that is, the children of the "new breeds" (*shinjinrui*), are no longer classifiable in marketing terminology as their parents and grandparents were. Contrary to what is sometimes claimed, they are not some kind of "new new breeds" (*shin-shinjinrui*), because they are not separated from previous generations solely or simply in relation to their mode of consumption. By the way, if they are no longer into consumption, it is also because they do not have the means to do so. Most often, it is not abstinence by choice, but by default (Furuichi 2015: 80–82).[1] As always, one is at risk to apply criteria and terms of description of the past to describe a young generation that has been formed in a very different socio-economic setting. For the current young generation, criteria such as consumption no longer have the same meaning or relevance (see Borggreen, this volume). Not understanding this is to misunderstand the young, a mistake that is frequently committed (see Ebihara 2010 for a detailed analysis). The generation of young Japanese today – and probably also the ones to follow them in the near future – can no longer be characterized on the basis of criteria pertaining to consumption or marketing. These criteria were developed for an immutable Japanese society, in which the generations were clearly distinguished by their behavior, however within a finite and set context. It was this set and shared context that perpetuated cross-generational continuity. It no longer exists. Different choices in products, lifestyles and cultural preferences alone no longer characterize the young generation. The very attitudes towards what is up for choice and what these choices imply have changed. Heinrich's study (this volume) of language use by the young generation shows that something deeper than "choice" has changed – the mechanism underlying choices are being made a subject of consumption, manipulation, and play because the young generation has gained a deeper awareness how choice defines individuals. This is the end of "youth fashion" or "youth culture" as we knew it, because it is about more than "choosing something". We are dealing with the savvy activities and expressions of "choice itself", and it is this meta-knowledge and these meta-practices that make up youth culture today (Maher 2005). The old stuff – Japan as Number One, regional characteristics, gendered stereotypes and so on – is not gone in the culture of young Japanese. It is joyfully recycled, highlighting in so doing the many transitions and changes from Shōwa to Heisei society. Innovation consists today also crucially in the purposeful perpetuation of "old stuff in new contexts" in order to create new meaning. This requires a distance as well as a critical sense towards Shōwa period Japanese society, and this, too, separates the generations in Japan.

"The crisis of Japan's youth" is not "the crisis of a generation". Japanese youth is the product of and the reaction to "the crisis of Japan" *tout court*. Japan's youth is the generation of Japan's economic and institutional crisis and of its political

222   *Christian Galan and Patrick Heinrich*

stasis (see e.g., Baldwin and Allison 2015; Chiavacci and Hommerich 2017; Satō and Imai 2011). To reduce this durable and permeating crisis to an antagonism towards the young, or to leave it for discussion only to the media, is an error of evaluation and analysis. It is a historical error, too. It is emblematic that policies addressing "youth problems" are not addressing the needs of the young per se but are simply meant to mobilize the young into the older layers of Japanese society in order to soften the ongoing crisis. This failure underlines the need to adequately and comprehensively grasp generation as an analytic concept in Japan. In the words of Mannheim (1998[1923]: 163), "[t]he problem of generations is important enough to merit serious consideration".

Japan's crisis does not disintegrate society – it recomposes it. The opposition between the "active" and the "inactive" part of the population pushes a large part of the old population and a large part of the young people, and a large part of women in one and the same camp – that of the "inactive" (in the literal sense of the word for the old, but more implicitly so for women and young people). In comparison to most other developed economies, the young "inactive" Japanese are not facing an economic situation where unemployment is the problem. They rather find themselves facing a situation of "quasi-employment", a kind of employment that affects not only the work-wage relationship but also the work-status of an adult (Toivonnen 2013). Hence, the situation of Japanese youth has deteriorated considerably not so much in terms of access to employment – there is always some kind of job for the young in a super-aged society – but in terms of quality and security of employment. This is no trivial change. Quality and security of employment have been the foundation for access to male adulthood in post-war Japan, and with this the foundation of family life and of generational reproduction (Imai, this volume). In this sense, most young people – especially young men – can no longer "become adult", even if they work. At least, they cannot be "adult" in the way it had been socially defined in post-war Japan. We are dealing with deep-rooted changes and although no new models of "maleness" are yet in sight, "old masculinity" or "default masculinity" is becoming exceptional for young Japanese. What is more, nothing hints at a return to this kind of masculinity. On the contrary, everything points to further change.

Japanese society is transforming, and the present young generation is the first who grew up in this changing society. This crucially distinguishes them from all other living generations in Japan, and this triggers the production of new values, new ways of living, and new ways of becoming an adult. This is not an easy process, especially in view of the fact that it is opposed by other parts of the population – the "classic adults", so to speak, who want to maintain the modus operandi because it profits them and because they know nothing else. This desire is totally unrealistic though. The young generation, arch-realists as they are, know this very well. Young Japanese have done nothing to want or to push for such change. Change simply occurred, chronologically and historically, at a specific juncture of time. They were born this way. Now it is up to them to live in this specific time and this specific situation – in this post-boom, nostalgic, unrealistic and therefore debt-ridden, demographically declining, super-aging society. It is up to Japanese

Social rejuvenation and change 223

youth to make the best out of this, to live and to act in a meaningful way in these circumstances. It is in this sense that we can clearly see that the Japanese society that defined itself as post-war (*sengo*) is over. All the while, the young generation has to face and live with the remnants of this literally "old society" (population, expectations, institutions, definitions, categories, etc.). They are not part thereof, nor will they ever be, because Japanese society today is both relationless (*muen*) and segregated (*kakusa*). Finding themselves being left out entails that they need to forge a new and meaningful path in new circumstances while, firstly, experiencing aspects of instability, discomfort, insecurity, doubts, and sometimes also despair and, secondly, being measured on the "post-war yardstick of success". This is the background from which the discourse on Japanese youth as either being pitiful (*kawaisō*) or weak (*yowai*) emerges. We can now clearly see that such kind of discourse lacks analytic depth. It does not do justice to what it means to be young in super-aging and economically stagnating Japan.

It was never easy to be young, but it is without doubt particularly difficult to be young in contemporary Japan. The changes in the access to adulthood, the ongoing economic stasis, the redefinition of work, the demographic crisis, the redefinition of roles within the family, the nuclear problem – the list of changes, tasks, and problems is long. The challenges that the current young generation is facing are unprecedented since 1945. Upon reflection, one cannot but admire how young Japanese are dealing with this situation.

A resilient generation

Contrary to what is often claimed about young Japanese (see e.g., Yamaoka 2009), young Japanese have not collectively resigned. Consider their cultural and emotional reactions to the difficulties that shaped them as a generation. According to the authors of our book, young Japanese seek to find their place in Japan's changing society (Coulmas, this volume); they find happiness in unexpected and novel things (Hommerich and Tiefenbach, this volume); they are better, deeper, and more phatically connected to one another (Masiko, this volume); they recycle with much fervor and skill abandoned dialects in order to (verbally) stylize themselves (Heinrich, this volume); they have more artistic prowess than any generation in contemporary Japan before (Fujiwara, this volume); and they engage in novel, reciprocal ways with the public (Borggreen, this volume). The young generation of Japan is not resigned – it is resilient.

Young Japanese have to find their place in a society that is not the society they had been promised, or the society for which they have been prepared in their families and in the education system (Galan 2011, this volume). They have to accept to not be able to "become adults" by following the trajectory that has been traced for them – a path that their parents and grandparents have taken "naturally" before. They are witnessing the blurring of old family landmarks such as masculinity, paternity, success, transmission, parental responsibility, filial love, etc. They have to live with the disappointments they "cause" to their parents, that is, the result of being unable to follow their path and the path that they had projected for them.

224 *Christian Galan and Patrick Heinrich*

Young Japanese are not fulfilling the dreams and hopes their parents have placed on them. Imai provides for a vignette that encapsulates all of this, and that reveals how hard it can be to deal with this.

> His parents [parents of an irregular employed men, CG & PH] did not directly show concern or anxiety, and they seemed to respect the life-course of their son. However, he says that "it [the parents' attitude, JI] hurts me somehow" (*chotto kizu tsuku*), knowing that the situation cannot be easily legitimated, and recognizing that his parents are aware of this.
>
> (Imai, this volume)

Being young in super-aged Japan involves having to accept being less wealthy than the older generations, to live less comfortably, and to live more precariously. Young Japanese know that the financial debt left to them by older generations is colossal, and they know that their interests have been traded for the material comfort of the older generations. They also know that the older generations did nothing to facilitate their lives, and their future has been sacrificed. They also know that even if they voted (which is not the case), they would be trapped in a minority position and would thus anyhow be subjected to the political choices of the older generations. The lowering of the age for the right of vote from 20 to 18 in 2016 changed nothing in that respect. Young Japanese live in a society where unpredictability has become the rule. They know that their country lives under a nuclear threat. They know that their own children – if they will have children – will have to live in conditions as difficult or even more difficult than those that they are facing themselves today.

After graduation from the education system, young people face the threat of poverty, adult criticism, difficulties of finding a job that allows them to live an independent and "adult life", and accordingly the difficulty or even impossibility of founding a family, etc. Yet, the majority of young Japanese carry on to live happily, although a number of studies show that they have no illusions about the grim outlook of their future and that of their country. That young Japanese state to be "happy" reveals an astonishing and unexpected resilience. Departing form the work of other researchers, Zolkoski and Bullock (2012: 2296) define resilience as "achieving positive outcomes in challenging or threatening circumstances [. . .], coping successfully with traumatic experiences, and avoiding negative paths with risks". Resilience is the ability of humans to overcome severe trauma, and adapt to painful situations or threats to live by all means and at all costs. By departing from such a definition of resilience, we can undoubtedly attribute Japan's young generation the feature of being resilient. In this sense, too, this generation is quite apart from previous (and future) generations. The generation born and raised in the Heisei period had to deal with multiple difficulties that the older generation did not face, and while subsequent generations may have to face similar difficulties, they will face them better prepared, and they will be provided with a model for how to live such a life without having to deal with the effects of shock, surprise and disillusionment that the Heisei generation experienced.

Social rejuvenation and change   225

Work on resilience show that among the protective phenomena that allow for resilience to emerge are all the biological, individual, familial, and environmental factors that are specific to the development of an individual (Werner 1995). Resilience is the quality of emotional relationships with the loved ones, and the ability of individuals to bounce back and to face reality as active agents. This last aspect is probably central to the phenomenon of collective resilience. In our opinion, resilience was unavoidable for a young generation facing obligations that differed from what had been promised to them and differed from what they had been prepared to deal with. Resilience allowed them to initiate a dynamic that enabled them to positively and actively participate in processes that vary from those their parents knew in their youth. These experiences and the reactions to them are entirely *theirs*. In having this trait of resilience, young Japanese form a social generation in a Mannheimian sense.

Of course, at an individual level the reactions may differ, due to the presence or absence of different protection layers and different resources existing at the level of personality, family, or the extended circle of friends. At the level of generation, though, we can identify a metamorphosis resulting in collective acts of resilience, because all of them have at a young age and at the same time been confronted with the same difficulties, contradictions, fears, and uncertainties. The young generation is both "a product" of the crisis as it is "an emancipation" of the backbreaking effects that the crisis could have had on them. Studies show that resilience involves a distancing from the upset and trauma, a reflection on it, and a development of objectives and exit strategies from the situation that caused the difficulties. Resilience leads to new activities – activities that result in a recovery and in a restoration of dignity (or in a new sense dignity). All of this necessitates processes of analysis, decision, autonomy, and action.

Unable to find a place in the "old society", and unable "to fit" into the secure and routinized pathways traced by older generations, Japan's young generation is confronted with the necessity to regain the capacity to think for themselves. Young Japanese have no choice if they want to break free from the image and the experiences of "failing" the expectations that are placed on them. The models proposed, the established frameworks of thought, and the benchmarks of previous generations have crumbled before their eyes. They have become zombie-institutions – they no longer work (are dead) but they continue to be in place (are alive). This generation has to "rethink" or "think differently" on every basic issue of their lives – their relationships to study, to work, to money, to partnership, to sexuality, to consumption, to family, etc. This book has made it abundantly clear that in all of these areas the old criteria of "success", "achievement", or "happiness" have become outdated if not obsolete. The young generation has to formulate and put into practice their very own criteria. This results in processes of social rejuvenation and change. On the one hand, life may be less "easy" and "comfortable" for the young, but on the other hand it may just as well be more "interesting", more "motivating", or simply more "lively" by having to gain the responsibility for one's own life, and by having been freed from choices on their behalf made by older generations.

226 *Christian Galan and Patrick Heinrich*

All of this implies that the young generation has to use its own intelligence and sensitivity to re-organize, re-prioritize, re-define and re-dimension the criteria and attributes of a "successful" personal life. More or less as a side effect thereof, they have to create new relationships with others and with society at large. Compared with previous generations, who had to limit their lives and achievements to a predefined framework spelled out by others, young Japanese are undoubtedly "winners" in the sense that they are (in contrasts to their parents) master of their lives. In this sense, young Japanese could develop more "real" relations to reality, i.e., more affect, more interaction with others, more personal commitment to act on the world. They could become more "social" than their parents and grandparents. The second part of our book suggests that they are already busy in doing exactly this.

The social, economic, financial and environmental crisis of the Heisei period brusquely exposed the contradictions of the "old" society. It rendered adults powerless, adrift on a course towards a destiny that no longer exists; it made them propose a destiny nobody believes in anymore. The young generation may be heading towards an uncertain and a somewhat somber destiny, but it is a destiny that depends on them – something that cannot be said of the older generations. The young generation has the chance to restore the agency over their lives and, on the basis of the chapters assembled in this book, we believe that they are already doing so. So maybe this is what is at the heart of the puzzling figure that is at the center of Furuichi's (2015) book – almost 80 percent of Japanese youth claims to be happy, an unprecedented number. One can imagine that this high rate of satisfaction is actually the consequence of the crisis. The young enjoy freedom and pleasure more because it can no longer be taken for granted. They have become like frail old people, for whom a sunny day in the park provides for "more happiness" than the exact same sunny day in the exact same park by a person in the middle of life's rush hour. This approach to and appreciation of the "little pleasures" of life in itself is an expression of new values, of new ways of living, and of new ways of being Japanese.

It appears as if the traumas that this generation has experienced are being processed. This gives rise to the possibility of finding new ways of being in the world (which some parts of Japanese society might find puzzling). Moreover, the phenomenon of resilience, that is, the young generation's new ability to withstand shocks and upsets, leaves them better prepared to deal with an insecure and unpredictable future in comparison with their parents and grandparents (who piled up public debt ultimately because they were unable to adapt to a changing world). We could thus hypothesize that the young generation is in this sense more "robust". This phenomenon of collective resilience among the young could well present itself as a range of new opportunities. How this will spell out on a large scale of topics such as sustainability, equality, multiculturalism and multilingualism, strong and trusted relations with neighboring nations, migration – issues in which the old generations have had and continue to have difficulties with – awaits to be seen. It seems to us that we need to keep an eye on the young generation if we are to study and discuss these fundamental and important issues for the future of Japan.

Social rejuvenation and change 227

Note

1 At the time of writing this chapter in November 2017, inserting the word *"wakamono"* in the Japanese Google site, resulted in the automatic suggestions of the following second search words: *kotoba* (language), *eigo* (English), *hanare* (distancing [from the parent generation]), *shi'in* (cause of death), *hinkon* [poverty], and *kuruma* (car [not buying one]).

References

Allision, Anne (2013) *Precarious Japan*. Durham: Duke University Press.

Baldwin, Frank and Anne Allison (2015) *Japan: The Precarious Future*. New York: New York University Press.

Cadicott, Helen (ed.) (2014) *Crisis Without End: The Medical and Environmental Consequences of the Fukushima Nuclear Catastrophe*. New York: The New Press.

Chiavacci, David and Carola Hommerich (2017) *Social Inequality in Post-Growth Japan*. London: Routledge.

Ebihara, Tsuguo (2010) *"Wakamono wa kawaisō-ron" no uso* [The Lies About "Youth Being Pitiful"]. Tokyo: Fusōsha.

Furuichi, Noritoshi (2015) *Zetsubō no kuni no kōfuku na wakamonotachi* [The Happy Youth in a Desperate Country]. Tokyo: Kōdansha Bunko.

Galan, Christian (2011) Out of this World, in This World, or Both? The Japanese School at a Threshold. In: *Language Life in Japan: Transformations and Prospects*. Patrick Heinrich and Christian Galan (eds.), 77–93. London: Routledge.

Genda, Yuji (2006) *A Nagging Sense of Job Insecurity*. Tokyo: I-House Press.

Karel, Ernst, Verena Paravel and Lucien Castaing-Taylor (2015) *Ah Humanity!* Cambridge and Paris: Harvard University Press.

Maher, John C. (2005) Metroethnicity, Language, and the Principle of Cool. *International Journal of the Sociology of Language* 175/176: 83–102.

Mannheim, Karl (1998 [1923]) The Sociological Problem of Generations. In: *Essays on the Sociology of Language*. Paul Kecskemeti (ed.), 163–195. London: Routledge.

Mizushima, Hiroki (2007) *Nettokafe nanmin to hinkon nihon* [Net-Café Refugees and Poverty in Japan]. Tokyo: Nihon Terebi Hōsō.

Murakami, Ryū (2002) *Kibō no kuni no ekosodasu* [The Exodus of a Country with Hope]. Tokyo: Bunshon Bunko.

Oguma, Eiji (2009) *1968*. Tokyo: Shin'yosha.

Satō, Yoshimichi and Jun Imai (2011) *Japan's New Inequality*. Melbourne: Trans Pacific Press.

Toivonnen, Tuukka (2013) *Japan's Emerging Youth Policy*. London: Routledge.

Tsutsui, William and Stefano Mazzotta (2014) The Bubble Economy and the Lost Decade. *Journal of Global Initiatives* 9(1): 57–74.

Werner, Emmy E. (1995) Resilience in Development. *Current Directions in Psychological Science* 4(3): 81–85.

Yamaoka, Taku (2009) *Hoshigaranai wakamonotachi* [Young People Without Desires]. Tokyo: Nihon Keizai Shinbun Shuppansha.

Zolkoski, Staci M. and Lyndal M. Bullock (2012) Resilience in Children and Youth: A Review. *Children and Youth Services Review* 34(12): 2295–2303.

Index

1.57 shock 20–21, 71–72, 75

adolescence 6–9, 11, 47, 63–64, 121–122, 157, 184–194
adulthood 6–11, 46, 56–57, 64–66, 86, 113, 122–126, 157, 192–193, 200, 218–220, 223

birthrate 17–24, 29, 64, 70–71, 119, 122
Bourdieu, Pierre 42, 47, 48, 106, 170
boyfriend 185, 191, 208
breadwinner 17, 19, 21, 71, 75, 84–88, 95–97
bubble economy 2, 39, 56, 96, 132, 135–139, 156, 198, 217; post-bubble 6–9, 69, 72, 79–80, 206, 209, 211

childhood 6, 7, 11, 38–39, 41, 47, 57, 157, 200
community 19, 21, 65, 74, 77, 113, 137–138, 178, 198, 203–205, 209–211; of destiny and experience 218–220; moral 107
consumption 3, 6, 7, 11, 126, 157–159, 200–203, 209, 211, 220–221, 225
cool 177–179

debt 2, 18, 45, 134, 218, 222–226
dream 46–47, 179, 192, 198, 206, 209–210, 224

egalitarianism 18–19, 29, 38, 45–46, 114, 226
elections 20–24, 105, 110, 124, 218

Facebook 104, 157, 161, 162
familism 19, 21, 28, 75
family 4, 9, 22, 29–30, 37, 39, 43–46, 56, 64, 86, 95–96, 104, 106, 111, 122–123, 136, 138–142, 152, 155, 166, 171, 176, 179, 200, 206–208, 220–225; breakdown 184–193; life 59; policy 69, 71–80; standard 17; work balance 19
fatherhood 69–80, 104, 106, 186–191, 218
femininity 58–59, 76, 86–87, 187, 193, 201
fertility 18–19, 51, 52, 55, 61–66, 69–71, 74–76, 79, 119–123, 126–127, 208
freeter (*furitā*) 4, 32, 46, 87, 97, 132, 201–202, 208, 211
friendship 185, 191, 208
Furuichi, Noritoshi 3, 10–11, 113, 134–137, 142, 144–145, 226

Galapagos syndrome 159–161
Genda, Yuji 56, 64, 130
gender equality 19, 21, 29, 53, 72–73
generation as an actuality 8–9, 12, 46
generation unit 9, 12, 39, 46, 102, 104
grandparents 2–3, 7–8, 54, 69, 79, 128, 137, 167, 171, 179, 206, 217–221, 223, 226

herbivore male (*sōshoku danshi*) 52, 54, 58, 59, 63, 66
hikikomori ("social withdrawal") 4, 11, 32, 42, 46, 47, 124, 132

identity 4, 9, 10, 37, 47, 80, 95, 98, 175–178, 193, 220
immaturity 192, 200
income 18, 20, 37–38, 42–47, 74, 80, 83, 90–91, 95, 125, 129, 139
independence 53, 56, 79, 86, 93, 97, 126, 207–208, 220, 224
inequality 18, 87–88, 92, 177, 218
information society 6, 153, 157–158

230   *Index*

inter-generational continuity 3–4, 11, 108, 217, 193, 199, 217–218
Internet 7, 87, 150–153, 156–157, 160–163, 193, 203, 205

job-hunting (*shūkatsu*) 200–201, 207

kawaii ("cute") 200–201, 207
Kinsella, Sharon 200–201

LDP (Liberal Democratic Party) 17, 20–24, 29, 103, 111, 114, 218
life expectancy 119–120, 127
lifestyle 3, 73, 126, 130, 135, 144, 152, 155, 199–203, 208–209, 218–221; choices 6, 132; female 26, 59; legitimate 86; minimalist 157
lost decade 2, 8, 10, 56, 135, 200–201, 211
lost generation 11, 132

Mannheim, Karl 8, 10, 46, 102–104, 110, 220, 222, 225
marriage 4, 6, 18–19, 21, 25–26, 54–57, 69–71, 79, 89, 94, 121–124
masculinity 58–59, 76, 85–88, 93–98
maturity 9, 10, 87, 124, 126, 183–184, 200, 222–223
Miura, Atsushi 199, 202–203, 211
Mixi 151, 156, 161
moratorium 93–94, 97, 124
motherhood 22, 64, 70–80, 107, 186–188
M-shaped curve 25, 71
Murakami, Ryū 4, 183, 219

neoliberalism 5, 9, 19–22, 32, 92, 126

Oguma, Eiji 109
otaku ("obsessive fandom") 6–7, 124, 190

parents 1–3, 6–10, 19, 21, 32, 37, 39, 75–80, 92, 134, 147, 152, 167, 171,

179; anxiety 106–108, 111–114; and demographic change 127–129; failed 184–187; and school education 40–47; social roles 70–72
pension 4, 18–19, 22, 25, 46, 74, 87, 91, 129, 218
population decline 1–5, 8–12, 17–22, 32–36, 43, 219
poverty 3, 7, 9, 20, 42–43, 47, 92, 123, 128, 133, 219, 224; *see also* precarity
precarity 7, 11, 201, 211, 218–219, 224; *see also* poverty
pregnancy 52, 57, 65

relationless society (*muen shakai*) 3, 19, 70, 219–223
resilience 46, 52, 63–66, 144–145, 223–226
retirement 11, 56, 79, 91, 96, 127
risk 17, 19, 22, 52, 56–57, 61, 107, 110–114, 126–128, 145, 175, 187, 224

segregated society (*kakusa shakai*) 3, 223
shinjinrui ("new breeds") 7–8, 199–200, 203, 206–209, 211, 221
silver democracy 23–25, 128
singles 6, 55–56, 59, 70, 124, 132, 208
social aging 2, 5, 17, 19, 23, 29, 69–71, 78–79, 120–121, 124–130, 218
spouses 69, 71–72, 76, 78, 80, 95–96, 139, 188–189, 208
stigma 23, 86, 93–97, 168, 172, 175, 177–178
stylization 178, 193, 201, 211
super-aging society 3, 120–130, 179, 222–224

teachers 63, 65, 75, 107, 184, 188–189, 193
Terayama Shūji 190
Twitter 109, 158, 161–162